LABOR RELATIONS AND PUBLIC POLICY SERIES

REPORT NO. 3

THE NLRB AND THE APPROPRIATE BARGAINING UNIT

by

JOHN E. ABODEELY

Published by

INDUSTRIAL RESEARCH UNIT, DEPARTMENT OF INDUSTRY
Wharton School of Finance and Commerce
University of Pennsylvania

Distributed by

University of Pennsylvania Press
Philadelphia, Pennsylvania 19104

Copyright © 1971 by the Trustees of the University of Pennsylvania
Library of Congress Catalog Card Number 70-150789
MANUFACTURED IN THE UNITED STATES OF AMERICA
ISBN: 0-8122-9072-0

Foreword

Governmental regulation of industrial relations gives rise to serious and complex questions of public policy. To encourage thoughtful discussion of such issues, the Industrial Research Unit, Wharton School of Finance and Commerce, University of Pennsylvania, has inaugurated a report series dealing with significant labor relations policy matters. The first two of these studies, *Compulsory Arbitration and the NLRB* and *Union Authorization Cards and the NLRB*, were published in February 1968 and January 1969, respectively. This, the third, deals with bargaining unit determinations by the NLRB.

The National Labor Relations Board's determination of the appropriate bargaining unit plays a vital role in determining overall labor relations policies. The delineation of the unit obviously affects the choice of which union, if any, will gain representation rights. It also defines the scope of collective bargaining and thus affects the freedom of employees and the operational capacity of employers. The literature contains many articles dealing with aspects of unit determination, but, despite the importance of the subject, there is a surprising scarcity of current literature dealing with all of the major problems. Mr. Abodeely's study undertakes an examination of these problems, emphasizing both their historical development and current application.

The author, John E. Abodeely, Esq., began work on this study while a student in the Graduate Division of the Wharton School of Finance and Commerce, University of Pennsylvania. Prior to receiving the degree of Master of Business Administration, Mr. Abodeely attended the Boston University College of Business and the Boston University School of Law, where he received the degree of *Juris Doctor*, magna cum laude. A member of the Massachusetts Bar, he is currently Director of the Labor Policy Section of the Industrial Research Unit. The study was financed through contributions by the Labor Policy Association, Inc., Washington, D.C., and by the Research Advisory Group of the Industrial Research Unit.

Thanks are due to the *Boston College Industrial and Commercial Law Review*, the *University of Pennsylvania Law Review*, and the *George Washington Law Review* for permission to reprint modified versions of Chapters III, IV, and V, respectively. The manuscript was typed by Mrs. Veronica M. Kent, Mrs. Rose K. Elkin, and Miss Mary McCutcheon. Mrs. Margaret E. Doyle, Administrative Assistant of the Industrial Research Unit, cared for the numerous administrative details and Mr. Bryson Cook provided the necessary technical assistance. Special thanks are due to Mrs. Marie R. Keeney for her exceptional diligence in the editing of the manuscript.

Finally, the author owes a heavy debt of gratitude to his family for their continued support and encouragement. Special appreciation is due to the author's wife, Evryklia, not only for her willingness to share the sacrifice, but for her patience and understanding.

Although many persons aided in this study, the author takes full responsibility for the errors, shortcomings, and conclusions contained herein.

HERBERT R. NORTHRUP, *Director*
Industrial Research Unit
Wharton School of Finance and Commerce
University of Pennsylvania

Philadelphia

February 1971

TABLE OF CONTENTS

PAGE

FOREWORD iii

CHAPTER

I. INTRODUCTION 1

The Divergent Philosophies 3
Congressional Action—and Inaction 5
The National Labor Relations Board 6

II. THE RELEVANT FACTORS: THEIR HISTORY AND APPLI-
CATION IN DETERMINING THE APPROPRIATE BAR-
GAINING UNIT 7

Community of Interests 7

Defining the Factor 9
Application of the Factor 12

Geography and Physical Proximity 15

Application of the Factor 16

Employer's Administrative or Territorial Divisions 22

New Use of the Factor 24
Judicial Reaction 28
The NLRB's Response 36

Functional Integration 39

Truck Drivers: Functional Separation or Integra-
tion 42
Application of the Factor 47

Interchange of Employees 48

Characteristics of the Factor 50
Application of the Factor 53

Bargaining History 54

The Factor and Its Rationale 54
The Relevant History 56
Summary 64

v

CHAPTER   PAGE

Employee Desires 65

Development of the Factor 65
Application of the Factor 70
A New Use? 74
The Tallying of Votes 75
Responsibilities of the NLRB 78

Extent of Organization 79

Interpretation and Use of the Factor 80

Concluding Remarks 85

III. NLRB CRAFT SEVERANCE POLICIES: PREEMINENCE OF
THE BARGAINING HISTORY FACTOR AFTER *Mal-
linckrodt* 87

The Historical Development 88

The *American Can* Doctrine 89
Section 9(b)(2) of the NLRA 90
The *National Tube* Doctrine 91
The *American Potash* Doctrine 92

The *Mallinckrodt* Doctrine 94

Application of the *Mallinckrodt* Doctrine 99

The *National Tube* Industries After *Mallinckrodt* 106

Concluding Remarks 110

IV. UNIT MODIFICATION: DEVELOPMENT AND USE OF THE
UNIT CLARIFICATION PETITION 113

History of the Unit Clarification Petition 114

Traditional Uses of the Unit Clarification Petition 119

Dispute Over Job Classifications 119
Traditional Problems of Jurisdiction in Job Classi-
fication Disputes 121
The Accretion Issue 124

Abuses of the Unit Clarification Procedure 128

CHAPTER   PAGE

New Use of the Unit Clarification Procedure 131
    Libbey-Owens-Ford 132
    The Question of Authority 136
    Aftermath of *Libbey-Owens-Ford* 141
    Concluding Remarks 146

V. THE EFFECT OF REORGANIZATION, MERGER, OR ACQUI-
    SITION ON THE APPROPRIATE BARGAINING UNIT...... 148

Corporate Reorganization 149
    Jurisdictional Work Disputes 153
    Expanding or Contracting Units............................... 155

The Accretion Issue 158
    The Doctrine Applied 162

Successor Employer Policy 168
    The *Wiley* Case 169
    Application of the *Wiley* Doctrine 170
    The *Wiley* Doctrine Extended 173
    Continuity of Employment 175
    Competing Union Claims.. 178
    Wiley on Remand 182

The NLRB's Successor Doctrine.................................... 185
    Burns International Detective Agency 186
    Companion Cases 189
    Application of the *Burns* Decision 191
    Concluding Remarks 196

VI. BARGAINING UNIT DETERMINATIONS UNDER SPECIAL
    CIRCUMSTANCES 198

Confidential and Clerical Employees 198
    Clerical Employees 202

Managerial and Supervisory Employees 204
    Managerial Employees 209

Professional Employees and Guards 211
    Professional Employees.. 211
    Guards 215

CHAPTER   PAGE

Multiemployer Bargaining Units 216
  Appropriateness of Multiemployer Units 218
  Withdrawal from Multiemployer Bargaining 220

VII. SUMMARY AND CONCLUSION 225

INDEX OF CASES 230

CHAPTER I

Introduction

The National Labor Relations Act,[1] the embodiment of our country's labor laws, provides that the national policy is "to eliminate the causes of certain substantial obstructions to the free flow of commerce . . . by protecting the exercise of workers of full freedom of association, self-organization, and designation of representatives of their own choosing. . . ." The task of implementing this policy was assigned to the National Labor Relations Board.[2] The Act provides the Board with a policy, statutory mandates, and considerable, although limited, discretion. One of the responsibilities assigned to the NLRB is to determine the appropriate unit for collective bargaining and to conduct an election within this unit to decide which union, if any, shall represent the employees.[3] The determination of the appropriate bargaining unit is the subject of this study.

The NLRB's delineation of an appropriate unit is one of the most important and yet most problematic areas of labor law. As Dean Derek C. Bok has observed, "[I]t is disturbing to note how few writers have paid attention to the problem of defining an appropriate unit, despite the fact that a unit determination may profoundly affect labor management relations and constitute a heavy proportion of the work of the NLRB." [4] These profound effects arise, in part, from the fact that the choice of a unit may well constitute the decisive factor between unionism and nonunionism. Moreover, the choice of one unit configuration over another may heavily influence which labor organization will gain representation rights. The early controversies between craft and industrial unionism provide acute evidence of the far-reaching effects of a unit determination.[5]

---

[1] National Labor Relations Act, 29 U.S.C. § 151 (1964).

[2] 29 U.S.C. § 160 (1964).

[3] 29 U.S.C. § 159 (1964).

[4] Discussion, *Proceedings of the 19th Annual Winter Meeting, Industrial Relations Research Association*, 1966, pp. 99-104.

[5] *See* J. Rayback, *A History of American Labor* (New York: Macmillan Co., 1964).

The consequences of an NLRB unit decision do not end, however, with the choice of which union, if any, will gain representation rights. Collective bargaining is a continuing relationship. The Board is thus called upon to determine appropriate units not only in the initial, organizing phase of unionization but in postbargaining situations as well. The chosen unit configuration has an immediate effect upon the scope of collective bargaining. An inappropriate grouping of employees may lead to an inefficient allocation of resources and to a disruption—if not destruction—of the collective bargaining process. The National Labor Relations Board recognized these continuing effects when it stated:

> In performing this function [unit determination], the Board must maintain the two-fold objective of insuring to employees their rights to self-organization and freedom of choice in collective bargaining and of fostering industrial peace and stability through collective bargaining. In determining the appropriate unit, the Board delineates the grouping of employees within which freedom of choice may be given collective expression. At the same time it creates the context within which . . . collective bargaining must function. Because the scope of the unit is basic to and permeates the whole of the collective bargaining relationship, each unit determination, in order to further effective expression of the statutory purposes, must have a direct relevancy to the circumstances within which collective bargaining is to take place. For, if the unit determination fails to relate to the factual situation with which the parties must deal, efficient and stable collective bargaining is undermined rather than fostered.[6]

The appropriate bargaining unit inevitably affects the structure of collective bargaining. The bargaining structure, however, encompasses more than the appropriate unit. The theorists in industrial relations contend that there are four types of "units" involved in every bargaining structure.[7] The basic unit is the *informal work group* whose members are unified by a set of common objectives and common interpretation of their environment. "However formed and whatever the cementing ties, the informal work group is the foundation of the bargaining structure."[8] The *election district* is the grouping which has become equated with the appropriate bargaining unit. It is the unit determined by

---

[6] Kalamazoo Paper Box Corp., 136 N.L.R.B. 134, 137 (1962).

[7] A. Weber (editor), *The Structure of Collective Bargaining* (New York: Free Press of Glencoe, 1961).

[8] B. Samoff, *Law School Education in NLRB Representation Cases*, 21 Labor Law Journal 691, 697 (1970).

the NLRB for purposes of employees' self-determination in regard to the question of union representation. The *negotiation unit*, the one in which collective bargaining actually takes place, may or may not coincide with the election unit. It is most frequently shaped by corporate and union structure and by alliances among employers or unions. The final element is the *unit of direct impact*, that grouping of separate units directly affected by a particular bargaining agreement. This unit is intricately associated with the concepts of pattern and coalition bargaining.[9]

The appropriate unit as defined by the NLRB affects the structure of collective bargaining; but does the NLRB consider the anticipated bargaining structure when it defines the appropriate unit? Former Secretary of Labor, George P. Shultz, has commented, "Board decisions on appropriate units, inevitably affecting the structure of collective bargaining, have primarily reflected considerations other than those having to do with structure." [10] Furthermore, NLRB Regional Director Bernard Samoff has accurately noted that "the number and frequency of shifts from appropriate units [as defined by the Board] to negotiating units [as established by the parties] . . . occurs regularly." [11] The question is apparent: why must the parties "regularly" redefine the appropriate unit so as to fit the needs of collective bargaining?

The problems involved in an appropriate unit determination should not be underestimated. They are both complex and voluminous. The presence of these problems can be attributed to the divergent philosophies of various labor groups, as well as to those between labor and management; to congressional action or inaction—whether intentional or inadvertent; and to the absence of consistent, objective, easily understood NLRB decisions.

THE DIVERGENT PHILOSOPHIES

It is not unreasonable to expect that a union seeking representation rights will petition only for a grouping of employees which it can successfully organize. Equally true, the employer will argue for that unit which is most difficult to organize. Al-

---

[9] W. Chernish, *Coalition Bargaining* (Philadelphia: Industrial Research Unit, Wharton School of Finance & Commerce, University of Pennsylvania, 1969).

[10] D. Brown and G. Shultz, "Public Policy and the Structure of Collective Bargaining," in A. Weber, *supra* note 7, at 311.

[11] Samoff, *supra* note 8, at 697.

though neither of these interests may be given controlling weight, they have certainly led to conflict and confusion. Cases involving competing unions have increased this confusion by adding a third interest to the situation. The bitter confrontations between the American Federation of Labor and the Congress of Industrial Organizations during the 1930's placed substantial burdens upon the National Labor Relations Board. As one labor historian has noted:

> Even under peaceful conditions [the NLRB's] task was not an easy one since the C.I.O. claimed all employees regardless of what work they did and the A.F.L. claimed all men who accomplished any task however faintly it resembled a craft. In the midst of bitter conflict the work of the N.L.R.B. became much more difficult.[12]

The chaos and confusion resulting from the divergent philosophies of the craft and industrial unions has not been dissipated by the passage of time.

The task of determining an appropriate unit has been further hindered by the fact that the union, while presumably representing the best interests of the employees, does have a life of its own. Its existence as an effective force in a dynamic society requires it to continually search for additional dues-paying members. One commentator has noted that "[the union] frequently has objectives independent of employee rights, so that in requesting a particular unit the union may be seeking not so much to vindicate employee interests as to sweep additional employees into its jurisdiction or simply to prevent a rival union from organizing a group of employees which it wants for itself." [13] Accepting this proposition, it then follows that the interests of the individual employees, certainly the intended beneficiaries of the nation's labor laws, are relegated to a position of minor importance. A former member of the NLRB staff recognized this when he concluded that "the unit decisions consistently encourage the growth of unionism as such, rather than protect the rights of employees." [14]

---

[12] Rayback, *supra* note 5, at 363.

[13] Hall, *The Appropriate Bargaining Unit: Striking a Balance Between Stable Labor Relations and Employee Free Choice*, 18 Western Reserve Law Review 479, 485 (1967).

[14] K. C. McGuiness, *The New Frontier NLRB* (Washington: Labor Policy Ass'n, 1963), p. 97.

CONGRESSIONAL ACTION—AND INACTION

In promulgating the National Labor Relations Act, Congress adopted the objectives of preserving the employees' freedom of association and maintaining a stable and harmonious system of labor relations. To implement these policies with respect to the appropriate bargaining unit, the legislature enacted section 9(b) which provides in part that:

> The Board shall decide in each case whether, in order to assure to employees the fullest freedom in exercising the rights guaranteed by this Act, the unit appropriate for the purposes of collective bargaining shall be the employer unit, craft unit, plant unit, or subdivision thereof. . . .

Despite the wide latitude and the importance of this delegation, section 9(b) contains the only affirmative standard to guide the Board's choice of bargaining units. A strict application of this standard—"to assure to employees the fullest freedom in exercising the rights guaranteed by this Act"—would require the Board to allow employees any grouping which they desired. This would promote their "fullest freedom" by allowing those who wish union representation to join while permitting the remaining employees to abstain from unionization. Although certainly enhancing employee freedom, such a scheme would be ruinous of long-run industrial relations stability. The rights of the unorganized would effectively be controlled by the actions of the organized.

To prevent such an occurrence, Congress enacted, as part of the Taft-Hartley Amendments, section 9(c)(5) which states that "In determining whether a unit is appropriate for [collective bargaining] the extent to which employees have organized shall not be controlling." Subsequent to the passing of this section, the Supreme Court ruled that the law only prevented the use of extent of organization as a *controlling* factor in determining unit size. Nevertheless, sections 9(b) and 9(c)(5) do represent conflicting mandates in terms of long-run policy considerations. This conflict, plus the absence of any other affirmative statutory requirement pertaining to unit configuration,[15] has resulted in placing the burden of unit determinations upon the National Labor Relations Board.

---

[15] Section 9(b) does contain a provision regarding special treatment for professional employees, guards, and craftsmen. See Chapters III and VI, *infra*.

THE NATIONAL LABOR RELATIONS BOARD

The absence of congressional guidance and the conflicting interests of the parties have caused serious problems for the members of the National Labor Relations Board. The vacilating trends and inconsistent results in many of the unit cases provide substantial evidence of the severity of this problem. An analysis of these same cases will reveal that much of the confusion in the area of unit determinations is attributable to the Board itself.

It is the thesis of this study that the appropriate bargaining unit determinations of the NLRB do not reflect the realities of labor management relations. Again quoting Bernard Samoff: "A unit is 'appropriate' if it is 'appropriate' for the purposes of bargaining." [16] Yet, current bargaining patterns indicate that the parties "regularly" shift from an "appropriate unit" as determined by the Board to a negotiating unit as dictated by the necessities of collective bargaining. If the unit configuration is so intricately involved in the structure of bargaining, why then is the bargaining structure not a factor in the determination of the appropriate unit?

The solutions to the problems are not easily ascertainable. Even the development of basic principles presents an unenviable task. Recognizing this complexity, Professor John T. Dunlop has made the following observation:

> People inherently try to develop some kind of understanding and basic axioms in this area of unit determinations. But as far as I can discover, there are no real principles in this area. It seems to me that this situation leaves us on quicksand when we talk about public policy.[17]

Notwithstanding the possibility of slowing sinking into the quicksand to which Dr. Dunlop refers, this study shall attempt to review and analyze the major unit decisions of the NLRB. The next chapter will examine the development and application of the "factors" utilized in delineating an initial unit configuration. The succeeding four chapters will concentrate primarily on post-bargaining unit issues. The final section shall briefly present some of the special unit situations confronted by the Board.

---

[16] Samoff, *supra* note 8, at 696.

[17] Weber, *supra* note 7, at 328.

CHAPTER II

The Relevant Factors: Their History and Application in Determining the Appropriate Bargaining Unit

The National Labor Relations Act, whether by design or by oversight, contains few standards which the NLRB may utilize in determining the appropriate bargaining unit. The provisos of section 9(b) covering professional employees, craftsmen and guards [1] provide little help in most unit cases. Consequently, the Board, in order to promote consistency, has developed certain "factors" to be applied in determining the appropriate bargaining unit. It is the objective of this chapter to examine these factors first, to see if the consideration is an appropriate one, and second, to determine the propriety of its application. Since the Board has adopted a case-by-case approach,[2] it will be necessary to adhere to a similar scheme. Although each of these cases generally involves more than one factor, the liberty of discussing each factor individually has been taken so as to facilitate an overall examination.

COMMUNITY OF INTERESTS

Of all the factors used in the determination of the appropriate bargaining unit, the community of interests factor is by far the most important and yet the most difficult to comprehend. The Board has stated that "first and foremost is the principle that mutuality of interest in wages, hours and working conditions is the prime determinant of whether a given group of employees constitutes an appropriate unit." [3] The importance of this com-

---

[1] Bargaining unit decisions affecting craftsmen are presented in Chapter III, *infra*. Unit placement of professional employees and guards is discussed in Chapter VI, *infra*.

[2] American Cyanamid Co., 131 N.L.R.B. 909 (1961).

[3] Continental Baking Co., 99 N.L.R.B. 777, 782 (1952). *Accord*, Chrysler Corp., 76 N.L.R.B. 55 (1948).

mon community of interests may well be attributed primarily to
the fact that the designated unit and its chosen representative
must operate for the mutual benefit of all employees. Should
there exist a dissimilarity of interests, then surely collective bargaining would be severely impeded. One union during one negotiation would be forced to bargain for several different sets of
wages, hours, and other working conditions. A single agreement
for a bargaining unit composed of employees with diverse interests would lead to unrest, chaos, and possibly disruption of production. Similarly, a unit so narrowly defined as to exclude employees of common interest would likewise lead to instability and
confusion. As early as 1938, the Board recognized the need for
an appropriate delineation of the extent of the common community of interests when it stated:

> Under the terms of the act, the Board, in determining the ap-
> propriate unit, attempts to insure to employees the full benefit of
> the right to self-organization and to collective bargaining. The
> *chief object of the Board, therefore, is to join in a single unit only
> such employees, and all such employees, as have a mutual interest
> in the objects of collective bargaining.* The appropriate unit se-
> lected must operate for the mutual benefit of all the employees in-
> cluded therein. To express it another way, the Board must consider
> whether there is that community of interest among the employees
> which is likely to further harmonious organization and facilitate
> collective bargaining.[4]

As the Board noted, the defining of the community of interests either too broadly or too narrowly would present a severe
impediment to harmonious industrial relations. An excessively
broad definition could lead to a grouping of employees so extensive as to make union organization an impossible task. Such a
unit would obviously contravene the NLRA's policy of promoting
the employees' full freedom of association. Furthermore, as previously noted, a commingling of distinct employee interest groups
would prevent an effective collective bargaining relationship. If,
on the other hand, the community is narrowly defined, the resulting relationships would be both inefficient and unstable. From
the employer's point of view, he would be forced to bargain with
many different unions and at many different times. A large
number of small units would greatly increase the danger of
whipsawing of the employer, and would be equally devastating

---

[4] 3 NLRB Annual Report 174 (1938) (emphasis supplied). *Accord,* Goodyear Tire & Rubber Co., 3 N.L.R.B. 431 (1937).

to the union. Inter-union rivalry and a sharp decrease in union bargaining power would surely result. As for the employees, the large number of small units, although seemingly maximizing their freedom of choice, would result in gross inequities in wages, hours, and working conditions.

The consequence of an improper definition of community of interests are easily recognized. The determination of an appropriate definition so as to avoid these consequences is considerably more difficult.

Defining the Factor

The NLRB's creation and use of the community of interests factor is undeniably a proper exercise of administrative expertise, but the definitions (and I emphasize the plurality of the word) given to this factor are somewhat questionable. In the most general terms, mutuality (community) of interests is defined in terms of similarity of working conditions, wages, terms of employment, and other common collective bargaining interests.[5] More specifically, however, early Board decisions indicated that such relevant considerations as medical, recreational, and parking facilities would bear strong weight in delineating the extent of the community of interests.[6] Furthermore, the "common community of life" of the employees has been held to evidence the presence or absence of common interests.[7] In one early case, the Board found as appropriate a single unit comprised of mining and milling employees located in three separate towns because the residents of the three communities shared common recreational, educational, and judicial facilities![8]

Fortunately, in further defining the community of interests factor, the Board did consider the working environment of the employees. It was reasoned that where employees were paid the same wage rate and where the conditions of work were substantially the same, the single unit would be proper.[9] Conversely,

---

[5] Continental Baking Co., 99 N.L.R.B. 777, 782 (1952).

[6] 3 NLRB Annual Report (1938).

[7] *Id.* at 175.

[8] Tennessee Copper Co., 5 N.L.R.B. 768 (1938). *See also* Aluminum Co. of America, 44 N.L.R.B. 1111 (1942); Pennsylvania Edison Co., 36 N.L.R.B. 432 (1941); Fisher Body Corp., 7 N.L.R.B. 1083 (1938); American Brass Co., 6 N.L.R.B. 723 (1938).

[9] American Brass Co., 6 N.L.R.B. 723 (1938); Standard Oil Co., 5 N.L.R.B. 750 (1938).

a substantial difference in wage rates [10] or in working conditions [11] would generally militate against the propriety of the single unit. In a number of early cases, the Board extended this definition to cover the manner of wage payment as well as the similarity of wage rates. In one of the annual Board reports it was reasoned that "The manner in which wages are paid may serve to identify a class of employees uniformly affected by wages, hours, and working conditions, and hence interested in bargaining as a unit." [12] This statement, however, does not necessarily mean that the method of wage payment may be effectively used to argue for or against a particular grouping of employees. In *Century Electric Co.*,[13] the NLRB granted a union petition and, contrary to the arguments of the employer, held that a "mere" difference in method of payment is no basis for excluding employees from a unit. How this decision affects the definition given to the mutuality of interests factor is, at best, confusing.

In one novel case decided in the early 1950's,[14] the Board was confronted with a request to apply an unusual definition to the community of interests factor. The petitioning union argued that mutuality of interests should be defined so as to favor that unit which would give the employees the greatest degree of bargaining power. Fortunately, the Board rejected this argument citing the following reasons:

> (1) . . . The Board has exclusively followed a mutuality of interests test in deciding what is an appropriate unit. The relevant portion of Section 9(b) of the Wagner Act was reenacted without substantial change in the present Act. There is not the slightest evidence that Congress intended to supplant or suppliment the mutuality of interest standard with a power factor test. Under such circumstances, it is a fair assumption that by reenacting Section 9(b), Congress accepted the Board's mutuality of interest standard for unit determination.

> (2) In the second place, we do not believe that, even considering Section 9(b) together with Section 1 of the Act, as urged by Continental Division, the inference is warranted that Congress

---

[10] *See* Zenite Metal Corp., 5 N.L.R.B. 509 (1938).

[11] *See* Bartlett & Snow Co., 4 N.L.R.B. 113 (1937).

[12] 3 NLRB Annual Report 177-178 (1938). *Accord,* Alabama Drydock & Shipbuilding Co., 5 N.L.R.B. 149 (1938).

[13] 146 N.L.R.B. 232 (1964).

[14] Continental Baking Co., 99 N.L.R.B. 777 (1952).

intended that the Board should consider the power factor in unit determination. Section 1 only discusses inequality of bargaining power between employers and "employees who do not possess full freedom of association or actual liberty of contract." That is not the case here.

(3) In the third place, the application of a power test would bring economic warfare to the forefront of collective bargaining, instead of keeping it in the background where it belongs. . . .

(4) Finally, the Board would be faced with an impossible administrative problem in trying to decide when equality of bargaining power does or does not exist.[15]

The reasons recited by the Board for rejecting the power test are indeed impressive. Unfortunately, the NLRB during the 1960's, while still professing an adherence to the policies expressed by the 1952 Board, issued unit decisions which raise serious questions as to the sincerity of this professed adherence.

In the more recent bargaining unit decisions, the Board has been somewhat hesitant in defining a community of interests. The decisions generally include a statement to the effect that since there exists (or does not exist) a similarity of "wages, hours and working conditions" a particular unit is appropriate (or inappropriate).[16] In reaching such a conclusion, the Board members usually undertake a relatively detailed examination of the skills and duties of the employees in issue.[17] One of the results of this broad definition is that in any given case a majority of the Board may rely on the community of interests factor to support a particular grouping of employees, while the minority may rely on this same factor to reach a diametrically opposed result. If the Board itself cannot agree on the effects of a given factor, then surely the parties involved in unit cases are left entirely without standards by which to guide their conduct.[18]

---

[15] *Id.* at 782 n.11.

[16] For cases relying on a similarity of wages, hours, and working conditions, see Metro Beverages, —— N.L.R.B. ——, 46 L.R.R.M. 1492 (1960); ACF-Wrigley Stores, 124 N.L.R.B. 200 (1959); and Shoe Corp. of America, 117 N.L.R.B. 1208 (1967). For cases involving a dissimilarity of wages, hours, and working conditions, see Wells Dairies Cooperative, 107 N.L.R.B. 1445 (1954); Clay & Bailey Mfg. Co., 106 N.L.R.B. 210 (1953); and R. L. Polk & Co., 91 N.L.R.B. 443 (1950).

[17] Diamond T. Utah, Inc., 124 N.L.R.B. 966 (1959).

[18] In a recent arbitration proceeding involving the placement of a new,

Application of the Factor

The community of interests factor is an appropriate, realistic consideration. When a standard is so loosely defined and applied as to allow it to be used to *support* a conclusion rather than to *reach* one, however, then its continued effectiveness must be questioned. An examination of the Board's recent unit decisions reveals that there no longer exists a common "community of interests." The Board has successfully used this factor to find appropriate units of such diverse groups as: all employees doing one job in a single store; [19] all employees in a store; [20] all employees in an employer's metropolitan area; [21] all employees in a state; [22] all employees of an employer throughout the nation; [23] and all of a particular craft or class of employees throughout a region. [24] Admittedly there cannot and should not be any one community of interests for all industrial settings. It would not be unreasonable, however, to require the NLRB, as is done with other administrative agencies, to provide a definition of the factor—and to apply that definition consistently—so as to further the possibility of predictability. [25]

---

clerical employee, the arbitrator considered the following factors to be important:

1. whether an office was shared by clerical employees in the same category;
2. the area in which the new job operated as compared to other workers;
3. whether the new job had supervision in common with unit jobs;
4. whether contact was more frequent with unit than non-unit workers;
5. whether there was any interchange between the new job and existing ones, and whether there was any similarity of duties.

United States Plywood-Champion Papers, Inc., 68-1 CCH Labor Arbitration Awards, ¶ 8273 at 3947 (1968) (Arbitrator Robert G. Howlett).

[19] Fox Co., 158 N.L.R.B. 320 (1966).

[20] Sav-On Drugs, Inc., 138 N.L.R.B. 1032 (1962).

[21] Father & Son Shoe Stores, Inc., 117 N.L.R.B. 1479 (1957).

[22] Allstate Ins. Co., 118 N.L.R.B. 855 (1957).

[23] Paxton Wholesale Grocery Co., 123 N.L.R.B. 316 (1959).

[24] Great Atlantic & Pacific Tea Co., 128 N.L.R.B. 342 (1960).

[25] Hall, *The Appropriate Bargaining Unit: Striking a Balance Between Stable Labor Relations and Employee Free Choice*, 18 Western Reserve Law Review 479, 486-489 (1967); Grooms, *The NLRB and Determination of the Appropriate Bargaining Unit: Need for a Workable Standard*, 6 William & Mary Law Review 13 (1965); Friendly, *The Federal Administrative Agencies: The Need for Better Definition of Standards*, 75 Harvard Law Review 863 (1962).

As noted above, one of the consequences of the Board's refusal to offer a consistent definition of the community of interests factor has been a plurality of communities. The problem becomes exceptionally acute when this plurality is found to exist in one particular employment pattern. Not only must the Board counterbalance the relevant factors but it must further decide which of several communities of interests is to be given credibility. For example, in the recent case of *Continental Can Co.*,[26] the union petitioned for a unit composed only of those employees engaged in the lithographic process. In denying the petition, the Board offered the following explanation:

> It is, of course, true that the Board has long recognized that employees engaged in the lithographic process may constitute an appropriate bargaining unit in appropriate circumstances. However, in this case, the separate community of interests flowing from their performance of lithographic functions is far outweighed by the larger community of interests they share with other employees in the plant by reason of shared supervision, common location in the production line, and shared responsibility for and participation in the operation of the non-printing machinery on the press line. Accordingly, we find that they do not by themselves constitute a unit appropriate for purposes of collective bargaining.[27]

The Board's decision to emphasize the larger of the two existing communities of interests cannot be severely criticized. The Board recognized that the choice of an appropriate bargaining unit has lasting effects on employees outside as well as within the unit. Thus, the emphasis on the more inclusive grouping. Had the Board chosen to rely on the "similarity of skills and duties" definition of the factor, however, a separate unit of lithographic employees would have been appropriate. The decision actually reached in the case appears, then, to have been based upon the "whim" of the Board members. As the political winds change and new members are appointed, the unit decisions may show drastic turnabouts.[28] It is highly doubtful that Congress, or even labor and management, ever intended or desired such a vacillation in national labor policies.

---

[26] 171 N.L.R.B. No. 99, 68 L.R.R.M. 1155 (1968).

[27] 171 N.L.R.B. No. 99, 68 L.R.R.M. at 1157.

[28] For an excellent study of the effects of political change in national labor policies, see K. C. McGuiness, *The New Frontier NLRB* (Washington: Labor Policy Ass'n, 1963).

Mention should also be made of the relationship between the community of interests factor—thought by some to be the most conceptual of the factors [29]—and the Board's other considerations. In a 1954 decision, the Fifth Circuit Court of Appeals offered the following description of this relationship:

> It is true that similarity of duties and working conditions are factors which are proper for consideration in the determination of an appropriate bargaining unit, however, *mutuality of interests is by no means the "primary and controlling" test to be applied.*[30]

Adopting the Court's position, it would appear, then, that the Board should weigh each factor in context with each other, giving controlling weight to no one factor. Unfortunately, recent unit decisions raise doubts as to whether the NLRB has consistently conducted this balancing process. In the case of *F. W. Woolworth Co.,*[31] the Board, in a three to two decision, held that a single department of a store was an appropriate bargaining unit. In support of its decision, the majority reasoned:

> Although it is apparent from the foregoing that there are some factors that would support a finding of the appropriateness of a store-wide unit, it is equally clear that the requested employees . . . have a sufficient mutuality of interests to justify their establishment in a bargaining unit, apart from other store employees.[32]

Contrary to the weighing of factors process advocated by the Fifth Circuit, the Board in *Woolworth* gave controlling weight to the mutuality of interests. Furthermore, an examination of unit decisions reveals that the NLRB has used the various factors in such a way as to reach inconsistent rulings. Each factor, taken by itself, can be the basis for a given result, but it is also true that if weight is given to one factor over another, a different or inconsistent result may be obtained. Add to this the absence of a definitive explanation of the meaning and use of such factors as the community of interests, and the problem of determining the appropriate bargaining unit becomes even more complex.

---

[29] Hall, *supra* note 25, at 486.

[30] NLRB v. Smythe, 212 F.2d 664, 667 (5th Cir. 1954) (emphasis supplied).

[31] 144 N.L.R.B. 307 (1963).

[32] *Id.* at 308. The decision in this case has added significance in that it directly contravenes the single store presumption created in *Sav-On Drugs,* discussed in a subsequent section of this chapter.

GEOGRAPHY AND PHYSICAL PROXIMITY

A factor which has been attributed varying degrees of importance in the determination of the appropriate bargaining unit is the physical location of the employees in question. Although a consideration in all unit cases, the physical proximity factor has been accorded its greatest significance in multilocation situations. As with a number of other factors, the Board has not seen fit to articulate specific reasons for the relevancy of location.

An awareness of the consequences of a unit determination can provide support for the use of this factor. For example, when the employees included in a particular unit configuration are separated by great physical distances, attempts at organization are more difficult and costly. The Board, however, is not authorized to consider geographic proximity as an aid to union organization.

Successful collective bargaining, being a continuing process, requires a certain homogeneity of employee interests, and geographical proximity may reasonably raise a presumption—albeit a rebuttable one—that this homogeneity exists. Implicit in physical proximity is a common labor market which encompasses similar wages, hours, and working conditions for like occupations. If collective bargaining is considered to be an alternative to individual bidding among competing employees, then certainly a common labor market is a relevant consideration.

Admittedly, the existence of a common market is dependent on far more than geographical location. As one commentator noted:

> whether two locations are in the same labor market depends not only on distance, but also on population density, distribution, and mobility; the availability of highways and mass transportation; and the presence of geographic obstacles. . . . Thus consideration of distance alone, apart from the relevant market considerations, is an unreliable guide.[33]

Recognition being given to these limitations, geographical location can serve a useful and necessary role in the determination of the appropriate bargaining unit. Thus, once again, the appropriateness of the factor depends upon its application.

---

[33] Note, *The Board and Section 9(c)(5): Multilocation and Single-Location Bargaining Units in the Insurance and Retail Industries*, 79 Harvard Law Review 811, 832 (1966).

Application of the Factor

When using the physical location factor, the Board normally distinguishes between geographical integration and separation. Although there is no mathematical formula for determining when integration ends and separation begins, a useful distinction can be based on the presence or absence of similar wages, hours, and working conditions among competing employees. The difference in actual physical location could reasonably be used as determining the existence of this common labor market. Should other considerations militate against such a finding, then the Board should so rule. Specific reference to these "other considerations" and their applicability, however, should be a requisite of the Board's opinion.

In the case of *Safeway Stores, Inc.,*[34] the NLRB was confronted with a situation in which an integrated, multilocation unit was requested despite substantial geographical separation. The petitioning labor organization requested representation rights for a unit composed of one of the employer's six administrative districts. The employer resisted the request, arguing that the unit was inappropriate because of, *inter alia,* substantial geographic separation within the district. The twenty-two stores requested by the union were located in a rectangular area which was approximately 200 miles from north to south and 45 miles from east to west. The average distance from one town to the nearest neighboring town within the district having one of the employer's stores was approximately 30 miles, while the average distance from each of them to the administrative center of the district was 61 miles. Despite these facts, the Board reached the following conclusion:

> Although there is a *substantial geographical separation of Employer's retail outlets* within its Waco District, it is clear that that factor does not present a barrier either to the successful functioning of the Employer's administrative organization or to an expression of the employees' unity of interests.[35]

In minimizing the effects of the geographical separation factor, the Board referred to the fact that the Waco District employees met once a year for a picnic and that "once or twice a

---

[34] 96 N.L.R.B. 998 (1951).

[35] *Id.* at 1000 (emphasis supplied).

year" the location managers and head meat cutters held a dinner meeting to discuss common problems.[36]

Admittedly, the social interaction of the employees involved in the proposed unit should be given some consideration. If employees are to intermingle, even on a social basis, then differences in wages and other working conditions might lead to bad feelings and, potentially, industrial strife. Social interaction may well constitute a viable reason for the use of the physical location factor. An annual picnic or dinner meeting, however, could hardly be considered sufficient social interaction to justify the Board's disregard of the "substantial geographical separation." [37]

Notwithstanding the decision in *Safeway*, the NLRB, prior to 1962, generally emphasized the geographical location factor in multilocation unit cases. Concurrent with this emphasis, the Board relied heavily on the employer's administrative divisions as a supplement to geographical location. This reliance evolved to the point where there was created a presumption in favor of the appropriateness of a unit which was coextensive with the administrative unit or geographical area. So emphatic was the Board's reliance on this presumption that the cases soon revealed a mechanistic application of the factors. Although offering consistency, this approach increased the possibility of an inappropriate bargaining unit being certified. Heavy criticism prompted the Board, in 1962, to abolish the presumption. In the now famous case of *Sav-On Drugs, Inc.,*[38] the Kennedy Board offered the following comments:

> Reviewing our experience under that policy we believe that too frequency [sic] it has operated to impede the exercise by employees in retail chain operations of their rights to self-organization guaranteed in Section 7 of the Act. . . . Therefore, whether a proposed unit which is confined to one of two or more retail establishments making up an employer's retail chain is appropriate will be determined in the light of all the circumstances of the case.[39]

---

[36] *Id.* at 1000 n.6.

[37] *See* Note, *The Board and Section 9(c)(5), supra* note 33, at 832 n.144. *Compare* Murray Corp. of America, 101 N.L.R.B. 313 (1952) (distance of 14 miles indicative of geographical proximity) *and* Textron, Inc., 117 N.L.R.B. 19 (1957) (distance of 18 miles indicative of integration), *with* Brown Equip. & Mfg. Co., 93 N.L.R.B. 1278 (1951), *enforced,* 205 F.2d 99 (1st Cir. 1953) (distance of 14 miles indicative of geographic separation).

[38] 138 N.L.R.B. 1032 (1962).

[39] *Id.* at 1033.

Although the decision in *Sav-On* has had the greatest impact on the administrative territories factor,[40] it has also affected the application of geographical location in determining the unit configuration. In *Sav-On*, for example, the petitioning union requested representation rights for a unit composed of employees at the company's Edison, New Jersey retail outlet. The employer argued that the appropriate unit should be all nine stores in its administrative subdivision or, alternatively, all the stores in the state of New Jersey. After alluding to those factors which supported the employer's contention, the Board reasoned that there were "other factors supporting units confined in scope to the Edison store, such as geographic separation of the Edison store . . . ."[41] With respect to this geographical separation, the Board found that the nine stores in the subdivision were separated by distances ranging from 5 miles to 65 miles, with all stores being served administratively by one central office. The Edison store, which the Board concluded did constitute a separate appropriate bargaining unit, was located 10 miles from the central office. Ten miles was thus held sufficient to constitute "geographical separation."[42]

It is again suggested that although there exists no mathematical formula for determining where geographical integration ends and separation begins, the Board should be required to articulate reasons for reaching conclusions such as that in *Sav-On*. The immediate need for this requirement is further illustrated by a comparison of the above holding in *Sav-On* with that in *Equitable Life Insurance Co.*,[43] a case decided a mere 15 days prior to *Sav-On*. In *Equitable*, the petitioner had requested a unit of two of the employer's district offices which were located 28 miles apart.[44] Applying the various factors, the Board reasoned

---

[40] A complete discussion of the Board's decision in *Sav-On* and subsequent cases is presented in the section on administrative divisions, *infra*.

[41] 138 N.L.R.B. at 1035.

[42] Shortly after its decision in *Sav-On*, the Board decided Dixie Belle Mills, Inc., 139 N.L.R.B. 629 (1962) in which a majority, over the bitter dissent of Member Rodgers, concluded that 20 miles was sufficient geographical separation to grant the union's request for a single plant unit.

[43] 138 N.L.R.B. 529 (1962).

[44] Although the two district offices were located within the state of Ohio, the Board has ruled that an appropriate unit may cross state lines or cover cities in more than one state. Paxton Wholesale Grocery Co., 123 N.L.R.B. 316 (1959); Jewel Food Stores, 111 N.L.R.B. 1368 (1955); *Crown Drug Co.*, 108 N.L.R.B. 1126 (1954); Busch Kredit Jewelry Co., 97 N.L.R.B. 1386 (1952).

that each of the district offices could constitute an appropriate bargaining unit. Notwithstanding this, however, the Board granted the union's request, offering the following analysis:

> Although we have found that the individual district offices may constitute separate appropriate units, we do not believe that such a finding should preclude the grouping of such offices *where such grouping is justified by cogent geographic considerations.*[45]

The Board thus held that a distance of 28 miles constituted *geographical integration* so as to justify the combining of district offices. Fifteen days later, this same Board held that 10 miles constituted *geographical separation!* Since the Board's manipulation of the factor led in each case to a granting of the union's requests, it is no wonder that the dissent in *Equitable* was forced to conclude that the majority's decision was "based upon extent of organization." [46]

A 1964 Board decision added further confusion about the proper role of the geographical location factor. In *Frisch's Big Boy Ill-Mar, Inc.,*[47] the petitioning union requested as a bargaining unit one of the employer's eleven restaurants—ten of which were located in Indianapolis, Indiana. In a three to two decision (Members Leedom and Jenkins dissenting), the Board granted the petition on the basis of the criteria set forth in *Sav-On.* The majority conspicuously neglected to consider the geographical location of the requested restaurant. The dissent, however, sharply noted that "all 10 of the Employer's 11 restaurants are located within a few blocks of one another." It concluded that the "very factors relied on by the Board in *Sav-On* require the conclusion here that the single-restaurant unit is inappropriate." [48] One need not be a labor economist to realize that restaurants located within a "few blocks of one another" would fall, in all probability, within the same labor market, characterized by similar wages, hours, and working conditions. Geographical proximity should have been a primary consideration in the Board's decision.

---

[45] 138 N.L.R.B. at 530 (emphasis supplied).

[46] *Id.* at 531.

[47] 147 N.L.R.B. 551 (1964), *reversed and remanded*, NLRB v. Frisch's Big Boy Ill-Mar, Inc., 356 F.2d 895 (7th Cir. 1966).

[48] 147 N.L.R.B. at 554.

In January of 1970, the NLRB was confronted with an unusual, although not entirely novel, unit request. The petitioner in *Drug Fair-Community Drug Co.*[49] asserted that an appropriate bargaining unit was composed of all the employer's stores located, with one exception, within the Washington "Standard Metropolitan Statistical Area." Disagreeing, the employer maintained that the only appropriate unit would be employer-wide.[50] In support of its position, the company noted that all the recruiting, hiring, firing, and disciplining of pharmacists was performed by the central office and that wages, hours of work, and fringe benefits were centrally determined and administered. All the pharmacists throughout the chain met once to several times per year to discuss wages and fringe benefits. The proposed unit would cause a division of certain of the company's administrative districts, entirely including some and excluding others. The company further pointed to a history of seventy-five permanent or temporary employee transfers. Finally, the company argued that the use of the Standard Metropolitan Statistical Area in this case would be "an irrelevant and arbitrary geographical standard" since it would include stores up to fifty miles apart while excluding others no more than one, two, five, or ten miles from unit stores. To grant the union's request, concluded the employer, would constitute a unit determination based solely on the extent of organization.

The petitioning union—which had in the past unsuccessfully attempted to organize on an employer-wide basis—contended that the requested pharmacists shared similar economic problems, and thus a similar community of interests, because of their presence within the Washington SMSA. In addition, the petitioner asserted, other factors favoring the requested unit were "its own small size, recent organization, lack of professional staff, and consequent inability to adequately represent employees on the broader basis." [51]

Agreeing with the union's contentions, a three-member panel of the Board [52] reached the following conclusion:

[49] 180 N.L.R.B. No. 94, 73 L.R.R.M. 1065 (1969).

[50] There were 116 stores in the employer's chain employing some 300 pharmacists. The requested unit would include about 82 stores employing some 200 pharmacists. *Id.*

[51] 180 N.L.R.B. No. 94, 73 L.R.R.M. at 1066.

[52] Chairman Frank McCulloch and Members John Fanning and Gerald Brown constituted the Board panel.

In sum, and after consideration of the Employer's arguments regarding its administrative centralization and the apparently minimal transfer and interchange experience throughout the chain, we find that the appropriateness of the metropolitan area unit here proposed is supported by substantial factors of economic, demographic, social and geographic integration, and shall direct an election therein.[53]

In reaching this conclusion, the Board discussed the single issue of the applicability of a Standard Metropolitan Statistical Area as a factor in unit determinations. Contrary to the employer's contentions, it was reasoned that a unit based on a metropolitan area was "supported by substantial nonorganizational factors." The members commented, "The Bureau of the Budget has concluded that the area encompassed by the proposed unit . . . is a separately definable metropolitan entity, *presumably sharing and facing those needs and problems peculiar to such a community, and enjoying a large measure of economic and environmental integration.*" [54]

The Board's use of the Standard Metropolitan Statistical Area as a definition of the geographical location factor may be reasonably justified. In addition to providing consistency, the use of the metropolitan area can properly raise the presumption of the existence of an integrated economic and social unit. The classification is generally used to delineate probable product markets, which to some extent would affect the similarities of the labor markets.[55] The presumptions raised by the use of the metropolitan area, however, should not be considered conclusive. Where the evidence reveals that in fact the employees both within and without the area are economically and socially integrated and that there exists an overall community of interests in wages, hours, and working conditions, then this factor should not be applicable. In *Drug Fair*, the wages, hours, and working conditions were centrally determined and administered; the fringe benefits were identical for all of the firm's employees; and all the pharmacists met to discuss wages and benefits. Geographical location did not to any extent affect rates of pay, job content, professional duties, or fringe benefits. The presumption created by the Standard Metropolitan Statistical Area seems to have been rebutted.

---

[53] 180 N.L.R.B. No. 94, 73 L.R.R.M. at 1067-1068.

[54] 180 N.L.R.B. No. 94, 73 L.R.R.M. at 1067 (emphasis supplied).

[55] Note, *The Board and Section 9(c)(5)*, *supra* note 33, at 831-832.

A serious problem with the Board's decision in *Drug Fair*, as well as in other unit cases, is the lack of correlation between the chosen unit and the anticipated scope of collective bargaining. The actions of the union as representative of the employees within a given unit would also affect the employment relationship of those employees outside the unit—even where a majority of employees in the overall company had previously rejected the union. This does not fulfill the mandate of assuring to employees the fullest freedom in exercising the rights guaranteed by the Act—including the right to refrain from unionization—unless, somehow, employee freedom is equated with extent of union organization.

The geographical location factor is an appropriate standard in the determination of the collective bargaining unit. As an indicator of the existence of a common labor market and of economic and social integration, geographical location can help to insure that the unit configuration promotes harmonious and effective collective bargaining. Defining the factor so as to distinguish geographical integration from separation and to provide a consistent, realistic standard is a difficult, but not impossible task. The use of the Standard Metropolitan Statistical Area, with a recognition of its limitations, may provide a viable solution. It is essential to the proper determination of the appropriate bargaining unit, however, that the NLRB recognize the continuing effect of the unit configuration upon the scope of collective bargaining.

EMPLOYER'S ADMINISTRATIVE OR TERRITORIAL DIVISIONS

In the early part of the 1950's, the NLRB's unit decisions in multilocation situations revealed a heavy reliance upon the extent of the company's administrative divisions.[56] As with the physical proximity factor, there is a noticeable lack of articulated reasons for the applicability of such a factor.

The realities of collective bargaining encourage having the bargaining unit correspond to the administrative division. Should an employer establish a highly integrated, centralized operation

---

[56] Drug Fair-Community Drug Co., 180 N.L.R.B. No. 94, 73 L.R.R.M. 1065 (1969); Jewel Food Stores, 111 N.L.R.B. 1368 (1955); Father & Son Shoe Stores, Inc., 117 N.L.R.B. 1479 (1957); Sparkle Markets Co., 113 N.L.R.B. 790 (1955); Safeway Stores, Inc., 96 N.L.R.B. 998 (1951).

in which decisions pertaining to wages, hours, and working conditions come from a single administrative office, it would be both reasonable and efficient to have the bargaining unit consist of those employees who are affected by such decisions.[57] If, as in many of the larger corporations and conglomerates, the organization is one of decentralized administrative subdivisions, then the appropriate bargaining unit should correspond to these divisional units. The most frequently encountered situation, however, usually involves neither of these clear extremes. Generally, there is an overlap of labor relations responsibilities between the division managers and the central office. In such a situation, the Board should compare the relative responsibilities and designate as appropriate that unit which most closely corresponds to the division having primary control over those matters which are subject to the collective bargaining process. This would again serve to align the size of the unit with the anticipated scope of collective bargaining.

Prior to the advent of the Kennedy Board, the administrative division factor was used with the realization of the interrelationship of unit configuration and effective, continuing collective bargaining. Illustrative of this is the frequently cited case of *Paxton Wholesale Grocery Co.*[58] Of the 38 retail food stores operated by the firm, the petitioning union requested 10 separate units, each limited to the meat department employees of the individual stores. The employer contended that the only appropriate unit should consist of the meat department employees in all the stores. Agreeing with this contention, the Board specifically noted that pricing and labor relations policies for the entire chain were determined and administered by the central office, which also controlled all hiring and discharges. Relying on these facts, the Board reached the following conclusion:

> In view of the highly centralized administration of all the Employer's stores, and as the single-store units sought by the Petitioner do not conform to any administrative division of the Employer's operations, we find that the single-store units sought are inappropriate and that a companywide unit is alone appropriate.[59]

---

[57] These considerations have been of considerable significance in the public utilities industry. *See* Western Electric Co., 98 N.L.R.B. 1018 (1952); Niagara Hudson Power Corp., 79 N.L.R.B. 1115 (1948).

[58] 123 N.L.R.B. 316 (1959).

[59] *Id.* at 317.

Decisions such as that in *Paxton* revealed an awareness of the applicability of the employer's administrative territory in the determination of the appropriate bargaining unit.

As the Board continued to make extensive use of the administrative division factor, a number of problems became apparent. When an employer establishes a territorial or administrative unit, he does so for purposes of administrative convenience and ease and not primarily for labor relations purposes. As a company's administrative and organizational needs change, so will its administrative divisions. The size of the bargaining unit cannot be expected to fluctuate as does the level of the employer's organizational units. Opponents of the use of the factor have argued that an employer could use his administrative structure to stifle union organization.

If the Board were to strictly adhere to the administrative division, the employer could structure his firm so as to keep the bargaining units large and thus impede union organization. This argument, however, finds little support in the realities of the market place. First, the organizational structure of today's large firms is so essential to efficient and economic management that to disregard all but the potential labor relations effects of the structure would be to place the firm in financial jeopardy. It would seem that such an employer would prefer the quick death of closing his firm to the slow, agonizing death of financial ruin. Secondly, the NLRB has not, and does not, use this factor as the sole criterion for establishing a particular bargaining unit. "Indeed, where common supervision is cogent, it is usually because other factors, such as common skills or conditions, proximity, or interchange, are present." [60] Nevertheless, in 1962, the Kennedy Board, allegedly in response to these criticisms, drastically altered the effects of the administrative division factor in the choice of bargaining units.

New Use of the Factor

The alteration of the applicability of the administrative division factor occurred in a case involving the retail chain store industry. The case, *Sav-On Drugs, Inc.*,[61] concerned a petition

---

[60] Hall, *supra* note 25, at 493. Illustrative of the Board's use of the administrative division factor in conjunction with other unit factors, see Father & Son Shoe Stores, Inc., 117 N.L.R.B. 1479 (1957).

[61] 138 N.L.R.B. 1032 (1962). The relevance of this case to the geographical location factor is discussed in the preceding section of this chapter.

filed by the Retail Clerks International requesting a unit comprised of all employees located at the employer's Edison, New Jersey store. Disagreeing, the employer contended that the appropriate unit should be all nine of its stores located in New Jersey and New York, which constituted an administrative subdivision of the parent corporation. Dismissing the petition, the regional director relied on earlier Board decisions and concluded that "in cases involving retail chainstore operations, absent unusual circumstances, the appropriate unit for collective bargaining should embrace employees of all stores located within an employer's administrative division or geographic area." [62] On review, a majority of the full Board reversed the regional director's decision on the basis that the earlier policy had frequently served to impede the employees' right of self-organization as guaranteed by section 7 of the NLRA. It was reasoned that the policy of adhering to the administrative division "has ignored completely as a factor the extent to which the claiming labor organization had sought to organize the employees of the retail chain." [63] Consequently, the future unit determinations in retail chain operations would be made "in the light of all the circumstances of the case." [64] In the circumstances of the present case, the majority felt compelled to grant the union's petition.

Member Rodgers, the lone dissenter in *Sav-On*, would have affirmed the regional director's decision and continued to adhere to earlier Board precedent. He perceptively commented:

> I certainly have no desire to frustrate the employees' right to self-organization. But that right must be accomodated by the Board to the prohibition in Section 9(c)(5) of the Act, that, in deciding the unit appropriate for the purposes of collective bargaining, "the extent to which employees have organized shall not be controlling." In short, what the present change specifies, in my opinion, is that the union's extent of organization has now become, and will be, a decisive factor in determining the appropriate unit for retail store operations. [65]

The fears expressed by Member Rodgers were soon to be proved well founded.

---

[62] *Id.* at 1033.

[63] *Id.*

[64] *Id.*

[65] *Id.* at 1037.

In the case of *Dixie Belle Mills, Inc.*,[66] the NLRB reduced even farther the applicability of the employer's administrative division in unit determinations. Based on facts similar to those in *Sav-On*, a majority of the Board, reversing the regional director, granted the union's petition and concluded that "a single-plant unit, being one of the unit types listed in the statute as appropriate for bargaining purposes, is presumptively appropriate." [67] Member Rodgers, again the lone dissenter, pointed out that the traditional factors used in unit determinations all indicated the propriety of the larger, integrated unit. Nevertheless, the majority reasoned that "even assuming that the unit urged by the Employer and found by the Regional Director here may be the most appropriate unit, this does not establish it as the only appropriate one." [68] If the traditional factors used in determining an appropriate bargaining unit dictate that the larger unit is most appropriate, on what basis could, or should, the Board find a different unit appropriate? Member Rodgers' prediction that extent of organization would become a controlling factor appears to find substantial support in the majority's decision.

The subsequent unit cases soon revealed that the Board firmly adopted the ruling in *Sav-On* that single-store units would be presumptively appropriate. The administrative division factor, it was thought, had been relegated to a position of minor importance. In May of 1963, however, the Board decided *Weis Markets, Inc.*,[69] which involved a union request for two separate bargaining units. One unit was to consist of employees at two of the employer's stores located in Lancaster, Pennsylvania, while the other unit was to include the employees located in four stores in York, Pennsylvania.

Contesting the appropriateness of these units, the employer relied on the holding in *Sav-On* that single-store units were presumptively appropriate in retail chain operations. The Board, however, disagreed with the employer and stated that its holding in *Sav-On* did not abandon the use of employer's administrative territory as a factor, but rather merely added other possible configurations as appropriate bargaining units. Administrative division, it concluded, has been and continues to be an important criterion in unit determinations.

---

[66] 139 N.L.R.B. 629 (1962).

[67] *Id.* at 631.

[68] *Id.*

[69] 142 N.L.R.B. 708 (1963).

The Board's decision in *Weis* created substantial problems and confusion. On one hand, the Board declared that administrative units were to be considered important factors. But on the other hand, the decision in *Weis* revealed a disregard for this criterion. The employer argued that his administrative chain consisted of all six stores and that there was no division in terms of administration between the York and Lancaster stores. While admitting this to be true, the Board concluded that the union's petitions should be granted because of geographical separation.[70] The factors, it would appear, were manipulated so as to support a desired conclusion.

The extent and consequences of this manipulation were revealed in the 1964 case of *Frisch's Big Boy Ill-Mar, Inc.*[71] The petitioner had requested representation rights at one of the employer's ten stores located in Indianapolis. Rejecting the employer's contention that all ten stores constituted an appropriate administrative unit, the Board stated that its decision in *Sav-On* had *abandoned* the policy of using this as a primary factor! It concluded that based on all the relevant circumstances the single restaurant—although not the most appropriate—was an appropriate unit. The union's petition was granted.

Members Leedom and Jenkins dissented, alleging that the "very factors relied on by the Board in *Sav-On* require the conclusion here that the single-restaurant unit is inappropriate." [72] After reviewing these various factors, the two dissenters concluded:

> But since, as we have shown, no other factors support the appropriateness of the single restaurant, this determination rests solely on the Petitioner's extent of organization, a result which is specifically forbidden by Section 9(c)(5) of the Act.[73]

Leedom and Jenkins were aware of the fact that the unit size chosen by the majority would have an effect on the interests of the employees in the remaining nine stores. The single unit was too narrow for the anticipated scope of collective bargaining. The NLRA's mandate of providing the "fullest freedom" applies to all employees and not just those that the petitioning union thinks it can successfully organize.

---

[70] *Id.* at 710.

[71] 147 N.L.R.B. 551 (1964), *reversed and remanded,* NLRB v. Frisch's Big Boy Ill-Mar, Inc., 356 F.2d 895 (7th Cir. 1966).

[72] 147 N.L.R.B. at 554.

[73] *Id.* at 556.

The alterations on the applicability of the administrative division factor have been of considerable significance in unit determinations. The evolution from *Sav-On* to *Frisch* appears to have firmly entrenched the presumption of the appropriateness of the single-store bargaining unit. In certain multilocation cases, however, such as *Weis Markets*, the Board, or at least a majority thereof, has seen fit to disregard the presumption. Furthermore, in a considerable number of single-location cases, the NLRB has been willing to "carve out" smaller units from the single-store unit. For example, in the 1963 case of *F. W. Woolworth Co.*,[74] the Board, in a three to two decision, granted the union's petition for representation rights in a unit composed of employees of one department of the employer's retail variety store. This request was granted despite the fact that all store employees were hired under the same processing procedure, received the same starting hourly wage, vacation period, sick leave, holidays, pensions and discount benefits, and punched the same timeclock. It is no wonder that the dissenters bitterly commented that

> It appears to us that this is simply the latest in a series of cases in which our colleagues have held that arbitrary groupings of employees, obviously based solely on the Union's extent of organization, constitute appropriate units for the purposes of collective bargaining.[75]

Notwithstanding these remarks, a majority of the Board continued to grant union requests by carving out units in spite of the single-store presumption.[76]

Judicial Reaction

The National Labor Relations Act provides that any party "aggrieved by a final order" of the NLRB may obtain review in any United States court of appeals.[77] Since bargaining unit determinations are not "final orders," however, the employer opposed to a Board ruling must first commit an unfair labor prac-

---

[74] 144 N.L.R.B. 307 (1963).

[75] *Id.* at 310. Members Rodgers and Leedom dissenting.

[76] In 1965, the Board decided three companion cases in which approval was given to separate units of selling, non-selling, restaurant, and clerical employees in retail department stores. Lord & Taylor, 150 N.L.R.B. 812 (1965); Allied Stores d/b/a Stern's, 150 N.L.R.B. 799 (1965); Arnold Constable Corp., 150 N.L.R.B. 788 (1965).

[77] 29 U.S.C.A. § 160(f).

tice by refusing to bargain with the union. Once in a proper judicial forum, the opponent of a Board unit ruling is faced with considerable obstacles. The Supreme Court has noted that a judicial forum is not well equipped to apply intensive review of bargaining unit decisions. Therefore, the high court has held that unit decisions, because they involve a "large measure of informed discretion" are "rarely to be disturbed." [78] Notwithstanding this stringent restriction, a number of circuit courts have provided close scrutiny of Board decisions. The Circuit Court for the District of Columbia recently set forth what may properly be considered the applicable standard of review with respect to bargaining unit determinations:

> A court obviously should not examine a unit determination of the Board with a disposition to substitute its own judgment for that of the Board if it finds that it might have preferred the selection of an alternative unit. Instead, a court must review the Board's decision to see, first, whether the Board has articulated the factors which underlie its choice of a unit; and, second, to see whether those factors, when viewed against the backdrop of other Board decisions and a statute which has given the agency broad discretion in the performance of a difficult task, are sufficiently substantial to dispel an impression of unreasoned arbitrariness and to negate an inference that "extent of organization" was the primary basis for the Board's action. [79]

The articulation of the relevant factors, the first criterion for the court to apply, obviously presents little problem for the Board. Recently, however, a growing number of circuit courts have begun to question the "arbitrariness" of the Board's unit decisions.

One of the most frequently referred to disputes between Board and court occurred in a case involving Purity Food Stores. The company consisted of seven supermarket operations all located in Massachusetts and characterized by a high degree of centralization. Relying on the single store presumption of *Sav-On*, the NLRB granted the union's petition for a unit comprised of one of the seven stores. [80] On appeal to the First Circuit Court of Appeals enforcement was denied. [81] The Court criticized the Board

---

[78] Packard Motor Car Co. v. NLRB, 330 U.S. 485, 491 (1947).

[79] NLRB v. Adams Drug Co., 414 F.2d 1194, 1201 (D.C. Cir. 1969).

[80] Purity Food Stores, Inc., 150 N.L.R.B. 1523 (1965).

[81] NLRB v. Purity Food Stores, Inc., 354 F.2d 926 (1st Cir. 1965).

for having misread and misused the facts (see Table, p. 31) and for having totally disregarded the importance of the centralized control. The Court sharply commented:

> If [the Board's opinion] was a singling out of those particular facts which, in [its] opinion, justified treating the Peabody store as a single unit, some of them were so expressed, or limited, as to give the wrong impression; . . . some of them were materially incomplete; . . . and some seem almost totally insignificant. Furthermore, to isolate some facts, and omit others some of them at least comparable, and some seemingly of much greater importance than some mentioned, is, *per se*, a failure to view even the recited facts in context.[82]

The Circuit Court referred the case back to the Board for reconsideration. The NLRB, with no new findings of fact nor admissions of error, reaffirmed the appropriateness of the single-store unit.[83] On appeal, the First Circuit Court again denied enforcement.[84] The Supreme Court subsequently denied the Board's writ of certiorari.[85]

Shortly after the First Circuit's decision in *Purity*, it was suggested that the decision constituted a rejection of the *Sav-On* presumption and a resurrection of the importance of the administrative division factor. The First Circuit, however, soon offered its own interpretation. In the case of *Banco Credito y Ahorro Ponceno*,[86] the NLRB found as appropriate one of the bank's twenty-nine branches. On appeal to the First Circuit, the employer argued that "the evidence of its island-wide, integrated centrally controlled system, with uniform policies and standards and corresponding lack of authority in local branch managers precluded the Board from making substantiated findings that one branch was an appropriate unit." [87] Disagreeing, the Court affirmed the Board's decision, stating, "Our own decision in *NLRB* v. *Purity Food Stores, Inc.* . . . does not stand for the proposition that central policy-making in a chain precludes a

---

[82] *Id.* at 930.

[83] Purity Food Stores, Inc., 160 N.L.R.B. 651 (1966).

[84] NLRB v. Purity Food Stores, Inc., 376 F.2d 497 (1st Cir. 1967).

[85] NLRB v. Purity Food Stores, Inc., 389 U.S. 959 (1968).

[86] 167 N.L.R.B. 397 (1967).

[87] Banco Credito y Ahorro Ponceno v. NLRB, 390 F.2d 110, 111 (1st Cir. 1968), *cert. denied*, 393 U.S. 832 (1968).

THE PURITY FOOD STORES CASE

Question: Is the Single Peabody Store of this Supermarket Chain an Appropriate Bargaining Unit?

The Facts as Alleged by the NLRB	*The Facts as Found by the U. S. Court of Appeals, First Circuit*
1. NLRB refers to "following relevant facts."	Court remarks that if this is a backhand ruling that all unmentioned facts are not relevant, it is clearly erroneous.
2. That employer advertises in different area newspapers which do not list name and location of all stores of the chain.	When advertising in Boston papers and radio stations all seven stores are listed.
3. Store hours vary among 7 stores.	Hours are determined exclusively by President who spends considerable time in each store.
4. Management of each store determines number of employees.	No basis for this finding. Determined jointly by store executive and local manager on a formula basis uniform for all stores and volume figures issued by central office.
5. Persons employed at Peabody store are hired there and must fill out application there.	Only for some persons is this true. Application is local only to extent employment may be, and application is uniform, supplied by central office.
6. Almost all part-time employees, who comprise 50 percent of Peabody store's work force, come from Peabody area.	Court feels the important corps of employees are the full-timers.
7. Operations of store under direct control of store manager and store supervisor.	Store supervisor a central office man with duties throughout chain. Meat, produce and delicatessen operators controlled by central office.
8. Store supervisor and manager have direct control over hiring.	Not so as mentioned above.

PURITY (*continued*)

The Facts as Alleged by the NLRB	The Facts as Found by the U. S. Court of Appeals, First Circuit
9. And over discharge.	Store supervisor, the central office executive does nearly all firing. None done at local level without at least consultation.
10. Vacation schedules are based on departmental seniority within the store.	Only partially true. *Length* of vacation based on company-wide system. All lists cleared through home office.
11. Time records of employees at Peabody store are kept and totaled there and forwarded to main office for payroll purposes.	"Significance of this escapes us."
12. Four office employees at Peabody store who perform clerical work for Peabody store only.	If this is of any significance, the correct number is three.
13. Other than fresh meat and dairy products, merchandise ordered by individual stores directly from vendors and warehouses with quantity ordered left to discretion of individual store management.	Other than produce also. Erroneous if this is to imply individual store discretion as to brands, quality etc. Determined by central office. Central office also determines placement, display and arrangement of merchandise in every store. Entire meaning of phrase is that local management is responsible to see that shelves do not get empty.
14. In a two-year period there were 118 employee transfers to or from Peabody store.	Neglects to include fact that some regularly divide work between two or more stores and work basic week in one and overtime in another.

Source: H. R. Northrup and G. R. Storholm, *Restrictive Labor Practices in the Supermarket Industry* (Philadelphia: Industrial Research Unit, Wharton School of Finance and Commerce, University of Pennsylvania, 1967), pp. 152-153.

single unit determination." [88] Although some commentators consider the Court's statement to constitute a serious deemphasis of the holding in *Purity*, a broad factual distinction between the two cases can be made. The branch bank involved in *Banco* was distinct from the other branches in that it was not involved in any employee transfers, maintained its own records, and was located a considerable distance away. Nevertheless, the decision of the First Circuit Court does leave open to question the future effects of the *Purity* decision. [89]

The opinion rendered by the NLRB in *Frisch*, discussed above, was appealed by the employer to the Seventh Circuit Court of Appeals. [90] Reversing the decision, the Court based its opinion on the invalidity of the Board's factual analysis. Contesting the credibility of the Board's conclusion that each restaurant manager had autonomous powers, it was found "that the decisions left to the managers do not involve any *significant element of judgement as to employment relations.*" [91]

The distinctions between the Board and Court decisions in *Frisch* readily illustrate the serious and extremely difficult problem of determining what powers the local manager must possess in order to support the appropriateness of the single-plant unit. Since in the majority of industrial settings control of industrial relations issues is diffused throughout various corporate levels, the Board will have no problem in pointing to "certain powers" justifying a particular administrative division so as to support a union requested unit. Such a situation was recently confronted by the Fifth Circuit Court in *NLRB* v. *Davis Cafeteria, Inc.* [92]

In *Davis*, the employer owned and operated eight restaurants in the Miami area, which constituted an administrative division. The NLRB had granted the union's request for representation rights in two of the eight stores. On appeal, the Fifth Circuit denied enforcement because the Board "has failed to disclose the

---

[88] 390 F.2d at 112.

[89] In *Banco*, the First Circuit made specific reference to the relationship between unit size and effective collective bargaining. Thus, although the Board and Court may have come to the same conclusion, it is doubtful that their reasoning was the same. See NLRB v. Capital Bakers, Inc., 351 F.2d 45 (3rd Cir. 1965) and the Board's decision on remand, Capital Bakers, Inc., 168 N.L.R.B. No. 119, 66 L.R.R.M. 1385 (1967).

[90] 356 F.2d 895 (7th Cir. 1966).

[91] *Id.* at 897 (emphasis supplied).

[92] 396 F.2d 18 (5th Cir. 1968).

basis for its order." [93] The Board, however, reaffirmed its earlier decision on the basis of the autonomous authority of the restaurant managers.[94] Again denying enforcement,[95] the Circuit Court commented that the important determinations pertaining to labor policies, wages, and working conditions were made by the central office. The Court concluded that "where local managers do not have authority to decide questions which would be subjects of collective bargaining, the two respondent cafeterias do not constitute an appropriate bargaining unit." [96] A comparison of the Board and Court decisions again reveal that the agency, by pointing to "certain powers" possessed by local managers, is able to support almost any unit configuration. The courts, unlike the Board, compare the *relative* responsibilities of the corporate officials to determine which group controls and administers those matters which are proper subjects of collective bargaining. This subtle but important distinction was clearly brought out in the recent case of *NLRB* v. *Solis Theatre Corp.*[97]

Interboro Circuit, Inc. owned fifteen theatres located throughout New York. Solis Theatre Corporation operated one of the three theatres located in the Bronx. The United Independent Theatre Employees Union requested representation rights for the employees of the one theatre operated by Solis. The Board's order granting the union's petition was appealed to the Second Circuit Court of Appeals which subsequently denied enforcement.

A comparison of the opinions offered by the Board and Court reveals, at best, negligible differences. In fact, not only did the Court espouse the same applicable principles as the Board, but it also agreed with the latter's findings of fact. Specifically, in ruling the single theatre to be an appropriate unit, the Board relied on the fact that the local manager had the right to discipline and reprimand employees, interview job applicants, and recommend vacation schedules. The Court, nevertheless, denied enforcement because "the Courts of Appeals have been reluctant to sanction bargaining units whose managers lack the authority to resolve issues which would be the subject of collective bargain-

---

[93] NLRB v. Davis Cafeteria, Inc., 358 F.2d 98, 100 (5th Cir. 1966).

[94] Davis Cafeteria, Inc., 160 N.L.R.B. 1141 (1966).

[95] 396 F.2d 18 (5th Cir. 1968).

[96] *Id.* at 21.

[97] 403 F.2d 381 (2nd Cir. 1968).

ing." [98] In this case, the Court noted, "It is of marked significance that Interboro sets a single labor policy for the entire circuit, which has resulted in similar wages, hours and working conditions for all of its employees." [99]

The decisions coming from the various courts of appeals [100] reveal what is submitted to be the basic problem with the Board's application of the administrative division factor. A proper application of the factor entails an examination, not of the employer's verbal delineation of territories, but rather of the existing corporate structure to determine where the control of labor policies is situated. Furthermore, labor policies should be defined in terms of wages, hours, and working conditions—that is, those issues which are the proper subjects of collective bargaining. It is at this juncture that the courts and Board have differed. The complexities of today's large corporate structures dictate that all levels of management have *some* control over labor relations issues. In its determination of the administrative division, the Board has consistently pointed to "certain powers" possessed by a particular manager to support its decisions. If the Board is allowed to designate a particular division on the basis of an arbitrary picking and choosing of powers, then, in effect, we are allowing the Board to predetermine a unit size and to justify it by the use of this factor.

If, however, the responsibilities and authority granted to each level of management are examined on a comparative basis—that is, the relative control of labor policies—and applied to determine which level has primary authority over those issues subject to collective bargaining, then the ultimate unit configuration will correspond more closely to the anticipated scope of collective bargaining. To say that a certain level of management has "managerial authority" is not sufficient. The arbitrary picking and choosing of powers and the consideration of authority in an absolute as opposed to a relative manner has allowed the Board to

---

[98] *Id.* at 383.

[99] *Id.* In April of 1969, the Second Circuit decided Continental Ins. Co. v. NLRB, 409 F.2d 727 (2nd Cir. 1969) in which the following analysis of the *Solis* decision was offered: "The holding of *Solis Theatres*, therefore, is that the Board may not, without substantial justification, fractionate a multi-unit operation whose labor policy is centrally directed and administered." *Id.* at 729.

[100] *See also* NLRB v. Harry T. Campbell Sons' Corp., 407 F.2d 969 (1st Cir. 1969), *denying enforcement of the Board's decision in* Harry T. Campbell Sons' Corp., 164 N.L.R.B. 247 (1967).

"substantiate" almost any unit size it desires. That such a power should not be given to an administrative agency was recognized by Chief Justice Hughes who said that "An unscrupulous administrator might be tempted to say 'Let me find the facts for the people of my country, and I care little who lays down the general principles.' " [101]

The NLRB's Response

Judicial criticism of the misuse of the administrative division factor has had little noticeable effect upon the National Labor Relations Board. In fact, the Board has noted that a majority of circuit courts have enforced the agency's rulings.[102] These statistics, it is argued, demonstrate judicial support for the expansion of the *Sav-On* doctrine.[103] The Board's contention is tenuous, at best. An analysis of the various favorable circuit court decisions reveals support not for the policies and rulings of the NLRB, but rather for the Supreme Court's mandate of a limited scope of judicial review.[104] Notwithstanding this, the controversy between support or nonsupport by the judiciary is somewhat moot. In late 1968, the Board decided *Haag Drug Co.*[105] in which it was specifically held that those court decisions which had denied enforcement of a Board award were unequivocally rejected.

Haag Drug involved a petition filed by the Hotel and Restaurant Employees and Bartenders Union, AFL-CIO, requesting a ruling that one of the employer's eleven restaurants constituted an appropriate bargaining unit. Sustaining the petition, the Board reviewed the development of its *Sav-On* policy and again concluded that a single-store unit in a retail chain "is presumptively an appropriate unit for bargaining." With respect to the

---

[101] Kostel Corp., 172 N.L.R.B. No. 167 (1968).

[102] NLRB v. Sun Drug Co., 359 F.2d 408 (3rd Cir. 1966), *enforcing* 147 N.L.R.B. 669 (1964); NLRB v. Merner Lumber & Hardware Co., 345 F.2d 770 (9th Cir. 1965), *enforcing* 145 N.L.R.B. 1024 (1964), *cert. denied*, 382 U.S. 942 (1966); NLRB v. Primrose Super Market, Inc., 353 F.2d 675 (1st Cir. 1965), *enforcing* 148 N.L.R.B. 610 (1964), *cert. denied*, 382 U.S. 830 (1966).

[103] J. H. Fanning, "Representation Law: A Responsive Approach to the Exercise of Employee Rights," delivered at the Pacific Coast Labor Law Conference, Seattle, April 18, 1969. Reported in *Daily Labor Report* No. 75 (April 18, 1969).

[104] Packard Motor Car Co. v. NLRB, 330 U.S. 485 (1947) wherein the Court ruled that Board unit decisions should be disturbed only if they are found to be arbitrary and unreasonable.

[105] 169 N.L.R.B. No. 111 (1968).

administrative division factor, it was reasoned that despite the holdings in *Purity* and *Frisch* centralized administration "is of little significance in determining the question," but that "substantial autonomy" in the local manager is extremely relevant. But does not the latter really affect the existence of the former? The Board, by defining centralized administration in terms of centralized bookkeeping, purchasing, merchandising, and other non-employee related activities, was able to divorce the two concepts. Indeed, should one adopt the definition proffered by the Board, then the conclusion that the factor is insignificant must logically follow. Previous Board and court decisions, however, have defined centralized administration, as it relates to bargaining unit determinations, in terms of wages, hours, and working conditions and other matters which are proper subjects of collective bargaining. The significance of the factor thus defined is undeniable. A proper application of this factor would help to delinate a unit coextensive with the scope of collective bargaining and not, as some unit cases indicate, with the extent of union organization.[106]

In *Haag Drug*, the NLRB also directed itself to the question of the degree of conclusiveness of the single store presumption. Specifically, it was held,

> That presumption is of course not a conclusive one and may be overcome where factors are present in a particular case which would counter the appropriateness of a single-store unit.[107]

Typical of the factors that could rebut the presumption of the single store would be: 1) an existing stable bargaining relationship; 2) no meaningful identity as a self-contained economic unit; 3) day-to-day supervision by central office officials; 4) there exists substantial employee interchange distinctive of homogeneity; or 5) a combination of these factors.

Thus, in holding the single store presumption to be a rebuttable one, the Board provided itself with flexibility and the em-

---

[106] The NLRB has generally adhered to the principles enumerated in *Haag*: U-Tote-Em Grocery Co., 185 N.L.R.B. No. 6 (1970) (3 of 11 stores held to be an appropriate unit); Kostel Corp., 172 N.L.R.B. No. 167 (1968) (one of seventeen retail stores was held to be an appropriate bargaining unit); May Dept. Stores, 175 N.L.R.B. No. 97 (1968) (each of three of the employer's twelve stores designated as appropriate units); Grand Union Co., 176 N.L.R.B. No. 28 (1968) (the Board relied on *Haag* to find one of six stores which constituted an administrative division to be an appropriate unit).

[107] 169 N.L.R.B. No. 111 (1968).

ployer with an opportunity to contest a requested unit configuration.[108] *Star Market Co.*[109] is illustrative of the elements necessary to defeat a representation position. The Amalgamated Meat Cutters requested as an appropriate unit one of the five retail food stores which together constituted the employer's New Hampshire division. Dismissing the petition, the Board held that the employer had successfully rebutted the *Sav-On* presumption. Specifically, it was found that the local store managers had very little authority in personnel matters, the division supervisors exercised direct supervision over the stores, and there was a high degree of geographical integration and employee interchange. In fact, the record in *Star Market* revealed that each of the employer's divisional headquarters had extensive control and direction of their divisions' labor policies.

The Board's decisions in *Star Market* and in subsequent cases holding the presumption to have been rebutted give little cause for exaltation.[110] As noted earlier, most of today's large corporations authorize different levels of management to decide different aspects of labor policy. Those companies which successfully overcame the *Sav-On* presumption were characterized by an exceptionally high degree of centralized control. Moreover, recent unit decisions of the NLRB indicate an attempt to expand the single store presumption to industries other than retail chain operations. The policies enunciated in *Sav-On* have since been held applicable to warehouse operations,[111] the photocopy indus-

---

[108] The rebuttable nature of the single store presumption has also proven to be useful to unions attempting to "carve out" units from a single store. In a recent presentation, Board Member John Fanning offered the following analysis:

> The statutory policy of assuring employees the fullest freedom to exercise their Section 7 rights has also led in the department store field to certification of smaller units and separate groups or departments of employees. For many years the Board has consistently held that storewide voting was the optimum in the industry and had carved out from the storewide unit only "homogeneous" groups of employees possessing a community of interests by reason of their distinctive skills.

Fanning, *supra* note 103, at D-2.

[109] 172 N.L.R.B. No. 130 (1968).

[110] The single store presumption was successfully rebutted in the following cases: Allied Stores, 175 N.L.R.B. No. 162 (1969); Frankel Shops, Inc., N.L.R.B. Case No. 29-RC-1139 (1969); Matt's Shop-Rite, Inc., 174 N.L.R.B. No. 157 (1969); Pep Boys, 172 N.L.R.B. No. 23 (1968).

[111] Amfac, Inc., —— N.L.R.B. ——. Reported in *Retail Labor Report* No. 1013 (November 29, 1969).

try,[112] the automobile service industry,[113] utilities,[114] and the banking industry.[115]

The NLRB's unit decisions reveal seemingly inconsistent applications of the administrative division factor. The Board's opinions have verbalized what the courts and Congress have demanded, but the application of the factor indicates a disregard for the practical problems of a continuing collective bargaining relationship. The "new use" of the administrative division factor combined with the complexities of the average corporate structure have allowed the Board to point to any given level of management and conclude that therein lies "substantial autonomy." This arbitrariness, or what the Board members might call "flexibility," has led many labor authorities to contend that unions are able to obtain any unit configuration they so desire. As one trial examiner sarcastically commented, "When and if the Board adopts a unit policy based on 'what the union wants, the union gets' the work of Trial Examiners will be expedited." [116]

FUNCTIONAL INTEGRATION

A frequently used factor in both multilocation and single-location unit determination cases is the degree of functional integration of the employer's operations. The nature of the particular production processes may have substantial impact on the overall employment pattern.

If an employer utilizes a continuous flow process, the employees at the end of the system may well have a strong community of interests with the employees at the beginning. For example, an employer may divide, for administrative purposes, his continuous flow production operation into separate departments, hypothetically Departments A and B. Under these circumstances, if the NLRB chose to ignore the high degree of functional integration and designated each department as a separate unit, the impact on harmonious industrial relations could be severe. The unionization of Department A would directly affect the employ-

---

[112] R.B.P., Inc., 176 N.L.R.B. No. 22 (1969).

[113] American Automobile Ass'n, 172 N.L.R.B. No. 131 (1968).

[114] Monongahela Power, 176 N.L.R.B. No. 123, 71 L.R.R.M. 1336 (1969).

[115] Wells Fargo Bank, 179 N.L.R.B. No. 79 (1969).

[116] Kostel Corp., 172 N.L.R.B. No. 167 (1968); decision of the Trial Examiner, Case No. 38-CA-375 (1968).

ment relationship of employees working in Department B. A lockout, strike, or even work slowdown by employees in A would have a similar effect on employees in B. The practical result is that the union representative controls the employment relationship for *all* employees, despite the fact that it was designated as representative only for employees of Department A. This hypothetical disregarding of the functional integration factor led to the creation of bargaining units which were not coextensive with the anticipated scope of collective bargaining and thus to an abridgement of employee freedom.

Fortunately, the unit decisions of the NLRB do reveal an awareness of the applicability of the functional integration factor. In *Borden Co.*,[117] the Board—despite the hiring and firing authority of plant managers, the lack of employee interchange, the prior bargaining history, and the variance of working hours based on local practices—designated as appropriate a unit consisting of twenty separate plants. The members justified their conclusion by stating that:

> Although it appears that individual plant units might well be appropriate, the integration of the Employer's operations bespeaks the appropriateness of the broad over-all unit.[118]

The integration to which the Board referred consisted of the manufacturing of the product by three of the plants, the distribution of the product to the remaining seventeen branch offices, and the final sale of the product by these branches.

Although it appears unlikely that the current members of the NLRB would affirm the results in *Borden*,[119] there are several recent cases which indicate an awareness of the functional integration factor. For example, in *Potter Aeronautical Corp.*,[120] the employer's operation—the manufacturing of electromechanical flowmeters—was comprised of two major departments, the machine shop and the electronics department. The machinists would first construct the outer shell of the meter and then forward it to the electronics department. The inner workings of the meter

---

[117] Borden Co., Hutchinson Ice Cream Div., 89 N.L.R.B. 227 (1950).

[118] *Id.* at 229.

[119] The decision in *Borden*, rendered in 1950, would be affected under current Board policies by the presence of the single plant presumption. See the preceding section of this chapter.

[120] 155 N.L.R.B. 1077 (1965).

would then be installed and returned to the machine shop for final processing. Pursuant to a petition requesting an election of machine shop employees only, the Board ruled that it was unable to find sufficient distinction between the two departments to justify separate bargaining units. This decision was based upon

> the high degree of functional integration of the Employer's machine shop department with its other production department, as evidenced by the fact that the various components of the Employer's products pass back and forth between employees in both the machine shop and electronics department in the normal course of manufacture and assembly. . . .[121]

The decisions in *Borden* and *Potter* illustrate the proper use of the functional integration factor. Not all Board cases, however, are consistent with this application. In *S. D. Warren Co.*,[122] a 1963 case, the International Association of Machinists (IAM) and the International Brotherhood of Electrical Workers (IBEW) requested a bargaining unit consisting of employees of the engineering division of the employer's paper mill operation. In a two to one decision, the Board granted the petition on the grounds that the requested unit constituted a distinct administrative division. Notwithstanding the fact that the entire plant operation worked on an assembly-line, continuous flow system, the majority concluded that the degree of integration was not such "as to preclude the establishment of a unit other than one plantwide in scope." [123]

Member Leedom, the lone dissenter, argued that the chosen unit configuration was completely without "functional homogeneity." He reasoned that the majority's use of the administrative division as the controlling factor was incorrect in that the unit chosen excluded certain employees who were part of the division.[124] The facts led the dissenter in *Warren* to conclude that his colleagues' decision represented "an arbitrary grouping with no rational foundation." [125]

---

[121] *Id.* at 1079.

[122] 144 N.L.R.B. 204 (1963), *aff'd on other grounds*, S. D. Warren Co. v. NLRB, 353 F.2d 494 (1st Cir. 1965).

[123] 144 N.L.R.B. at 208.

[124] The majority's reliance on the administrative division factor is also questionable in view of the Board's earlier decision in *Sav-On Drugs*, discussed in the preceding section.

[125] 144 N.L.R.B. at 209.

The majority decision in *S. D. Warren* failed to consider a basic purpose in utilizing functional integration as a factor in bargaining unit determinations. As one commentator recently contended: "It is submitted that what is really behind the functional integration factor is the possibility that a work stoppage by one group will tie up the employees in the other groups." [126] In *Warren*, should the IAM and IBEW call for a strike, the company would be forced to cease all operations. Moreover, the wages, hours, and working conditions negotiated with the union for the unit employees would most certainly affect the employment relationship for nonunit employees. The result of the Board's narrow unit determination was that all employees, including those who were *not* provided with full freedom of choice, were affected by the unionization of some of the employees. The high degree of functional integration dictated that the scope of bargaining be plantwide. The Board's choice of units in the *Warren* case was not coextensive with that scope.[127]

Truck Drivers: Functional Separation or Integration

The converse of functional integration is functional separation. As with the physical location factor, there is no precise delineation of when integration ends and separation begins. The Board apparently has used the former terminology to support an overall unit determination, and the latter to substantiate a separate unit designation.[128] Nevertheless, the functional separation factor has found some degree of importance in cases involving an attempted organization of a firm's truck drivers. Board policy in these cases has had, to say the least, a vacillating history.

Prior to 1947 and the enactment of the Taft-Hartley Amendments, the NLRB adhered to a policy which favored the overall integrated bargaining unit.[129] Severance of distinct groups, such as truck drivers, from a larger unit was generally disfavored

---

[126] Hall, *supra* note 25, at 485.

[127] For other recent cases involving the functional integration factor see: Sears, Roebuck & Co., 172 N.L.R.B. No. 132 (1968); Republican Co., 169 N.L.R.B. No. 167 (1968).

[128] General Elec. Co., 173 N.L.R.B. No. 64 (1968); Carson Pirie Scott & Co., 173 N.L.R.B. No. 48 (1968).

[129] American Can Co., 13 N.L.R.B. 1252 (1939). The policies of *American Can* and its successors are primarily applicable in craft severance cases. *See generally* Cohen, *Two Years Under Mallinckrodt: A Review of the Board's Latest Craft Unit Policy,* 20 Labor Law Journal 195 (1969).

especially when there existed a history of bargaining in a broader unit. As with most policies, the Board began to "tack on" exceptions to the general rule and allowed the severance of truck drivers from the established unit "where circumstances justified" such a severance. As it was later noted, "[I]t was the functional rather than organizational or craft skill distinctions which formed the basis for separate units of truck drivers . . . ."[130] In deciding if separate representation were warranted, the Board would examine such factors as: different compensation and fringe benefits, separate supervision, lack of integration with other employees, dissimilar training and skills, and differences in job functions.[131]

With the enactment of the Taft-Hartley Amendments in 1947, the NLRB found what it contended to be legislative approval of its liberalized exceptions to the nonseverance policy. In more readily granting separate units of truck drivers, the Board relied on section 9(b)(2) of the Amendments which provides, in part, that:

> the Board shall not . . . decide that any craft unit is inappropriate for such purposes [collective bargaining] on the ground that a different unit has been established by a prior Board determination, unless a majority of the employees in the proposed craft unit vote against separate representation.

This legislative mandate, the Board contended, represented congressional approval of separate units for distinct groupings of employees and of the use of self-determination elections.[132] On the contrary, opponents contended, section 9(b)(2) gave approval to separate units only where there existed an identifiable craft group and truck drivers could not be considered skilled craftsmen. Furthermore, such an explicit mandate was meant to be a *limitation* on the granting of severances and on the use of self-determination elections.[133]

---

[130] Kalamazoo Paper Box Corp., 136 N.L.R.B. 134, 136 (1962).

[131] Lockheed Aircraft Corp., 73 N.L.R.B. 220 (1947); Radio Corp. of America, 66 N.L.R.B. 1014 (1946); Sioux City Brewing Co., 63 N.L.R.B. 964 (1945); Sutherland Paper Co., 55 N.L.R.B. 38 (1944).

[132] Truck drivers were frequently granted self-determination elections: Star Union Products Co., 127 N.L.R.B. 1173 (1960); Reichold Chems., Inc., 126 N.L.R.B. 619 (1960); International Furniture Co., 119 N.L.R.B. 1462 (1958).

[133] The evolution and use of self-determination elections is discussed in a subsequent section of this chapter.

Notwithstanding this legal debate, the Board continued to grant separate units of truck drivers. All that was required was a showing that the requested employees constituted a true grouping of truck drivers.[134] The exceptions had become the general rule. In retrospect, one cannot help but wonder whether this "rubber stamping" of separate representation for truck drivers aided the Teamsters Union in their search for increasing economic bargaining power.

The situation continued to worsen until, in 1962, the Board undertook a major policy revision. The case, *Kalamazoo Paper Box Corp.*,[135] involved a petition filed by the International Brotherhood of Teamsters requesting severance of a unit of drivers from an existing production and maintenance unit, historically represented by the International Brotherhood of Pulp, Sulphite and Paper Mill Workers. Dismissing the petition, a majority of the Board (Chairman McCulloch and Members Brown and Fanning) reviewed the historical development of severance cases and concluded:

> In more recent times, while the Board has occasionally made references to the existence of some of these factors [differences in wages, job responsibilities, etc.] in granting severance of truck drivers from more comprehensive units, it has, for the most part, not required an affirmative showing in each case that their interests and conditions of employment substantially differed from those of other employees in the established unit. *The net result, in effect, has been tantamount to a practice of automatically granting severance to truck drivers whenever requested.*[136]

This, the majority reasoned, "is not a salutory approach toward achieving the purposes of the Act . . . ." The propriety of a separate unit of truck drivers should be determined by an examination of the various factors to assertain if the requested grouping was truly functionally distinct. Such a determination, the majority contended, should be based upon the factual situation existing in each case and not upon title, tradition, or practice.

---

[134] Beechnut Foods Div. of the Beechnut Life Savers Co., 118 N.L.R.B. 123 (1957); Allied Chem. & Dye Corp., 116 N.L.R.B. 1784 (1956); Interchemical Corp., 116 N.L.R.B. 1443 (1956); United States Smelting, Refining & Mining Co., 116 N.L.R.B. 661 (1956).

[135] 136 N.L.R.B. 134 (1962).

[136] *Id.* at 137 (emphasis supplied).

Members Leedom and Rodgers dissented, reasoning that the majority was reversing sound and settled Board policy "without coming forward with any persuasive reason for doing so."[137] The argument that prior Board decisions had failed to consider the community of interests between truck drivers and other employees was rejected by the dissenters on the grounds that neither the truck drivers nor the Teamsters Union had ever protested those rulings. (The dissenting members did not address themselves to the question of why either the union or the drivers would object to obviously favorable rulings!) In their opinion, the "predominant community of interests" was merely a reflection of the "predominant" duties and responsibilities of the employees. In *Kalamazoo*, the requested employees performed driving duties more than 50 percent of their time and thus, their predominant community of interests was distinct from nondriving personnel.

The policies proposed by the majority in *Kalamazoo* are indeed commendable.[138] Where the truck drivers and the production employees share a common community of interests as indicated by a high degree of functional integration, the overall bargaining unit should be deemed appropriate. The interrelated operations of an employer would require a plantwide scope of collective bargaining. The appropriate unit should, in such a situation, be coextensive with that scope. Alternatively, where the facts reveal a high degree of functional separation and thus separate communities of interests, the mandate of guaranteeing employee freedom of choice requires a finding of separate units. Admittedly, the Board is confronted with a delicate balancing process with the outcome dependent upon the factual situation existing in each case. Nevertheless, consistency could and should be required. Consistency of appropriate unit determinations can result from an objective application of the relevant factors within an overall policy of maintaining a coextensive relationship between unit size and scope of bargaining. The principles espoused in *Kalamazoo* could potentially provide the means for implementing this objective. Whether this potential has been realized is still doubtful.

---

[137] *Id.* at 141.

[138] What effect the bitter conflict between the AFL-CIO and the Teamsters Union had on the results in *Kalamazoo* is a matter left to conjecture.

In *Olinkraft, Inc.*,[139] decided in October of 1969, a Board majority, relying on *Kalamazoo*, denied a requested severance of truck drivers.[140] The majority found that the requested employees drove trucks 80 percent of their time and "performed nondriving functions for a substantial portion" of their remaining time. In addition, the drivers were included on a plant seniority list, had the same fringe benefits as other employees, and had the same use of plant facilities. On the basis of these facts and the considerations set forth in *Kalamazoo*, the majority in *Olinkraft* was "unable to conclude that the truck drivers herein constitute a functionally distinct group with special interests sufficiently distinguishable from those of the Employer's other employees to warrant severing them from the existing unit." [141]

Member Fanning, the lone dissenter, would have granted the union's request for severance. Factually he found that the drivers worked different hours from other employees, were away from the plant 80 percent of their time, and "normally" had enough driving to keep them busy away from the plant. With respect to the considerations of *Kalamazoo*, in which Member Fanning was in the majority, he reasoned:

> It was our stated purpose to require an affirmative showing other than job classification before granting a separate unit to truck-drivers seeking severance. Automatic severance from established units was to be avoided. However, it was also our avowed purpose *not* to *deny* severance to functionally distinct groups of drivers.[142]

From the facts presented in *Olinkraft*, it would appear that severance might properly have been granted. The opinion of the majority indicates a policy which would appear to favor the denial of most severance requests.[143] Although a policy disfavoring severance may be justified by the problems created by fragmented bargaining units,[144] a compromise is necessary. The pro-

---

139 179 N.L.R.B. No. 61, 72 L.R.R.M. 1337 (1969).

140 This request was made pursuant to a petition filed by the Miscellaneous Drivers and Helpers Union, an affiliate of the International Brotherhood of Teamsters

141 179 N.L.R.B. No. 61, 72 L.R.R.M. at 1337.

142 179 N.L.R.B. No. 61, 72 L.R.R.M. at 1338.

143 The related issue of craft severances is discussed in Chapter III, *infra*.

144 The disastrous consequences of fragmented bargaining units can be seen by an examination of the newspaper, maritime, or railroad industries.

motion of effective collective bargaining must be viewed in light of the need to preserve employee freedom of association.

Application of the Factor

The functional integration factor should play a significant role in the determination of the appropriate bargaining unit. It was initially believed that the 1962 decision in *Kalamazoo* constituted a recognition of this significance, not only with respect to truck drivers, but in all unit determination cases. Unfortunately, this has not been the situation. Decisions such as in *Olinkraft* create serious doubt as to the Board's application of the factor. Furthermore, other recent unit cases reveal a questionable adherence to the functional integration factor in situations involving production employees.

In 1967, for example, the Board was confronted with a unit determination involving a highly integrated stone quarry operation.[145] The petitioning union had requested an election to be held in a unit composed of employees in the calcite operation of the Harry T. Campbell Sons' Corporation. In opposition, the employer argued that the requested unit was inappropriate because of the high degree of integration of the entire quarry operations. The NLRB disagreed with the employer and granted the union's petition. On review, the Fourth Circuit Court of Appeals denied enforcement.[146] After criticizing the Board for both deemphasizing and disregarding important factual considerations, the Court concluded:

> Because of the integrated and interdependent nature of the Texas operations a labor dispute at calcite would undoubtedly severely disrupt the operations of the remaining facilities, causing economic hardship to employees not involved in the dispute but dependent upon the uninterrupted functioning of the quarry operations. This is neither the encouragement of stable collective bargaining nor is it collective freedom of choice as contemplated by the Act.[147]

The Fourth Circuit's decision, unlike the Board's, considered the applicability of the functional integration factor. The Court realized that a primary objective of the factor is to eliminate

---

[145] Harry T. Campbell Sons' Corp., 164 N.L.R.B. 247 (1967).

[146] NLRB v. Harry T. Campbell Sons' Corp., 407 F.2d 969 (4th Cir. 1969).

[147] *Id.* at 979.

the possibility that a work stoppage by one group of employees would seriously affect other groups. The National Labor Relations Act specifically forbids most forms of secondary boycotts.[148] The NLRB, by disregarding functional integration in their unit decisions, is indirectly promoting secondary effects of labor disputes. The Act's policy of promoting employee freedom of choice cannot be used to justify this result. As the Court of Appeals noted, the nation's labor laws contemplate the protection of *all* employees and not merely those requested by the petitioning union. The NLRB's decision in *Campbell* created a "fictional mold" and, in the language of the Court, "such a determination 'could only create a state of chaos rather than foster stable collective bargaining' because in the 'fictional mold' the prospects of fruitful bargaining are overshadowed by the prospects of a breakdown in bargaining." [149] The Congress of the United States could never have intended such a result.

INTERCHANGE OF EMPLOYEES

The frequency of employee interchange between various locations is also considered in the determination of the appropriate bargaining unit. Where there is found to exist "some" or "substantial" interchange, a bargaining unit of these combined localities is generally deemed to be appropriate. For example, in *Texas Pipe Line Co.*,[150] the NLRB granted the union's request for a unit comprised of three of the seven plants involved, basing this delineation on the presence of "some interchange of personnel" among the three plants.[151] Alternatively, a finding of "minimal" or no employee interchange would evidence the appropriateness of the smaller, single unit. In *Gerber Products Co.*,[152] the Board relied on the lack of interchange to grant the union's request for a unit of salesmen located in Rochester, New

---

[148] The prohibition against so-called secondary boycotts is set forth in section 8(b)(4) of the Act, 29 U.S.C.A. § 141 *et seq.*

[149] 407 F.2d at 979.

[150] 129 N.L.R.B. 705 (1961), *aff'd*, 296 F.2d 208 (5th Cir. 1961).

[151] *Accord*, El Paso Elec. Co., 168 N.L.R.B. No. 136 (1967) ; Air California, 170 N.L.R.B. No. 1, 67 L.R.R.M. 1385 (1968).

[152] 172 N.L.R.B. No. 195, 69 L.R.R.M. 1017 (1968).

York, despite the employer's allegations that the only appropriate unit was his overall administrative division.[153]

Once again, there is a noticeable lack of articulated reasons for the utilization of employee interchange as a factor in unit determinations. Certain reasons may be suggested. First, employees who continually work together for repeated periods of time are certain to develop a common community of interests. Furthermore, substantial interchange would provide significant evidence that the employer's operations are functionally coordinated and that the combined groupings constitute an administratively coherent unit. Finally, frequent transfers of employees in and out of a unit would make the unit ineffective for purposes of collective bargaining. The employee's wages and hours would fluctuate from unit to unit; the pension fund, insurance plans and seniority system would become chaotic; and the overall administration of the collective bargaining agreement would be disorderly. Thus, in principle, the employee interchange factor can help to delineate a bargaining unit which is, and which will continue to be, coextensive with the scope of collective bargaining.

Opposition to the use of the factor, however, has not been lacking. A number of labor organizations have contended that an emphasis upon employee interchange could provide management with an effective weapon for stifling organizational attempts. The frequent transfer of employees between plants, stores, or departments could force the NLRB to find the larger group as the appropriate bargaining unit. Consequently, the unit may be so extensive as to offer serious impediments to the union's organizational attempts. This, the labor groups argue, would contravene the national policy of promoting the employees' rights to bargain collectively. Theoretically, these contentions are sound. However, the economics of the market place and the realities of industrial relations raise serious doubt as to their practical validity.[154] First, the economic inefficiencies resulting from such "artificial" transfers would be sufficient to deter most profit-oriented organizations. Secondly, management would run the risk of so vexing and annoying the union that increased, concentrated organizational efforts would result. And finally, the practice of examining the various factors in each unit decision

---

[153] *Accord*, NLRB v. Moss Amber Mfg. Co., 264 F.2d 107 (9th Cir. 1959).

[154] Hall, *supra* note 25, at 497.

would negate any potential harm created by an artificial transferring of employees.

The employee interchange factor is a relevant consideration,
which if properly applied, can aid in the determination of an
appropriate bargaining unit. The decisions of the NLRB reveal
an expressed adherence to the relevance of the factor; unfortunately, these same decisions indicate that the Board has defined
the factor in terms of apparently inconsistent characteristics.
The nature of these inconsistencies and their effects are next
to be considered.

Characteristics of the Factor

When applying employee interchange, the Board generally distinguishes among various types of interchanges. Transfers of
employees resulting from the occurrence of an emergency, or
other such nonrecurring events, are usually considered to be of
minor significance.[155] On the other hand, where the interchang-
ing of employees involves a situation in which a large number
of employees work regularly at two locations, spending a portion
of their work week at each, then the factor is of considerable
importance.

Another characteristic frequently referred to is the length of
the particular transfers. Conflicts in recent Board decisions as
to the relative importance of "temporary" and "permanent"
employee transfers have been the cause of serious concern.

In the 1963 case of *Liebman Breweries, Inc.*,[156] the petitioning
union requested as an appropriate unit all the salesmen located
in the company's Orange, New Jersey office. The employer opposed the petition contending that the only appropriate unit
should comprise all of the firm's sales personnel. A majority of
a Board panel (Members Fanning and Brown) granted the
union's request and held that the complete absence of employee
interchange strongly reinforced the presumptive appropriateness
of the single unit. The Board's opinion revealed that although
there had not been any permanent employee transfers there had
existed substantial temporary ones. In so ruling, the majority

---

[155] Sav-On Drugs, Inc., 138 N.L.R.B. 1032 (1962); Central Wisconsin Motor
Trans. Co., 85 N.L.R.B. 287 (1949).

[156] 142 N.L.R.B. 121 (1963).

reasoned that only interchanges of a permanent nature would be significant.[157]

One year later, Members Fanning and Brown, joined by Member Jenkins, rendered an opinion which was inconsistent with the holding in *Liebman.*[158] A petition by the International Brotherhood of Teamsters requested representation rights for employees located at one of two of the employer's manufacturing plants. Rejecting the contention that the two plants were functionally integrated as indicated by a high degree of employee interchange, the Board panel granted the petition. The members noted that although the evidence indicated a history of 136 interplant transfers in a one-year period, only 83 of these transfers were for thirty days or less. In an accompanying note, the Board reasoned that:

> As transfers of more than 30 days in length approach a semipermanent change of status, we find the shorter transfer periods more significant in determining the integrated nature of the two plants.[159]

This inconsistent treatment of the employee interchange factor was recently criticized in a decision rendered by the Seventh Circuit Court of Appeals. The case, *NLRB* v. *Pinkerton's, Inc.,*[160] involved a request by the United Plant Guard Workers for a unit of guards located at the Pinkerton Company's Peru, Logansport, and Kokomo, Indiana plants. The NLRB, affirming the decision of the regional director, determined that the Peru and Kokomo plants together constituted one appropriate unit while the Logansport plant was a separate bargaining unit. The Circuit Court, reversing the Board, disagreed with the agency's application of the employee interchange factor.[161] Specifically, the Board found that the three plants together could not constitute an appropriate unit because of, *inter alia*, the minimal amount of em-

---

[157] Member Rodgers, the lone dissenter, contended that the majority's decision was based upon the extent of union organization and thus violated section 9(c)(5).

[158] Black & Decker Mfg. Co., 147 N.L.R.B. 825 (1964).

[159] *Id.* at 827 n.3.

[160] 416 F.2d 627 (7th Cir. 1969).

[161] In addition to the conflict regarding the employee interchange factor, the Court also disagreed with certain factual determinations, as well as with the effect of the geographical location.

ployee transfers. To the contrary, the Court reasoned, "one hundred thirteen transfers in a sixteen-month period cannot be considered a minimum amount of transfer when you are dealing with thirty-one guards." [162] The discrepancy between Board and Court decisions can be traced to the fact that although there were only two *permanent* transfers, there were 113 *temporary* ones. Furthermore, the Court noted that the Board, in holding the Kokomo and Peru plants to be a single appropriate unit, relied on the large number of *temporary* transfers between the two plants. It thus became obvious that the Board would use either permanent or temporary transfers depending on which classification would substantiate its conclusion. The factor was used not to *reach* a determination but rather to *support* one.

A final consideration with respect to the employee interchange factor concerns the appropriate standard of measurement to be used. Once again, NLRB decisions appear to be in conflict. The most frequently used standard is a percentage of the number of employees located at the unit in question. Five transfers into and out of a location should be considered significantly more important if the location employs ten workers than if it has a complement of 100 employees. The relevancy of employee interchange, however, has also been measured by the average numbr of transfers per week for a given grouping of employees.[163] Furthermore, recognizing that the degree of employee interchange is a relative consideration, the Board has used differential rates of interchange. For example, in *Weis Markets, Inc.*,[164] the Board compared the quantity of transfers among the stores within the requested bargaining unit with the number of transfers between such stores and those outside the requested unit. Although these varying standards of measurement provide the Board with a necessary degree of flexibility, consistency in application should be an important objective. It would not be unreasonable to require the Board to provide specific rationalizations for the use of a particular standard. Consistency in application or an explanation of an apparently inconsistent application would enhance the opportunities for better results in the determination of the appropriate bargaining unit.

---

[162] 416 F.2d at 631.

[163] Star Market Co., 172 N.L.R.B. No. 130, 68 L.R.R.M. 1497 (1968), wherein the Board held 1.9 transfers per week to be a significant interchange of employees.

[164] 142 N.L.R.B. 708, 710 (1963).

Application of the Factor

The use of employee interchange as a factor in determining the appropriate bargaining unit can be justified by the realities of the collective bargaining process. An attempt, however, to determine the propriety of the NLRB's application of the factor is beset with severe obstacles. First, most of the Board opinions dealing with the factor refer to "some" or "substantial" interchange, or merely that "employee interchange" has occurred, without specifying the quantity or nature of the transfers.[165] Moreover, inconsistent treatment of temporary and permanent transfers as well as the use of a varying standard of measurement prevent a meaningful comparison of decisions. Add to this the relative importance of the other factors and the fact that the Board need only determine *an* appropriate unit—and not *the* most appropriate unit—and the Herculean problems confronting the parties become obvious.

The result of this great "flexibility" has been, once again, to allow the NLRB to use employee interchange as *support* for its decisions rather than as reasons for them. For example, in *Hot Shoppes, Inc.*,[166] the Board pointed to 16 transfers among locations employing 304 employees to show significant employee interchange; but in *KVP Sutherland Paper Co.*,[167] 105 transfers in and out of a unit of 84 employees was not considered a substantial amount. Moreover, the Board has approved multilocation units in the retail chain industry where there existed minimal interchange [168] and in the insurance industry where there was a complete absence of interchange.[169] It is no wonder that one commentator reached the following lamentable conclusion:

> the support the Board can derive from the factor of employee interchange is gravely weakened by its perpetual failure to explain how much weight it has given it, what different weight it has given it in approving single location—and in approving multilocation units, what kinds of interchange are significant, and why interchange is relevant to unit determinations at all.[170]

---

[165] *See, e.g.,* Meijer Supermarkets, Inc., 142 N.L.R.B. 513 (1963).

[166] 130 N.L.R.B. 144, 146 (1961).

[167] 146 N.L.R.B. 1553, 1554 n.6 (1964).

[168] Spartan Department Stores, 140 N.L.R.B. 608 (1963).

[169] Metropolitan Life Ins. Co., 138 N.L.R.B. 512 (1962), *enforced*, 330 F.2d 62 (6th Cir. 1964), *vacated and remanded*, 380 U.S. 525 (1965).

[170] Note, *The Board and Section 9(c)(5), supra* note 33, at 831.

BARGAINING HISTORY

A traditionally significant factor in bargaining unit determinations is the presence, or absence, of a history of collective bargaining.[171] "Although the past history of bargaining is not considered binding, a prior finding as to the appropriate unit is not disturbed if collective bargaining has followed the pattern of the prior unit for any appreciable length of time." [172] The bargaining history which may be considered relevant is that of the industry, the geographical area, or the particular employer. The history of the industry's bargaining may demonstrate what has proven workable for other firms, while the bargaining history in a geographical area indicates the local or community practices. Neither of these, however, have been, or should be, as important as the history of bargaining of the particular employer and employees involved. The distinctive characteristics of each employment relationship considerably lessen the importance of any bargaining history other than that of the specific relationship in question. Nevertheless, consideration has been given to the established bargaining practices of similar groups of employees both in the geographical locality and in the industry.[173]

The Factor and Its Rationale

The relevance of the bargaining history of a particular grouping of employees in a unit determination may be grounded on a number of considerations. First, where there has existed successful and harmonious collective bargaining, there is strong, empirical evidence of a workable relationship. That the continuance of a harmonious relationship is congressional policy is indeed gainsay. That a successful bargaining history is indicative of this is undeniable. Second, the very existence of a history of bargaining creates a community of interests among employees, even where such a community might not have existed at the commencement of the bargaining relationship. The existence of a common seniority system, pension plan, and other conditions of

---

[171] Meijer Supermarkets, Inc., 142 N.L.R.B. 513 (1963); Eaton Mfg. Co., 121 N.L.R.B. 813 (1958); General Motors Corp., 120 N.L.R.B. 1215 (1958).

[172] 2 CCH Labor Law Reports, ¶ 2605 at 6707 (1968).

[173] Lockheed Aircraft Corp., 100 N.L.R.B. No. 147, 30 L.R.R.M. 1378 (1952); Foreman & Clark, Inc., 97 N.L.R.B. 1080 (1952).

employment create an intermingling of employee interests and needs. Disregard of this relationship could well create serious industrial relations problems.

A third rationale for the NLRB's use of the bargaining history factor is based upon the potential problems arising from inter-union rivalries. Where, for example, the bargaining unit consists of an overall production and maintenance unit, the incumbent union may be confronted with conflicting employee demands, as well as with conflicts between long and short run interests. The presence of such conflicts can create a considerable dissenting faction of employees. This faction then becomes a prime target for an outside union's organizational attempts. The application of the bargaining history factor offers the incumbent union a buffer against such outside interference. Accordingly, the Board has denied severance of a single plant where there existed a five-year history of multiplant bargaining,[174] and granted a unit of all seventeen of the firm's stores where there had been a twelve-year, employer-wide bargaining history.[175]

In their unit determinations, the Board must consider conflicting legislative policies. The bargaining history factor, while protecting the interests of the incumbent union, may also have the effect of severely limiting the "free choice" guaranteed to the employees by the National Labor Relations Act. The relevant factors which evidenced the propriety of the initial unit determination may have long since dissipated. Moreover, the employees presently included in the unit may be different individuals from those who voted in the initial representation election. As to the needs of the incumbent union, a number of protective devices are available. The existence of employee apathy, as well as the incumbent representative's greater opportunity to communicate with the workers, offers significant protection. Furthermore, section 9(c)(3) of the Act requires that at least one year must transpire between representation elections.[176] Internally, the AFL-CIO has enacted a number of no-raid agreements including the 1961 Internal Disputes Plan. This plan, which has

---

[174] Firestone Tire & Rubber Co., 103 N.L.R.B. 1749 (1953).

[175] Meijer Supermarkets, Inc., 142 N.L.R.B. 513 (1963).

[176] Section 9(c)(3) provides, in part, that: "No election shall be directed in any bargaining unit or any subdivision within which, in the preceding twelve-month period, a valid election shall have been held. . . ."

been adopted as Article XX of the AFL-CIO Constitution, provides that:

> Section 2: Each affiliate shall respect the established collective bargaining relationship of every other affiliate. No affiliate shall organize or attempt to represent employees as to whom an established collective bargaining relationship exists with any other affiliate. . . .
>
> Section 3: Each affiliate shall respect the established working relationship of every other affiliate. For purposes of this Article, an "established working relationship" shall be deemed to exist as to any work of the kind which the members of an organization have customarily performed at a particular plant or work site, whether their employer is the plant operator, a contractor, or other employer. . . .

The Internal Disputes Plan, although not applicable to non-affiliates,[177] does afford a large degree of protection from rival union raids. The Board's application of the bargaining history factor must consider these varying, and sometimes conflicting, industrial relations policies.

The Relevant History

Although the courts, the Board, and most labor authorities agree on the advisability of using the bargaining history factor, considerable conflict surrounds the issue of what history of bargaining should be given the greatest significance. As noted above, the NLRB has given consideration to the history of collective bargaining in the geographical area, in the industry, and in the particular employment relationship involved.

The first of these three "histories" has generally been accorded the least amount of probative value. Although the history of bargaining in the geographical area is frequently used to support a conclusion, it is seldom used to reach one. In one recent case, for example, a Board majority denied the petitioning union's request to sever the meat department employees from an overall, storewide unit, despite a geographical history to the contrary. It was reasoned that even though other grocery stores in the local community had been organized in separate units, this particular firm's employees had historically been represented in a

---

[177] Affiliates of the rival Alliance for Labor Action and other independent unions are, of course, not covered by the Internal Disputes Plan.

single unit.[178] A similar degree of relevance has been accorded to the industry's history of collective bargaining.[179]

The most important bargaining history to which the Board will refer is that of the particular employer and employees involved. Generally, where there has been bargaining without a written contract, or under a "member only" agreement, or where the earlier unit was contrary to a prior Board determination, the history will be of minimal significance.[180] Furthermore, it has been held that units stipulated by the parties for purposes of consent elections are not binding upon the Board in later determinations.[181] Adherence has also been given to the somewhat questionable policy that where there has been a history of collective bargaining for one group of an employer's organized employees, such history is not controlling with respect to the employer's unorganized employees. Recently, this principle was applied in *International Paper Co.*,[182] wherein the employer's ten plants historically constituted a single bargaining unit. After the opening of a new plant, a petition was filed requesting separate representation rights for the new employees. Granting the petition, Chairman McCulloch, joined by Members Fanning and Zagoria, reasoned that the new plant did not constitute an accretion and that the history of bargaining of the ten-plant unit was inapplicable because the new plant was not functionally integrated.

A recent case involving a similar application of the bargaining history factor was *Maryland Cup Corp.*[183] District 50, for-

---

[178] Buckeye Village Market, Inc., 175 N.L.R.B. No. 46, 70 L.R.R.M. 1529, 1532 (1969).

[179] The history of bargaining in the industry has been of considerable significance in cases involving the craft versus industrial union issue. The "integration of operations" theory set forth in *National Tube Co.*, 76 NLRB 1199 (1948), relied heavily upon the industry's history of bargaining. For a full discussion of the craft severance issue, see Chapter III, *infra*.

[180] In *Safety Cabs, Inc.*, the Board held that a combined unit of taxicab drivers employed by two companies constituting a single employer was the only appropriate bargaining unit. The history of separate unit bargaining was disregarded since the earlier pattern of bargaining was established and continued on the basis of race discrimination. 173 N.L.R.B. No. 4, 69 L.R.R.M. 1199 (1968).

[181] Coca Cola Bottling Co., 156 N.L.R.B. 450 (1965); Kaiser Alum. & Chem. Corp., 100 N.L.R.B 107, 113 (1952)

[182] 171 N.L.R.B. No. 89, 68 L.R.R.M. 1113 (1968).

[183] 171 N.L.R.B. No. 71, 68 L.R.R.M. 1081 (1968).

merly United Mine Workers, requested representation rights for employees at one of the company's plants in the Baltimore area. The employer opposed the petition on the grounds of centralized control, integration of operations, and employee interchange. In finding for the union, the Board reasoned that although there was some employee interchange, some centralized control, and some functional integration, these were not sufficient to rebut the presumption in favor of a single-plant unit. Without specifying the degree of the interchange, control, and integration, it concluded that "for the foregoing reasons, and particularly in view of the absence of a bargaining history . . ." the single-plant unit was alone appropriate.[184] With respect to this absent bargaining history, the Board noted that:

> the fact that elections have been conducted in stipulated multi-plant units involving some of [the employer's] facilities does not establish a bargaining history; those elections did not result in collective bargaining. Nor does the scope of the units established in bargaining for the Employer's plants in Illinois and California determine the scope of the unit required for the Maryland plants.[185]

Accepting the policy that the size of the bargaining unit should be coextensive with the expected scope of collective bargaining, the propriety of the Board's application of the bargaining history factor becomes doubtful. A finding that the plants and employees in issue are similar to those of the previously existing multiplant unit would surely indicate the primary importance of the bargaining history factor. Thus, in *Maryland Cup*, if the history of multiplant bargaining in both Illinois and California revealed a workable relationship leading to industrial relations stability, then such a history, barring any dissimilar relevant characteristics, would evidence the appropriateness of a multiplant unit in Maryland.

In *Bowman Transportation, Inc.*,[186] a 1967 case, the Board provided a revealing analysis of the process used in determining the relevant history of bargaining. The petition requested a unit composed of one of the employer's twenty-one terminal facilities. Holding this to be an appropriate unit, a Board panel relied on the geographic separation, the autonomy in day-to-day

---

[184] 171 N.L.R.B. No. 71, 68 L.R.R.M. at 1083.

[185] 171 N.L.R.B. No. 71, 68 L.R.R.M. at 1082 n.2.

[186] 166 N.L.R.B. 982 (1967).

operations, the lack of employee interchange, and the absence of any "controlling" bargaining history. With regard to the bargaining history, the Board made the following findings of fact:

1958-1964—the firm's employees were covered by a collective bargaining agreement negotiated by District 50, formerly United Mine Workers, for a systemwide unit which had been agreed to by the parties;

1961—a systemwide election was held (by consent) in which the Teamsters Union won recognition;

1961-1964—negotiations between the Teamsters Union and the company continued unsuccessfully;

1964—the NLRB ordered a systemwide unit election which resulted in a majority vote for no union representation.

Applying these findings, the Board reasoned that since the 1958 and 1961 systemwide elections resulted from stipulations— mutual consent of the parties—this unit size was not binding upon the Board in a subsequent unit determination proceeding. As to the 1964 certification of the employer-wide unit, it was held that this too was not binding because the election resulted in a vote for no union and thus there was never any history of collective bargaining. As to the 1961 to 1964 period, it was reasoned that although a representative was designated and negotiations were conducted, there never existed a contractual relationship and thus no relevant history of bargaining.

Technically, the analysis offered by the Board appears to be correct. Logically, it is questionable. The industrial relations history of the Bowman Company reveals that both the management and the unions believed that an employer-wide unit was a workable situation, and that in fact, from 1958 to 1961, there did exist industrial stability. Moreover, in 1964, the Board itself substantiated the propriety of the integrated unit when it granted certification to the systemwide bargaining unit. Why now does the Board reach an opposite conclusion? Disagreeing with the employer's reliance on the earlier certification, the NLRB members reasoned that the presence of additional facts prevented the earlier decision from being either conclusive or binding. Additional facts which accounted for the contrary results were: (1) the 1964 systemwide unit election resulted in a majority vote in favor of no union; and (2) for the first time, a union had requested representation rights in a single-terminal unit. To rest a bargaining unit determination on either or both facts would surely constitute a violation of the NLRA's mandate that "the extent to which the employees have organized shall not be controlling." [187]

In October of 1969, the Board was confronted with another situation involving a transportation firm's terminal facilities. *Transcontinental Bus System, Inc.*,[188] unlike the situation in *Bowman*, involved a joint petition requesting a systemwide bargaining unit, while the employer, in opposition, alleged the appropriateness of the existing single-terminal units. The company operated a series of terminal facilities of which the Amalgamated Transit Union represented eleven separate units, the Brotherhood of Railroad Trainmen represented nine separate units, and seven units were unrepresented. Attempting to increase their economic bargaining power and enlarge their membership roles, the two unions jointly petitioned for an employer-wide unit. In a three to two decision, the Board majority dismissed the petition relying on the "long and extensive history of collective bargaining on a separate unit basis." [189] The majority reasoned that the twenty-year history disrupted by only three work stoppages was strong evidence of a workable relationship leading to industrial stability.

Member Brown, joined in part by Chairman McCulloch, dissented, arguing that the result of the majority's decision was to "freeze" the current bargaining units. He contended that there existed no reasonable predicate for holding that the units as now established must continue to be the only appropriate basis for bargaining.

> The joint petitioners seek a unit which, in the absence of any bargaining history on a lesser basis, the Members of this Board would in all probability find at least presumptively appropriate for purposes of conducting a representation election. I would reach the same result in a situation such as the instant one, where the incumbent unions are seeking an election among all the bus operators employed throughout the entire system, thus placing in jeopardy their current representative status and facing the possibility of rejection as the employees' representative.[190]

---

[187] Act, § 9 (c) (5).

[188] 178 N.L.R.B. No. 110, 72 L.R.R.M. 1214 (1969).

[189] 178 N.L.R.B. No. 110, 72 L.R.R.M. at 1216.

[190] 178 N.L.R.B. No. 110, 72 L.R.R.M. at 1218.

The opinion offered by Member Brown raises a number of serious questions. Does he advocate diminishing or abolishing the relevance of the bargaining history factor? Why does the dissent choose to ignore the fact that seven of the requested units have never been unionized? Might it not be that the petitioning unions have been unable to organize any one of these seven terminals and that by consolidating them with the represented units the new employees would be "swept in" to union representation regardless of their desires?

Member Brown's justification for disregarding the bargaining history—the incumbent union's willingness to place in jeopardy their current representative status—ignores the realities of industrial relations. It would be highly unrealistic to assume that the incumbent unions, prior to filing their petition, did not thoroughly examine the extent of employee support. As noted above, the position of the incumbent representative is generally far superior to that of any challengers. The use of the bargaining history factor in unit determinations may be rationalized, in part, as the need to protect the incumbent union's representative status. The Board, however, should not be free to disregard the factor whenever a union expresses a willingness to risk its position. Furthermore, the NLRA guarantees to all employees certain protected rights—including the right to refrain from unionization. The effects of the decision advocated by the dissent would be to impinge upon this right and to grant the union whatever unit configuration would enhance its economic bargaining power. Congress never intended such a result.

One of the sharpest conflicts between Board members over the application of the bargaining history factor occurred in *Buckeye Village Market, Inc.*[191] The Retail Clerks International requested a unit of all employees located at the employer's retail grocery store in Alliance, Ohio, excluding employees in the meat and delicatessen department. Simultaneously, the Amalgamated Meat Cutters petitioned for a unit of all employees in that store's meat and delicatessen department. Opposing both petitions, the Buckeye Village Local Union intervened on the grounds that it had an existing collective bargaining agreement covering in one unit both of the requested employee groupings. Alternatively, the intervenor contended that the only appropriate unit would be all the employees, with specific exclusions, working in the Alliance store.

---

[191] 175 N.L.R.B. No. 46, 70 L.R.R.M. 1529 (1969).

In a two to one decision, the Board panel dismissed the petitions. After ruling that both petitions were timely filed with respect to the original contract expiration date,[192] the Board addressed itself to the appropriate unit delineation. In holding the storewide unit to be appropriate, the majority relied on the high degree of employee interchange, the centralized control of operations, and the twenty-two month history of storewide bargaining. Opposing the use of this bargaining history, the petitioners offered the following contentions:

> [T]his bargaining history is not controlling because it is of too short a duration; Intervenor has not enforced or administered its contracts; its officers have not complied with the requirements of the Labor-Management Reporting and Disclosure Act; its president allegedly is a supervisor; a single overall unit is contrary to area practice; and the separate units requested are appropriate craft or departmental units.[193]

The Board majority, over the bitter dissent of Member Fanning, found no merit in any of the petitioners' contentions. Relying on precedent, the majority first noted that a twenty-two month bargaining history was "substantial, if not controlling, in determining the appropriate unit." [194] Moreover, the intervenor's failure to comply with the requirements of the Labor-Management Reporting and Disclosure Act did not affect the evidential value of the history of bargaining. After disagreeing with the contention that the incumbent had not enforced or administered its agreement, the majority refused to rule on the key allegation that the union was employer controlled. Rather, it was reasoned, that where, as here, it is contended that there exists employer control of a recognized bargaining representative, the incumbent's "capacity to continue as such a representative can be determined only in unfair labor practice proceedings." [195] To this, Member Fanning issued a strong dissent.

Alleging that the majority has ignored the "patent contract defects," the dissenter contended that a unit combining a supervisor with rank and file employees is certainly not indicative of

---

192 The intervenor and the employer had attempted to prematurely extend the existing contract thus blocking the representation petitions. As noted, the Board disallowed this attempt.

193 175 N.L.R.B. No. 46, 70 L.R.R.M. at 1531.

194 *Id.*

195 175 N.L.R.B. No. 46, 70 L.R.R.M. at 1532.

a meaningful bargaining history. Relying on prior Board decisions which had disallowed employer controlled unions from acting as employee representatives, Member Fanning reasoned that the majority

> by closing their minds to the evidence that the incumbent intervenor is supervisory controlled pave the way for a possible certification of it as the employees' bargaining representative even though that will inescapably place the Employer on both sides of the bargaining table.[196]

Since the NLRA would prohibit certifying such a labor organization as bargaining representative, the dissenter concluded that allowing the incumbent to participate in the election would merely serve to "confuse" the employees.

It is submitted that while both sides attempted to apply the prevailing laws, neither considered the true essence of the problem. The history of bargaining provides empirical evidence of a workable collective bargaining relationship and creates a community of interests among the unit members. If there has been a stable and harmonious history, as did exist in *Buckeye,* then this should be sufficient to indicate the propriety of the existing unit configuration. The effectiveness or ineffectiveness of the incumbent union should be considered beyond the scope of the Board's review in the determination of the appropriate bargaining unit. Member Fanning's paternalistic attitude of protecting the employees from "confusion" would have the effect of denying to these men the opportunity to choose between alternative representatives. The dissenter was attempting to replace the freedom of the election process with the restrictions of administrative fiat.

Turning next to the petitioners' allegation that the "area practice" favored separate bargaining units, the majority held that while the evidence substantiated this contention, the history of bargaining of the employees here involved revealed the use of a single, overall unit. The majority properly subordinated the relevance of the bargaining history of the geographical area to that of the bargaining history of the particular employees. Once again, however, Member Fanning disagreed with his colleagues. He contended that this subordination was not proper under the present circumstances due "to the defect in [the incumbent] or-

---

[196] 175 N.L.R.B. No. 46, 70 L.R.R.M. at 1535.

ganization which these contracts patently show." [197] The dissenter again based his argument on the alleged ineffectiveness of the current representative and upon his interpretation of the collective bargaining agreement.

As to the last of the petitioners' contentions, the Board majority ruled that the requested units were neither departmental nor craft units such as would come within the criteria established in *Mallinckrodt Chemical Works*.[198] The meat and delicatessen department employees were neither sufficiently departmentalized nor skilled to warrant severance from the overall unit. In thus denying the last of the petitioners' arguments, the majority dismissed the request for separate bargaining units. It granted the alternate request of the Retail Clerks and the Meat Cutters to represent the employees jointly in a storewide unit. Despite Member Fanning's protestations over this "forced marriage of the Petitioners," the majority's decision offered the employees the opportunity to choose between alternative representatives. The effectiveness of the incumbent union as a representative would be determined by all employees through a secret ballot election and not by administrative fiat.

Summary

Traditionally, the NLRB has properly considered the history of collective bargaining as a factor in the determination of the appropriate bargaining unit. As well as providing evidence of a workable relationship, the factor indicates the presence of a strong community of interests. Disregarding the bargaining history of the employees could disrupt an otherwise harmonious relationship. On the other hand, the factor should not be used to "freeze" any existing unit configuration. The dynamics of the employment relationship may well dictate the need for change. Furthermore, the congressional mandate of guaranteeing to employees their freedom of choice, within the context of the process of collective bargaining, must be preserved. The Board's responsibility for conducting this delicate balancing process is facilitated by the use of the bargaining history factor. If the factor is objectively applied within the overall policy of conforming the unit configuration to the scope of collective bargaining, the resulting unit will truly be an appropriate one.

---

[197] *Id.*

[198] 162 N.L.R.B. 387 (1966). See Chapter III, *infra*.

EMPLOYEE DESIRES

A Board-created factor which has found significant use in the determination of the appropriate bargaining unit is the desires of the employees. Whether this may properly be considered a "factor" is questionable in that the NLRB has contended that employee desires only become relevant after there has been a determination of alternatively appropriate bargaining units. This question, however, is more academic than real. Certainly, the self-determination election procedure developed by the Board has come to play an important role in determining unit configurations. With certain qualifications, the Board and the courts have generally agreed that the desires of the employees involved is a proper consideration in deciding unit placement, subject only to the requirement that the Board consider all other legally relevant factors.[199] The Supreme Court has specifically sanctioned the Board's use of self-determination elections in bargaining unit determinations.[200] After reviewing the historical development of the factor, this section will undertake an examination of the applications of the self-determination election and the tallying of votes resulting therefrom.

Development of the Factor

An examination of the historical development of the use of self-determination elections reveals a conflict which involved the NLRB, the courts, and even Congress. A brief review of this development should provide added insight into the conflict currently existing over the proper use of such elections.

The Globe Doctrine. The first significant use of the self-determination election occurred in the 1937 case of *Globe Machine & Stamping Co.*[201] The case involved a dispute between three craft unions and an industrial union over alternative bargaining unit boundaries. The United Automobile Workers of America (an affiliate of the then Committee for Industrial Organization) contended that the appropriate unit should be plantwide and, in fact, on May 20, 1937, negotiated an agreement covering all industrial employees. Simultaneously, the Machinists, an affiliate

---

[199] NLRB v. Ideal Laundry & Dry Cleaning Co., 330 F.2d 712 (10th Cir. 1964).

[200] Pittsburgh Plate Glass Co. v. NLRB, 313 U.S. 146 (1941).

[201] 3 N.L.R.B. 294 (1937).

of the AFL, claimed jurisdiction over the punch press operators; while the Polishers Union, AFL, had organized the polishers and buffers. Jurisdiction over the remaining employees was claimed by an AFL Federal Union.

Prior to a UAW-CIO strike and the agreement of May 20, 1937, each of the four unions had negotiated oral, informal agreements covering their respective members and each had separately handled their own grievances. Moreover, the factors favoring a single plantwide unit were about equal to those favoring separate craft units: successful collective bargaining had been conducted on both a plantwide and craft unit basis; the plant was departmentalized but all work flowed through more than one department; and the punch press operators and the polishers had some skill but could not be considered true skilled craftsmen. Reviewing the considerations favoring each alternative, the NLRB reached the following conclusion:

> *In such a case where the considerations are so evenly balanced, the determining factor is the desire of the men themselves.* On this point, the record affords no help. There has been a swing toward U.A.W.A. and then away from it. The only documentary proof is completely contradictory. We will therefore order elections to be held separately for the men engaged in polishing and those engaged in punch press work. We will also order an election for the employees of the Company engaged in production and maintenance, exclusive of the polishers and punch press workers and of clerical and supervisory employees.
>
> *On the results of these elections will depend the determination of the appropriate unit for the purposes of collective bargaining.* Such of the groups as do not choose the U.A.W.A. will constitute separate and distinct appropriate units, and such as do choose the U.A.W.A. will together constitute a single appropriate unit.[202]

The practical consequences flowing from the application of the "Globe" election procedure were twofold.[203] First, a considerable portion of the decision making responsibility was shifted away from the Board and onto the employees. Secondly, the use of the self-determination election served to support the organizational efforts of the craft and other unions seeking to organize the

---

[202] *Id.* at 300 (emphasis supplied). The Board has subsequently held that the Globe election will not be ordered where the evidence sufficiently reveals the employee desires. Armour & Co., 5 N.L.R.B. 535 (1938); Worthington Pump & Machine Corp., 4 N.L.R.B. 448 (1937).

[203] City Auto Stamping Co., 3 N.L.R.B. 307 (1937) is generally considered as a companion case to *Globe Machine.*

smaller bargaining units. These effects formed the basis for the bitter criticisms raised by Member Edwin Smith. Although concurring with his colleagues in the *Globe* decision, Smith did not agree that the doctrine should have general applicability. The extent of this difference was soon to become apparent.

The Allis-Chalmers Case. In *Allis-Chalmers*,[204] the UAW was once again petitioning for a plantwide unit, while several craft unions requested groupings of certain skilled employees. As in *Globe*, there existed no problem of craft representation or no representation. Rather, the central issue involved unit configuration and the conflicting interests of labor groups. A majority of the Board applied the *Globe* doctrine and ordered separate elections for the power house employees, the maintenance electricians, and the draftsmen. The members again reasoned that where the considerations are "evenly balanced" a self-determination election is appropriate.

Member Smith, dissenting in part, disagreed with the majority's universal application of the *Globe* election. Criticizing the Board's abdication of its responsibilities, he stated,

> I feel the Board is here abandoning its necessary judicial function under the Act of making a reasonable determination of the appropriate bargaining unit in accordance with the facts of the particular case.[205]

He further contended that this "pseudo-democratic" device served only to protect the rights of the minority at the expense of disregarding the interests of the majority.

The main thrust of Smith's dissent, however, was based on more practical considerations. The dissenter was very much aware of the fact that the separation of bargaining units could seriously undermine the economic bargaining power of the industrial union. The majority's decision in *Allis-Chalmers* would potentially deprive the industrial unit of the skilled craftsmen's power to shut down the employer's entire operations and, at the same time, would raise the employer's "cost of agreeing" relative to his "cost of disagreeing." [206] To Smith, comprehensive em-

---

[204] Allis-Chalmers Mfg. Co., 4 N.L.R.B. 159 (1937).

[205] *Id.* at 175.

[206] J. C. Winfrey, "The Appropriate Bargaining Unit Decisions of the National Labor Relations Board," Ph.D. dissertation, Duke University, 1965, p. 159 n.1.

ployee bargaining units were necessary to offset the ever-increasing size of the American business organization. He commented:

> The workers who compose this group [oilers and firemen] form the great majority of the plant's two power houses. This gives them in their separate craft union a strike weapon of great potential force. Without doubt, the employer's *pro tem* recognition of the oilers and firemen in its existing contract was conditioned by the threat of economic power inherent in their separate form of organization. It is obvious that a group capable, by strike action, of shutting down completely a large manufacturing plant would be of the greatest assistance to the great mass of the employees in their bargaining efforts. Conversely, by remaining aloof from the general picture of collective bargaining, by not identifying the interests of its members with the great majority of the employees, this particular craft group could, *in its own interest,* take action which would throw thousands of persons out of work and hamper greatly the attempt of the majority to achieve stable employment under collective bargaining. Again, if the interests of the craft group and the industrial group are not welded in the collective bargaining process, it might well happen that if the major group sought to exercise economic pressure by means of strike, this minority group, through its ability to keep power flowing in the plant by abstaining from strike, would tend to weaken joint action.
> If the oilers and firemen and the skilled maintenance electricians bargain separately, by so much is the united economic strength of the employees as a whole weakened. Anything which weakens the bargaining power of the employees will tend to lessen reliance upon peaceful collective bargaining as the means for achieving the workers' economic ends. Such a tendency is plainly contrary to the purposes of the Act.[207]

To Member Smith, the proper use of the *Globe* election procedure would depend upon the extent of the interdependency of the relative economic bargaining power of the various unit configurations. Where the separation of employees would not seriously affect the strength of the comprehensive unit, the self-determination election should be allowed. Thus, in *Allis-Chalmers,* Smith's concurrence with his colleagues' decision to allow the draftsmen and technical engineers separate representation was explained by his comment that:

> Nor would the economic strength of these draftsmen and technical engineers contribute materially to the welfare of their fellow employees if they were added to the industrial unit.[208]

---

[207] 4 N.L.R.B. at 176-177 (emphasis supplied).

[208] *Id.* at 177.

Furthermore, Member Smith's concurrence with the decision in *Globe* would be consistent with his opinion in *Allis-Chalmers* in that a separation of units in *Globe* would not materially affect the bargaining power of the industrial unit.

American Can and the Taft-Hartley Amendments. Two years after the formation of the *Globe* doctrine, the NLRB was confronted with the novel issue of a requested craft severance. The case, *American Can Co.*,[209] involved a request for a unit of craft employees who had historically been represented in an overall bargaining unit. In dismissing the petition, a majority of the Board reasoned that:

> The Board is not authorized by the Act to split the appropriate unit thus established by collective bargaining and embodied in a valid, exclusive bargaining contract.[210]

Member Smith concurred, basing his decision on the lack of justification "for weakening the bargaining strength of the employees as a whole . . . ."[211] Chairman Madden, the lone dissenter, would have held the *Globe* doctrine to be applicable and granted a self-determination election.

The *American Can* decision, although having primary significance in craft severance cases,[212] did serve to substantially lessen the importance of self-determination elections in unit determinations. From 1939 until 1947, the *Globe* doctrine found only moderate application.[213] With the Taft-Hartley Amendments of 1947, the legislature gave specific recognition to the Board-created procedure of self-determination elections. In section 9(b)(1) of the Act, it was provided that:

> the Board shall not . . . decide that any unit is appropriate for [collective bargaining] purposes if such unit includes both professional employees and employees who are not professional employees *unless a majority of such professional employees vote for inclusion in such unit* . . . . (Emphasis supplied.)

---

[209] 13 N.L.R.B. 1252 (1939).

[210] *Id.* at 1256.

[211] *Id.* at 1258.

[212] The craft severance policies of the NLRB are fully discussed in Chapter III, *infra*.

[213] *Accord,* International Minerals & Chem. Corp., 71 N.L.R.B. 878 (1946); and General Elec. Co., 58 N.L.R.B. 57 (1944).

Furthermore, in reaction to adverse feelings about the *American Can* decision, Congress promulgated section 9(b)(2) which states that:

> ... the Board shall not ... decide that any craft unit is inappropriate for [collective bargaining] purposes on the ground that a different unit has been established by a prior Board determination, *unless a majority of the employees in the proposed craft unit vote against separate representation.* (Emphasis supplied.)

These statutory mandates do give recognition and thus sanction to the use of self-determination elections. A conflict now arises as to what extent Congress intended to sanction the *Globe* doctrine. Do these sections of the Act indicate unlimited congressional approval of the procedure whenever the other factors are "evenly balanced"? Or should they be interpreted as being *limitations* upon the Board's use of the election procedure? Generally, the NLRB has contended that the legislature gave an unqualified endorsement of the *Globe* doctrine, since sections 9(b) (1) and (2) assume that the Board may, and in some cases must, conduct self-determination elections. As a result, it has been held that such elections may be the controlling factor in unit determinations.[214] The Board has since found proper application of the *Globe* doctrine in a variety of factual situations.

Application of the Factor

As originally developed in the *Globe* case,[215] the self-determination election has been primarily used where the Board has found, after applying the other relevant factors, two (or more) potentially appropriate bargaining units. The NLRB has consistently reasoned that the National Labor Relations Act does not require a finding of *the* appropriate bargaining unit, but only of *an* appropriate unit.[216] The result has been a number of unit deci-

---

[214] J. I. Case Co., 87 N.L.R.B. 692, 698 n.8 (1949).

[215] 3 N.L.R.B. 294 (1937).

[216] Black & Decker Mfg. Co., 147 N.L.R.B. 825, 828 (1964) wherein the Board stated that:

> It has been our declared policy to consider only whether the requested unit is an appropriate one even though it may not be the optimum or most appropriate unit for collective bargaining. We are convinced that such a policy is compatible with the objectives of the Act which seeks to encourage rather than impede the collective-bargaining process.

Accord, Morand Bros. Beverage Co., 91 N.L.R.B. 409, 412 (1950).

sions which find as appropriate either of two or more unit configurations. In lieu of choosing which grouping is *more* appropriate, the Board has utilized the self-determination election to ascertain the desires of the employees, which then become the controlling factor.[217]

Where there has been an earlier determination of an appropriate bargaining unit, those employees excluded from that unit will not, as a general rule, be entitled to a self-determination election unless they can independently constitute an appropriate unit. Such a situation occurred in the *Boeing Co.* case.[218] The International Association of Machinists, which had represented the production and maintenance unit employees for twenty-nine years, requested the Board to grant a self-determination election in a unit of tool liaison employees. Dismissing the petition, the NLRB ruled that since the requested group was merely a "small segment" of a larger grouping of employees it could not independently constitute an appropriate bargaining unit. Pursuant to the general policy, the *Globe* election procedure was held to be inapplicable.

It should be noted that the presence of a history of bargaining for one grouping of employees does not, *per se*, affect the applicability of the self-determination election. Where there has been an existing bargaining unit the Board has readily granted an election to the unrepresented employees to determine if they wish to be separately represented or added to the existing unit.[219] Furthermore, *Globe* elections have been granted to employees who were previously excluded from an existing unit but who may now appropriately constitute a separate unit or an addition to the existing unit.[220]

A special area in which the *Globe* doctrine has found applicability is that of fringe or residual employees. In the early 1950's, the NLRB was confronted with a request for a self-determination election in a group of fringe employees which would not constitute a separate appropriate bargaining unit.

[217] Hilton-Burns Hotel Co., 167 N.L.R.B. 221 (1967); Myers Drum Co., 165 N.L.R.B. 1060 (1967).

[218] 169 N.L.R.B. No. 33, 67 L.R.R.M. 1284 (1968).

[219] Cities Service Oil Co., 145 N.L.R.B. 467 (1963); Montana-Dakota Utilities Co., 110 N.L.R.B. 1056 (1954).

[220] Krambo Food Stores, Inc., 119 N.L.R.B. 369 (1957); Fort Worth Stockyards, 109 N.L.R.B. 1452 (1954).

The Board ruled in *Zia Co.*[221] that the employees could properly be allowed to determine whether they wished to be added to the existing unit, notwithstanding that the fringe group would not constitute a separate appropriate unit.[222]

In 1961, with the advent of the Kennedy Board, the *Zia* rule was substantially modified by the decision in *D. V. Displays Corp.*[223] Chairman McCulloch, along with Members Fanning and Brown, decided that where there was a question of representation in the historical unit and the incumbent union sought to add the previously unrepresented fringe group (which no other union was seeking to represent on a different basis), only one election would be directed in which the fringe group would be included with the historical unit. The majority reasoned that the exclusion of the fringe group was a historical accident which would only be perpetuated by allowing a self-determination election. Furthermore, it was argued that the *Zia* rule constituted an abdication of the Board's responsibility to determine the appropriate bargaining unit, and that the new rule was more democratic in that all employees would have an equal voice. Members Rodgers and Leedom dissented, arguing that the majority's decision did not provide adequate protection of the rights of both groups of employees. A majority of the Board, however, has continued to follow the rule enunciated in *D. V. Displays.*[224]

An area in which the *Globe* procedure has found increasing applicability is when there occurs an expansion of the employer's existing labor force.[225] Such an expansion will generally occur through the creation of a new department or the acquisition of a new plant—either by purchase or merger. In such situations, the NLRB must determine whether the additional employees constitute an accretion to the existing bargaining unit or a new grouping of employees which requires a section 9(c)(1) representation election.

The determination of the status of the additional employees centers upon an examination of certain factors in order to as-

---

[221] 108 N.L.R.B. 1134 (1954).

[222] *Accord*, Mountain State Woodworkers Ass'n, 118 N.L.R.B. 806 (1957); Sperry Rand Corp., 116 N.L.R.B. 137 (1956).

[223] 134 N.L.R.B. 568 (1961).

[224] Century Elec. Co., 146 N.L.R.B. 232 (1964).

[225] The effects of an expanding labor force in an existing bargaining unit are considered in Chapter V, *infra*.

certain the presence or absence of a common community of interests.[226] Consideration is given to such factors as the history of the bargaining unit,[227] the geographic proximity or isolation of the new employees,[228] the functions, duties, and skills of the entire work force,[229] and the administrative territories or subdivisions of the employer.[230] Should the Board determine that an accretion has occurred the new employees will immediately become members of the existing unit. On the other hand, if no accretion is found, a section 9(c)(1) representation election will be directed. It is this latter situation in which the *Globe* doctrine may find applicability. For example, when an employer creates a new department and the Board, through an examination of the relevant factors, determines that the new department could appropriately be a separate unit or an addition to the existing unit, a self-determination election will become the controlling determinant.[231] Should the Board conclude that the new department could not separately constitute an appropriate bargaining unit, the *Globe* election would be inapplicable.[232] Similar results have been reached in cases involving "new operations" [233] and "new plants."[234]

The case of *Fruehauf Corp.*[235] presented a situation similar to that of a labor force expansion. The petitioning union had rep-

---

[226] Westinghouse Elec. Corp., 162 N.L.R.B. 768 (1967).

[227] ACF Industries, Inc., 136 N.L.R.B. 594 (1962); Brockton-Taunton Gas Co., 132 N.L.R.B. 940 (1961).

[228] Fox Co., 158 N.L.R.B. 320 (1966); Gas Service Co., 140 N.L.R.B. 445 (1963).

[229] Worthington Corp., 155 N.L.R.B. 222 (1965); Gas Service Co., 140 N.L.R.B. 445 (1963).

[230] Westinghouse Elec. Corp., 173 N.L.R.B. No. 51, 69 LRRM 1326 (1968); Pacific States Steel Corp., 134 N.L.R.B. 1325 (1961).

[231] Ware Laboratories, Inc., 98 N.L.R.B. 1141 (1952).

[232] Hudson Pulp & Paper Corp., 117 N.L.R.B. 416 (1957).

[233] Morgan Transfer & Storage Co., 131 N.L.R.B. 1434 (1961); Fleming & Sons, Inc., 118 N.L.R.B. 1451 (1957).

[234] Ryan Industries, Inc., 100 N.L.R.B. 1455 (1952). It should be noted that the Board has held that the mere establishment of a new plant does not of itself justify separate elections. Saco-Lowell Shops, 107 N.L.R.B. 590 (1953).

[235] 157 N.L.R.B. 28 (1966).

resented employees at one of the employer's plants for ten years. The employees at the company's nearby plant had remained unrepresented. In granting the union's request to represent these employees, the Board held that where the relevant factors favor either the multiplant or single-plant unit, the unrepresented employees would be entitled to decide in a self-determination election whether they desired to be included in the previously unrepresented unit. A similar result was reached in a recent case in which both groups of employees had had separate unit bargaining histories.[236]

The inverse of the merger of units would be the severance of units. Here also, the *Globe* election procedure finds applicability. The issue of a requested severance of employees has traditionally arisen in the context of the controversy between craft and industrial unionism.[237] The industrial union may well represent an entire complement of an employer's employees, including a small number of highly skilled craftsmen. The conflict arises when a craft union petitions the NLRB for separate representation rights for these skilled workmen. When confronted with such a request, the Board will examine certain "areas of inquiry"—developed in the case of *Mallinckrodt Chemical Works*[238]—to determine if the employees are a definable craft group entitled to separate representation.[239] Where such a finding is warranted, the Board will generally direct a self-determination election in the craft group.[240]

A New Use?

In January of 1968, the NLRB decided the case of *Libbey-Owens-Ford Glass Co.*[241] The case involved the filing of a unit clarification petition which requested the merger of two separate single-plant units with one multiplant unit, all represented by the United Glass and Ceramic Workers. Unlike the cases discussed above, *Libbey-Owens-Ford* presented a bargaining unit

---

[236] Community Publications, Inc., 162 N.L.R.B. 855 (1967).

[237] See Chapter III, *infra*.

[238] 162 N.L.R.B. 387 (1966); Chapter III, *infra*.

[239] *See* National Labor Relations Act, section 9(b)(2).

[240] Buddy L Corp., 167 N.L.R.B. 808 (1967); Jay Kay Metal Specialties Corp., 163 N.L.R.B. 719 (1967); Royal McBee Corp., 117 N.L.R.B. 741 (1957).

[241] 169 N.L.R.B. No. 2, 67 L.R.R.M. 1096 (1968).

issue in which there was no question of representation. Despite the absence of this critical factor, a three-member majority of the NLRB granted the union's request and directed self-determination elections in each of the two single-plant units. These elections were not held to determine whether the employees desired to be represented and by whom, as were all previous *Globe* elections. Rather, the employees were to decide whether or not they favored consolidation of units. This result, the majority contended, can be based on the theory that the NLRA contains no prohibition against giving "some weight to employee preference. . . ." [242] On the contrary, they argued, Congress implicitly approved the use of such *Globe* elections as exhibited by sections 9(b)(1) and (2).

Members Fanning and Jenkins dissented, stating that "there simply is no present statutory authority for permitting employees to decide, in a representational vacuum, which *contract* unit they wish." [243] The dissenters correctly noted that *Globe* elections have only been used in connection with the selection of a bargaining representative which in turn arose out of a section 9(c)(1) representation proceeding. Furthermore, the Taft-Hartley Amendments which allowed self-determination elections by professionals and craft employees were actually *limitations* imposed by Congress on the Board's power to define units. These congressional limitations are further exemplified by section 9(e)(1) which requires a secret ballot election to determine whether a labor organization's authority to negotiate a union shop agreement should be rescinded. The dissent accurately concluded that "these statutory realities are ignored by the majority." [244] The majority's decision in *Libbey-Owens-Ford* effectively contravened the intentions of the *Globe* doctrine and ignored the traditional uses of the self-determination election.[245]

The Tallying of Votes

The self-determination election generally finds applicability in a situation involving two or more appropriate bargaining units as well as two or more competing labor organizations. The various

---

[242] 169 N.L.R.B. No. 2, 67 L.R.R.M. at 1098.

[243] 169 N.L.R.B. No. 2, 67 L.R.R.M. at 1099.

[244] *Id.*

[245] The unit clarification petition is treated in detail in Chapter IV, *infra.*

combinations of these units and unions have led to complex problems as to how to tally the votes derived from the elections. In response to these problems, the NLRB has divided the use of *Globe* elections into three areas and devised a tallying method for each.

The first of these areas involves the situation wherein two unions are seeking initial representation rights. The units requested are generally a small, separate unit and a larger, comprehensive one. The Board will direct separate elections in each of the units and then utilize the so-called "pooling method" of tallying votes. If a majority of the group sought as a separate unit does not vote for the union seeking such separate unit, the votes will be pooled with those in the more comprehensive group. The votes will then be tallied as follows: votes for the union seeking the separate unit shall be counted among the valid votes cast, but shall not be counted for or against the union seeking the more comprehensive unit.[246] The result of this pooling method is to allow the smaller grouping of employees the right to choose separate representation, representation in an overall unit, or no representation.

The pooling method of tallying votes gained general acceptance and, as a result, the NLRB applied the same rule to the second area—that of craft severance cases.[247] In the mid-1950's, a number of craft unions offered strong opposition to the use of the pooling method. It was argued that this procedure deprived the separate unit employees (the craftsmen) the full freedom of association guaranteed by the Act. The overwhelming number of votes cast in the comprehensive unit could possibly serve to "sweep in" the craft employees despite their desires to the contrary. The NLRB rejected these arguments reasoning that the pooling method of tallying votes found strong justification in the need for labor relations stability.[248]

The last of the three areas in which *Globe* elections have been used has proven to be the most controversial. This controversy has centered over the conflicting interests of an incumbent union seeking to maintain its position and a challenging union seeking representation rights for a combined unit of previously unrepre-

---

[246] Westinghouse Elec. Corp., 108 N.L.R.B. 556 (1954).

[247] American Potash & Chem. Corp., 107 N.L.R.B. 1418 (1954); *reversed on other grounds by* Mallinckrodt Chem. Works, 162 N.L.R.B. 387 (1966).

[248] Stauffer Chem. Co., 113 N.L.R.B. 1255 (1955).

sented employees and employees of the existing unit. Confronted with such a situation in the 1960 case of *Waikiki Biltmore Inc.*,[249] the Board majority refused to apply the pooling method of tallying votes. Rather, it directed separate elections for the existing unit and for the unrepresented employees. An overall unit would be allowed only if the petitioning union won representation rights for both groups.[250]

The rule of *Waikiki* was short lived. For in 1961, the Kennedy Board decided *Felix Half & Brothers, Inc.*,[251] in which it overruled the earlier decision and adopted the pooling method of tallying votes. The case involved a petition filed by the International Brotherhood of Teamsters which requested a unit comprised of all office employees of the employer, including the porter-clerk and inside salesman who had previously been unrepresented. The employer and the Office Employees International Union, the incumbent intervenor, contended that the only appropriate unit was the existing one.

Reviewing the functions, duties, and responsibilities of the two unrepresented employees, the Board majority concluded that the two men "may properly be included in the same unit with the previously represented office employees." [252] The majority went on to say:

> However, as the Intervenor does not seek to add them to the existing unit, we shall not make a final unit determination at this time. Rather, we shall conduct an election among the employees in the existing unit to ascertain whether they desire to continue to be represented by the Intervenor.[253]

Accordingly, the majority directed two separate elections—one in the existing unit and one in the unrepresented unit. If the intervenor obtained a majority of the existing unit votes, it would then be certified. If a majority of the unrepresented employees then voted for the petitioner, this unit would be separately appropriate. Should the intervenor not obtain a majority in the existing unit, then the two units would be combined into

---

[249] 127 N.L.R.B. 82 (1960).

[250] *Accord*, Cook Paint & Varnish Co., 127 N.L.R.B. 1098 (1960).

[251] 132 N.L.R.B. 1523 (1961).

[252] *Id.* at 1524.

[253] *Id.*

a single, overall unit and all the votes would be pooled—that is, "the votes for Intervenor shall be counted as valid votes, but neither for nor against the Petitioner which is seeking the more comprehensive unit. All other votes are to be accorded their face value, whether for representation by the Petitioner or for no union." [254]

In thus ruling, the majority expressly overruled *Waikiki* and adopted the position advocated by Member Fanning in his dissent in that case. This reversal was based upon the belief that this was "necessary in order to insure that, in all cases, the will of the majority of employees in the appropriate unit or units, as the case may be, will be given effect." [255]

Members Leedom and Rodgers in dissent argued that the effects of the majority's decisison would be to promote "rigidity" in labor relations. The pooling of votes, the dissenters reasoned, would tend to prevent the unseating of an incumbent union at the expense of the employees' wishes, and would sacrifice equity and fairness of treatment to the incumbent's dictates. Members Rodgers and Leedom had argued in *Waikiki* that the pooling of votes led to a discrepancy of treatment which unduly weighted the scales in favor of the incumbent. Since the votes would only be pooled if the incumbent *lost* in the existing unit, the result was that the votes of the unrepresented employees could be used to give an incumbent union a second chance of retaining its status among the previously represented employees. At the same time, the votes of the unrepresented employees would have no effect in unseating the incumbent. To the dissenters, fairness required that the unions establish a representative status in both groups before a consolidation would be allowed. Moreover, the pooling method may well result in the certification of the incumbent as the representative for the overall unit, even though this same union lost the election in the separate, existing unit. It is indeed doubtful that this result conforms to the statutory mandate of providing the employees with the "fullest freedom" of engaging in collective bargaining or refraining therefrom.

Responsibilities of the NLRB

The evolution of the use of employee desires as a factor in the determination of the appropriate bargaining unit reveals certain

---

[254] *Id.* at 1525 n.6.

[255] *Id.* at 1525.

inherent advantages. By far one of the most basic foundations upon which our national labor policies rest is that employment disputes are reconcilable by the mutual consent of the parties. The consent to lose is an essential pillar in the structure of collective bargaining. Consent and acquiescence must pervade the entire collective bargaining process. The self-determination election injects this acquiescence into the bargaining unit determinations and into the choice of union representation. Without it, unionization, collective bargaining, and the overall employment relationship are severely impeded.

The use of the self-determination election must be viewed, however, with some degree of caution. The responsibilities for determining the appropriate bargaining unit lie with the NLRB. An excessive abuse of the *Globe* election procedure could constitute an abdication of this vital responsibility. Furthermore, the delineation of that unit configuration which best promotes harmonious industrial relations is not a proper function for the employees. Once again, it is submitted that the full freedom of association guaranteed to the employees by the NLRA must be preserved within the overall policy of promoting stable, effective, and efficient collective bargaining. Dr. George P. Shultz, the current Secretary of Labor, has offered the following comments:

> Self-determination has been an important, sometimes dominant theme of issues related to establishment of appropriate units. In part, this has been a result of the concept of the exclusive bargaining agent with its attendant philosophy of "unions of their own choosing." We adhere firmly to this concept, which has made a major contribution to orderliness in collective bargaining. But the notion of self-determination, when carried to the problems of recognition for occupational groups within an industry, is really not very useful. Self-determination for a small group is a denial of self-determination for the larger group.[256]

EXTENT OF ORGANIZATION

The most controversial consideration in the NLRB's determination of the appropriate bargaining unit is the extent to which the employees have organized. Prior to the enactment of the Taft-Hartley Amendments in 1947, the Board had consistently

---

[256] D. Brown and G. Shultz, "Public Policy and the Structure of Collective Bargaining," in A. Weber (ed.), *The Structure of Collective Bargaining* (New York: Free Press of Glencoe, 1961), pp. 319-320.

placed heavy reliance upon the extent of organization. Decisions, however, did note that unit determinations were not to rely *solely* upon organizational factors. As the Board commented in *Hudson Hosiery Co.:* [257]

> Extent of organization can be most important, but it can never be controlling in the full sense of that term. It must also appear that the unit sought is composed of a well-delineated and functionally coherent group of employees, and that it has some objective support over and above the petitioning union's momentary preference. Where the unit sought has not met such prerequisites, petitions have been dismissed, despite the limited extent of organization.[258]

Notwithstanding these comments, many of the Board's unit decisions prior to 1947 revealed an almost controlling emphasis upon the union's extent of organization. This reliance did find some support in the Wagner Act's (1935) expressed policy of promoting employees' organizational efforts.

Reacting to these unit determinations, Congress promulgated section 9(c)(5) of the Taft-Hartley Amendments. This legislative mandate cautions the Board that "in determining whether a unit is appropriate . . . the extent to which the employees have organized shall not be controlling." Admittedly, the thrust of the Taft-Hartley Amendments was to deemphasize unionization and to statutorily recognize the right of employees to remain unrepresented. Congress charged the Board with the obligation of assuring to all employees the "fullest freedom in exercising the rights guaranteed by this Act," including the right to refrain from union organization. The prohibition against using extent of organization as a controlling factor in unit determinations was to be one means of implementing these policies. Unfortunately, the NLRB's interpretation and use of section 9(c)(5) raises serious doubts as to its adherence to these congressional mandates.

Interpretation and Use of the Factor

Shortly after the promulgation of section 9(c)(5), the NLRB ruled that notwithstanding this mandate the extent of a union's organization may be properly considered in bargaining unit de-

---

[257] 74 N.L.R.B. 250 (1947).

[258] *Id.* at 252.

terminations.[259] The circuit courts have generally agreed[260] and, in 1965, the Supreme Court ruled that extent of organization is a permissible factor.[261] The consequences of these Board and court decisions has been to eliminate one possible interpretation of section 9(c)(5)—that no unit decision shall center on the extent to which employees have been organized. Such an interpretation would, in effect, require the Board to completely disregard the factor. Where nonorganizational criteria favor alternative unit configurations, the extent of organization would, by necessity, become the determinative factor. If Congress wished to prohibit such a result, a mandate so stating could have been promulgated. Moreover, the report of the House of Representatives accompanying the amendments specifically noted that "the Board may take into consideration the extent to which employees have organized, [but] this evidence should have little weight, and as [section 9(c)(5)] provides, is not to be controlling."[262]

There currently exists little conflict as to whether or not the Board may consider extent of organization. There are, however, two distinct views regarding the relative significance of the factor. The NLRB and most circuit courts contend that the only limitation upon the use of the factor is that it should not be the "sole" or "controlling" determinant of unit size. This, the Board argues, implies that section 9(c)(5) only prohibits a unit determination supported by no valid criteria other than extent of organization.[263] Generally, however, the courts require that the Board's decision indicate the presence of nonorganizational factors carrying some relatively substantial weight. That the courts should require the presence of substantial nonorganizational factors finds support in the House report accompanying section 9(c)(5) which warns that, occasionally, "the Board pretends to find reasons other than extent to which the employees have organized"[264] to support unit determinations.[265] Moreover, adopting

---

259 Thalhimer Bros. Inc., 83 N.L.R.B. 664 (1949).

260 *E.g.*, General Instrument Corp. v. NLRB, 319 F.2d 420 (4th Cir. 1963); Foreman & Clark v. NLRB, 215 F.2d 396 (9th Cir. 1954).

261 NLRB v. Metropolitan Life Insurance Co., 380 U.S. 438 (1965).

262 H. R. Rep. No. 245, 80th Cong., 1st Sess. 37 at 328 (1948).

263 *E.g.*, Abbotts Dairies, Inc., 97 N.L.R.B. 1064 (1952).

264 Note, *The Board and Section 9(c)(5)*, *supra* note 33, at 821.

265 H. R. Rep. No. 245, 80th Cong., 1st Sess. 37 at 328 (1948).

the position advocated by the Board would serve to completely nullify the effects of 9(c)(5). As noted above, even prior to the Taft-Hartley Amendments, the Board required unit configurations to have "some objective support" other than extent of organization.[266] The congressional enactment of the section would thus amount to an exercise in futility.

A second interpretation as to the relative significance of section 9(c)(5) has been proffered by the Third Circuit Court of Appeals. In *Metropolitan Life Insurance*,[267] the Court argued that the legislature intended that the Board should decide unit appropriateness on the basis of nonorganizational factors alone. Without rejecting the use of extent of organization, it was reasoned that section 9(c)(5) would only allow the Board to use organizational criteria to choose among alternatively appropriate units. Accordingly, after the traditional factors have been applied and the result is a determination of the appropriateness of more than one unit configuration, extent of organization could then become a consideration. In addition to more closely conforming to the policy of neutrality expressed in the Taft-Hartley Amendments, this interpretation would considerably lessen the burdens of judicial review of unit decisions.[268] Alternatively, it is suggested that where the Board finds as appropriate more than one unit configuration, the determinative factor should be the employees' desires—as expressed through a *Globe* election—and not the extent of union organization.[269]

Closely related to the varying interpretations of, and ambiguities in, section 9(c)(5) is the question of whether the NLRA requires a finding of the *most* appropriate unit for purposes of collective bargaining. The Board has long reasoned that the primary objective of the Act is industrial peace, that collective bargaining is essential to this peace, that to promote collective bargaining *some* organization among employees is preferable to none, and that to foster organization "any" appropriate unit will be certified rather than the optimum unit.[270] The result of this

---

[266] Hudson Hosiery Co., 74 N.L.R.B. 250 (1947).

[267] Metropolitan Life Ins. Co. v. NLRB, 328 F.2d 820, 825-826 (3rd Cir. 1964).

[268] *See* Leedom v. Kyne, 358 U.S. 184 (1958).

[269] For a full discussion of the *Globe* doctrine, see text accompanying note 201 *supra*.

[270] See note 216 *supra*.

Board policy has been to provide the unions a certain "limited alternative choice" in selecting among several overlapping appropriate units of different sizes.[271]

When Congress promulgated the Taft-Hartley Amendments, it did not indicate any specific awareness of this problem.[272] A number of leading commentators, however, have presented complex legal arguments concluding that the current national labor policies implicitly require a finding of the most appropriate unit.[273] Aside from the strict legality of the issue, it would appear that the extensive manipulation of the unit determination factors combined with the discretion to choose "any" appropriate unit would allow the Board to sustain most union petitions. Moreover, it as yet remains unclear "whether section 9 (c) (5) was intended to apply not only in the determination that a unit is possibly 'appropriate' but also in the final decision that a unit is that one appropriate unit in which the election will be ordered." [274] If 9 (c) (5) applies only to the initial determination and not to the final decision, then the extent of union organization may be the controlling determinant of the ultimate bargaining unit. Alternatively, an application of the mandate, in view of the Board's interpretation, would allow the factor to be a consideration in the unit choice but not to the extent of being controlling. Adopting this latter position, the question arises as to exactly what factors would dictate the ultimate unit configuration. If it appears that the various unit sizes all conform to the expected scope of collective bargaining, the employees' desires could then properly be determinative. Such a solution would require the Board to be cognizant of the fact that the guarantee of employee freedom of choice must be considered within the overall policy of promoting successful collective bargaining.

The controversies surrounding section 9 (c) (5) are indeed extensive and Board decisions provide sound justification for this conflict. For example, a comparison of the two *P. Ballantine*

---

[271] Morand Bros. Beverage Co., 91 N.L.R.B. 409, 418 (1950).

[272] Note, *The Board and Section 9(c)(5), supra* note 33, at 822.

[273] Rains, *Determination of the Appropriate Bargaining Unit by the NLRB: A Lack of Objectivity Perceived*, 8 Boston College Industrial and Commercial Law Review 175, 177-181 (1967).

[274] Note, *The Board and Section 9(c)(5), supra* note 33 at 822.

& Sons cases [275] reveals what is considered to be an almost controlling reliance upon extent of organization.

In the first of these cases, decided in 1958, the Office Employees International Union, AFL-CIO, petitioned for an election in a unit consisting of all outside salesmen working out of the company's Newark, New Jersey and New York City sales offices. Opposing the petition, the employer contended that the only appropriate unit would include the outside salesmen of all of its ten branch offices. Dismissing the union's petition, the Board made the following findings of fact: branch sales quotas were set by the home office; personnel and payroll records were kept both in the central office and in the branch offices; all payroll checks were prepared at the home office; hiring and firing were actively exercised by a central sales manager; *all major labor relations policies were formulated by the home office;* vacations, holidays, fringe benefits, and methods of compensation were centrally determined and administered; grievance and arbitration proceedings were handled by the home office; and there was some history of employee interchange between the branches and the regions. Relying on these facts, the Board concluded that the requested unit was "too narrow" in scope to constitute an appropriate bargaining unit.[276]

In the second *P. Ballantine & Sons* case, decided by the Kennedy Board in 1963, the same union petitioned for representation rights for the same salesmen of the same employer in a unit confined to the Newark sales office. The Board, referring to the earlier decision, again noted that "there is a substantial degree of centralization and integration in the Employer's sales organization." [277] Nevertheless, without pointing to any factual distinctions, the Board reversed its earlier decision and granted the union's petition. Attempting to justify this result, it offered the following analysis:

> Although the Board necessarily has wide discretion in the exercise of [its] authority, the statute does provide certain explicit guidelines. First and foremost is the requirement that each appropriate unit determination should "assure to employees the fullest freedom in exercising the rights guaranteed by this Act," i.e., the rights to self-organization and to collective bargaining. In order

---

[275] 120 N.L.R.B. 86 (1958); 141 N.L.R.B. 1103 (1963).

[276] 120 N.L.R.B. 86, 88 (1958).

[277] 141 N.L.R.B. 1103, 1104 (1963).

to effectuate this fundamental policy declaration of the Congress, the Board must be wary lest its unit determinations unnecessarily impede the exercise by employees of these rights. Such would be the result in the instant case if the Board were to continue . . . as it did in [the 1958 case].[278]

The decision in the second of the *P. Ballantine & Sons* cases and the analysis offered therein reveal that the Board has, in fact, equated employee freedom of choice with union organization. The result is a total disregard of the rights of the employees to refrain from collective bargaining, of the rights of the employer, of the requisites of successful collective bargaining, and of the neutrality demanded by the Taft-Hartley Amendments. As one commentator accurately noted: "It clearly appears that the Board's action in specifically overruling the first Ballantine case was based solely on the fact that the union had been unable to organize the larger unit." [279] This result, regardless of the interpretation accorded section 9(c)(5), obviously contravenes the objectives of the congressional mandate.

CONCLUDING REMARKS

When Congress enacted the Wagner Act of 1935, the need to protect the employees' right to organize was indeed apparent. The tremendous economic power enjoyed by the employer and the violent confrontations between labor and management provide ample justification for the policies enunciated in the Wagner Act. During this period, the bargaining unit decisions of the NLRB reflected these policies. As unions continued to grow in both size and power, however, Congress saw a need to more evenly balance the scales. The Taft-Hartley Amendments of 1947, with its policy of maintaining equality between employers and unions, was to be the implementation of this balancing process. Unfortunately, Board unit decisions, especially in the 1960's, reveal an adherence to the outdated principles enunciated under the Wagner Act.

The significance to be accorded extent of organization in bargaining unit determinations is a highly controversial issue. Undeniably, section 9(c)(5) prohibits the Board from giving controlling weight to the factor, and cases such as *P. Ballentine &*

---

[278] *Id.* at 1106.

[279] Rains, *supra* note 273, at 191.

Sons raise serious doubt as to the Board's adherence to this mandate. Moreover, the NLRB's broad discretion, as well as the great "flexibility" provided by the use of the various unit factors, present serious obstacles in determining precisely what relative significance has been accorded the extent of organization. As one commentator aptly noted:

> Indeed, the hollowness of these opinions may cause some concern for the integrity of the administrative process, concern not only that "parties all over the country are playing games with the units that are determined by the NLRB," but also that the Board itself is doing so.[280]

---

[280] Note, *The Board and Section 9(c)(5), supra* note 33, at 840 (footnote omitted).

CHAPTER III

NLRB Craft Serverance Policies: Preeminence of the Bargaining History Factor after Mallinckrodt

The entrustment to the NLRB of the right to designate appropriate bargaining units has created numerous problems. One of the most controversial and complex problems is the choice which the Board often is required to make between a craft and an industrial unit. Unlike most unit determination cases, it involves the overt conflict between employee interest groups.

The various skilled craft groups have raised a number of cogent arguments in favor of separate representation. First, being a minority in an industrial unit creates the feeling among craftsmen that their particular interests are being ignored. Second, the high degree of skill possessed by these "labor aristocrats" provides their representatives with greater economic bargaining power, thus allowing them to command higher wages and benefits for members of the unit. The mixing of skilled and unskilled employees tends to dilute this bargaining power, thereby lessening the benefits which the employer is willing to offer. On the other hand, the industrial unions forcefully argue that separate bargaining units jeopardize the rights of all employees, in that a strike by the skilled workers could effectively shut down the employer's entire operations. Industrial unions also argue that the larger unit enhances their bargaining power with employers. Further, it is claimed that the separation of employees into different units leads to competitive animosity with the concomitant disruption of industrial harmony.

The employers involved in these craft disputes usually concur in the position taken by the industrial unions. First, it is felt

Originally published in *Boston College Industrial and Commercial Law Review*, Vol. XI, No. 3. Copyright 1970 Boston College Law School. Reprinted by permission.

that bargaining with one unit is less formidable than dealing with two or more units. Second, employers fear bargaining separately with several different unions, particularly when each union possesses the power to disrupt their entire operations. Because of these diverse and often competing interests, it has been particularly difficult for the NLRB to formulate a policy which recognizes these interests as well as the interest of the public in maintaining labor stability. This difficulty has been reflected in the decisions of the Board during the past thirty-five years, a period during which the Board has unsuccessfully attempted to balance these interests in a way which would effectuate the broad policies of the Act. The purpose of this chapter is to examine the NLRB's past and present craft unit policies and the application of these policies. This, it is submitted, will reveal an existing dichotomy between current Board policy and practice. While the Board has articulated a policy which professes to examine all relevant factors in the determination of an appropriate unit, it has, in fact, emphasized only those factors which are supportive of its apparent preference for the industrial unit.

THE HISTORICAL DEVELOPMENT

When Congress enacted the National Labor Relations Act of 1935, the subsequent, extended controversy involving the determination of the appropriate industrial or craft unit was not foreseen. It was generally assumed that the American Federation of Labor's (AFL) policy of recognizing craft units would alleviate this problem.[1] During the first few cases before the Board, how-

---

[1] From the late 1800's until the mid-1930's, the AFL was concerned only with organizing the skilled labor force. It was not until after enactment of the National Labor Relations Act in 1935 that the craft versus industrial unit conflict surfaced. During 1936 and 1937, the then Committee for Industrial Organization conducted a spectacular organizing drive in the mass production industries. Shortly thereafter, in May 1938, the Committee transformed itself into the Congress of Industrial Organizations and pledged itself to the advancement of industrial unionism. After an attempt to unite the organizations failed, the nation found itself in the midst of a war for control of the labor force. This conflict resulted in modification of the objectives of both labor organizations and the placement of substantial burdens upon the NLRB. One labor historian has noted:

> The government became involved through the NLRB, which was inevitably called upon to settle the problems of proper bargaining units in industry after industry. Even under peaceful conditions its task was not an easy one since the CIO claimed all employees regardless of what

ever, there developed a noticeable trend toward favoring the larger integrated industrial units over the smaller craft units.[2] In 1937 the Board modified this position and instituted a policy which granted self-determination elections to craft units during the period of initial organization.[3] Under this policy the employees in the craft were allowed, when all other factors were "evenly balanced," to choose in an election between the union contending for the comprehensive unit and the union contending for the craft unit.[4]

The American Can Doctrine

In *American Can Co.*[5] the Board was confronted for the first time with a situation in which there had been an earlier determination in favor of an industrial bargaining unit. In dismissing the petition for severance a majority of the Board stated:

> The Board is not authorized by the Act to split the appropriate unit thus established by collective bargaining and embodied in a valid exclusive bargaining contract.[6]

---

work they did and the AFL claimed all men who accomplished any task however faintly it resembled a craft. In the midst of bitter conflict the work of the NLRB became much more difficult.

J. Rayback, *A History of American Labor* (New York: Macmillan Co., 1964), p. 363. *See also* J. Winfrey, "The Appropriate Bargaining Unit Decisions of the National Labor Relations Board," Ph.D. dissertation, Duke University, 1965, pp. 141-151.

[2] *See, e.g.,* Portland Gas & Coke Co., 2 N.L.R.B. 552 (1937); S. L. Allen & Co., 1 N.L.R.B. 714 (1936).

[3] Globe Mach. & Stamping Co., 3 N.L.R.B. 294 (1937).
The NLRB's determination of the appropriate unit for collective bargaining arises in the context of either an initial organization or a craft severance. Craft severance is "a process by which a group of skilled workers, recognized as a definable craft group, splits off from the union representing both themselves and a larger group of less skilled workers in order to establish a separate craft unit." Memorandum of the Legislative Reference Service, Library of Congress, March 20, 1968, reported in *Daily Labor Report* No. 39 (February 27, 1969).

[4] Globe Mach. & Stamping Co., 3 N.L.R.B. 294, 300 (1937).
The use of these "Globe" elections was heavily criticized by Board Member Edwin Smith. Member Smith argued that by allowing minorities to vote for separate representation, the Board disregarded the interests of the majority and magnified the risk of strikes by powerful craft units which could effectively shut down an entire operation. Allis-Chalmers Mfg. Co., 4 N.L.R.B. 159, 175-177 (1937).

[5] 13 N.L.R.B. 1252 (1939).

[6] *Id.* at 1256.

This decision established a Board policy of denying craft severance where there existed a stable history of collective bargaining. From 1939 to 1947 the Board generally continued to adhere to its decision in *American Can* and to deny most severance requests.[7] In the early 1940's, however, the Board developed the "craft-identity" exception to the *American Can* doctrine. Under this exception craft severance could be granted where the craft had maintained its separate identity, in spite of its inclusion in an industrial unit. The Board articulated this "craft-identity" exception in the *General Electric Co.*[8] case.

> [1] The group must demonstrate that it is a true craft, [2] that it has not been a mere dissident faction but has maintained its identity as a craft group throughout the period of bargaining upon a more comprehensive unit basis, and [3] that it has protested inclusion in the more comprehensive unit . . . .[9]

Eventually the Board liberalized its "craft-identity" exception and, in some cases, granted severance even where the craft had not satisfied the third test—protestation against inclusion in the larger unit.[10]

Section 9(b)(2) of the NLRA

Despite the increased use of the "craft-identity" exception, the *American Can* doctrine was bitterly protested by the AFL. In response to the AFL's appeal for remedial action, Congress enacted Section 9(b)(2) of the National Labor Relations Act. It was provided therein that

> the Board shall not . . . decide that any craft unit is inappropriate for [collective bargaining] on the ground that a different unit has been established by a prior Board determination, unless a majority

---

[7] *See, e.g.*, Pacific Tel. & Tel. Co., 23 N.L.R.B. 280 (1940) (toll maintenance employees denied separate unit); Todd-Johnson Dry Docks, Inc., 18 N.L.R.B. 973 (1939) (9 craft groups denied separate units); West Coast Wood Preserving Co., 15 N.L.R.B. 1 (1939) (boommen and rafters denied separate units).

[8] 58 N.L.R.B. 57 (1944).

[9] *Id.* at 59. The Board further noted that "[a]s alternative [to the craft identity exception], a craft group may show that the production and maintenance unit was established without its knowledge, or that there has been no previous consideration of the merits of a separate unit." *Id.*

[10] *See, e.g.*, Allied Chem. & Dye Corp., 71 N.L.R.B. 1217 (1946); International Minerals & Chem. Corp., 71 N.L.R.B. 878 (1946).

of the employees in the proposed craft unit vote against separate representation . . . .[11]

The legislative history of this amendment reveals the existence of a widespread feeling that the *American Can* doctrine, even as modified by the "craft-identity" exception, effectively precluded craftsmen from exercising the free choice guaranteed by the Act.[12]

After enactment of section 9(b)(2), officials of the Congress of Industrial Organizations (CIO) asserted that the provision would allow craft groups to obtain severance regardless of the consequences to the more comprehensive unit. This fear proved unfounded, for one year after this enactment the Board decided the *National Tube Co.*[13] case in which it rendered its first interpretation of section 9(b)(2).

The National Tube Doctrine

In *National Tube Co.* the petitioner requested severance of certain bricklayers who had been part of a production and maintenance unit. In dismissing the petition the Board reasoned that section 9(b) only prohibited using a prior unit determination as the *sole* basis for disallowing craft severance.[14] It maintained that a history of stable collective bargaining could still be used as a factor in determining the propriety of the requested severance.[15] Applying these principles to the facts in *National Tube*, the Board held that the high degree of functional integration when combined with the history of successful industry bargaining in the basic steel industry constituted an overwhelming argument in favor of the more comprehensive unit.[16]

In each of the three years from 1948 through 1950, the NLRB reaffirmed its interpretation of section 9(b)(2) and extended the *National Tube* doctrine to other industries. Thus the denial of

---

[11] The procedure for determining the appropriateness of a craft unit under § 9(b)(2) is outlined in detail in § 9(c) of the Act and in the NLRB's Statement of Procedure, 29 C.F.R. §§ 101.17-.21 (1969).

[12] S. Rep. No. 105, 80th Cong., 1st Sess. 12 (1947).

[13] 76 N.L.R.B. 1199 (1948).

[14] *Id.* at 1205.

[15] *Id.* at 1205-1206.

[16] *Id.* at 1207-1208.

craft severance was extended to the wet milling,[17] lumber,[18] and aluminum [19] industries which, like basic steel, were characterized by both highly integrated production methods and a stable history of collective bargaining.

The American Potash Doctrine

It was not until 1954 in the *American Potash & Chemical Corp.*[20] case that *National Tube's* "integration of operations" theory was seriously challenged. In a three to two decision, the Board again reviewed the legislative history of section 9(b)(2) and concluded that

> the right of separate representation should not be denied the members of a craft group merely because they are employed in an industry which involves highly integrated production processes and in which the prevailing pattern of bargaining is industrial in character. We shall, therefore, not extend the practice of denying craft severance on an industry-wide basis.[21]

Although rejecting the use of functional integration and a history of industry bargaining as a basis for denying craft severance, the Board refused to upset the application of the "integration of operations" theory in the *National Tube* industries (basic steel, lumber, aluminum, and wet milling) because it was not deemed "wise or feasible" to upset patterns of bargaining which had become firmly established after *National Tube.*[22]

Under the NLRB's new interpretation of section 9(b)(2), the principle was established that a self-determination election should be granted where the petitioning union can meet a dual burden of proof: "(1) the departmental group is functionally distinct and separate and (2) the petitioner is a union which has traditionally devoted itself to serving the special interest of the em-

---

[17] Corn Products Ref. Co., 80 N.L.R.B. 362 (1948).

[18] Weyerhaeuser Timber Co., 87 N.L.R.B. 1076 (1949).

[19] Permanente Metals Corp., 89 N.L.R.B. 804 (1950).

[20] 107 N.L.R.B. 1418 (1954).

[21] *Id.* at 1421-1422.

[22] *Id.* at 1422.

ployees in question." [23] The *American Potash* doctrine constituted a drastic change from *National Tube* in that it greatly favored craft severance and effectively disregarded the interests of the employer and the industrial union. [24] Despite this apparent favoritism and the inconsistency of using a double standard (one for the *National Tube* industries and a second for other industries), the Board's decision in *American Potash* was, with one exception, [25] never seriously challenged.

---

[23] *Id.* at 1424. The majority explained:

> If millions of employees today feel that their interests are better served by craft unionism, it is not for us to say that they can only be represented on an industrial basis or for that matter that they must bargain on strict craft lines. All that we are considering here is whether two craft groups should have an opportunity to decide the issue for themselves. We conclude that we must afford them that choice in order to give effect to the statute.

Id. at 1422-1423. Subsequent Board decisions established the necessary elements of a "true craft," Diamond T. Utah, Inc., 124 N.L.R.B. 966 (1959); International Harvester Co., 119 N.L.R.B. 1709 (1958); Reynolds Metals Co., 108 N.L.R.B. 821 (1954), and of a "traditional representative," Industrial Rayon Corp., 128 N.L.R.B. 514 (1960), *enforcement denied*, 291 F.2d 809 (4th Cir. 1961).

[24] *See* 107 N.L.R.B. at 1433 (dissenting opinion of Member Peterson).

[25] This exception occurred in NLRB v. Pittsburgh Plate Glass Co., 270 F.2d 167 (4th Cir. 1959). The United States Court of Appeals for the Fourth Circuit refused to enforce an order to bargain with a craft unit which had been determined appropriate pursuant to the *American Potash* rule.

The court criticized the NLRB's decision in *American Potash* on two grounds. First, it maintained that the Board's new test effectively permitted the craft unit to determine the issue of severance for itself, and thus constituted an abrogation of the Board's statutory duty to determine the appropriate unit. *Id.* at 172. Furthermore, by applying a rule which disregards the interests of the plant or industrial unit, the Board will frequently arrive at results which will be arbitrary and unreasonable, and thus subject to reversal by the courts. *Id.* at 174.

Second, the court held that the result was in fact arbitrary and discriminatory in the case at bar because the flat glass industry is indistinguishable from the *National Tube* industries in which, even after *American Potash*, the Board has persisted in denying severance by applying a different rule. *Id.* The court thus objected not only to the general substantive rule of *American Potash*, but also to the exception which continued the *National Tube* policy in the aluminum, unit milling, steel, and lumber industries. The court observed that this exception is subject to independent attack because all future cases involving the *National Tube* industries will be determined solely on the basis of prior Board determinations—a clear violation of the mandate of section 9(b). *Id.* at 175.

See also Royal McBee Corp. v. NLRB, 302 F.2d 330 (4th Cir. 1962), in which the Fourth Circuit Court of Appeals again refused to enforce a Board order on the ground that the Board's severance policies were arbitrary and discriminatory. *Id.* at 332.

Although the Board proclaimed that *American Potash* was only a "new interpretation" of section 9(b)(2), it is submitted that the Board which decided *American Potash* adopted a pro-craft unit philosophy which was diametrically opposed to the earlier Board's pro-industrial unit philosophy. At the same time, however, the *American Potash* Board was hesitant to overrule the deeply entrenched "integration of operations" theory. Thus, the Board attempted a political compromise by allowing the *National Tube* industries to retain their status while refusing to extend this privilege to other industries. The NLRB, however, was undaunted by this criticism,[26] for it was not until 1966 that the Board undertook a complete review of the policies established in *American Potash.*

THE MALLINCKRODT DOCTRINE

In December 1966, the NLRB was presented with a petition which requested severance of a group of instrument mechanics from an existing production and maintenance unit. It was in this case, *Mallinckrodt Chemical Works,*[27] that the Board instituted a major policy change with respect to the craft severance issue. In a four to one decision the Board rejected *American Potash* with regard to the standards developed therein and the favored treatment accorded the *National Tube* industries.[28]

At the outset of its opinion the majority examined the employer's operations—the manufacture of uranium metal—and concluded that it constituted a highly integrated process which was dependent upon a continuous flow system.[29] Then, using the first of the *American Potash* tests, the Board determined that the instrument mechanics were skilled workmen with identifiable interests and thus constituted a "true craft group."[30] The Board, however, found that the second of the *American Potash* tests was not met, for the petitioner did not qualify as a traditional repre-

---

[26] *See, e.g.,* E.I. duPont de Nemours & Co., 126 N.L.R.B. 885, 886 n.3 (1960). However, a short time after the decision in *Pittsburgh Plate Glass,* Member Fanning did call for a review of the Board's severance policies. Mallinckrodt Chem. Works, Uranium Div., 129 N.L.R.B. 312, 315 n.3 (1960).

[27] 162 N.L.R.B. 387 (1966).

[28] *Id.* at 396-397.

[29] *Id.* at 389.

[30] *Id.* at 390.

sentative of this particular craft.[31] At this point the Board could have dismissed the petition on the ground that the second *American Potash* standard was not met. Rejecting this approach, the majority stated that a mere failure to show that the petitioner was a traditional representative of the craft group was not sufficient, in and of itself, to constitute a ground for dismissal.[32]

Examining the historical development of the craft severance rules, the Board reasoned that the *American Potash* decision neglected to consider "all the relevant factors" and, as a result, only the desires of the craftsmen were being considered.[33] Recognizing the impropriety of this, the majority commented:

> Underlying [craft severance] determinations is the need to balance the interest of the employer and the total employee complement in maintaining the industrial stability and resulting benefits of an historical plant wide bargaining unit as against the interest of a portion of such complement in having an opportunity to break away from the historical unit by a vote for separate representation.[34]

After once again reviewing section 9(b)(2) and concluding that the legislature intended to give the Board broad discretion, the majority rejected the *American Potash* doctrine, admitting that it had prevented the Board from "discharging its statutory responsibility to make its unit determinations on the basis of all relevant factors, including those factors which weigh against severance."[35] Furthermore, the Board continued, the decision in *American Potash* created an arbitrary distinction between industries by continuing the *National Tube* policy in certain favored industries while rejecting it in other integrated industries.[36]

The majority in *Mallinckrodt* specifically overruled both *American Potash* and *National Tube* to the extent that those cases granted or denied craft severance without considering *all* relevant factors. The new approach outlined in *Mallinckrodt* involves an examination of all relevant "areas of inquiry" including, but not limited to, the following:

---

[31] *Id.* at 391.

[32] *Id.*

[33] *Id.* at 396.

[34] *Id.* at 392.

[35] *Id.* at 396.

[36] *Id.*

1. Whether or not the proposed unit consists of a distinct and homogeneous group of skilled journeymen craftsmen performing the functions of their craft on a nonrepetitive basis, or of employees constituting a functionally distinct department, working in trades or occupations for which a tradition of separate representation exists.

2. The history of collective bargaining of the employees sought at the plant involved, and at other plants of the employer, with emphasis on whether the existing patterns of bargaining are productive of stability in labor relations, and whether such stability will be unduly disrupted by the destruction of the existing patterns of representation.

3. The extent to which the employees in the proposed unit have established and maintained their separate identity during the period of inclusion in a broader unit, and the extent of their participation or lack of participation in the establishment and maintenance of the existing pattern of representation and the prior opportunities, if any, afforded them to obtain separate representation.

4. The history and pattern of collective bargaining in the industry involved.

5. The degree of integration of the employer's production processes, including the extent to which the continued normal operation of the production processes is dependent upon the performance of the assigned functions of the employees in the proposed unit.

6. The qualifications of the union seeking to "carve out" a separate unit, including that union's experience in representing employees like those involved in the severance action.[37]

The Board applied these new standards to the facts of the case, and concluded that the policies of the Act would not be effectuated by allowing the petitioner to "carve out" a separate bargaining unit.[38] The majority based its dismissal of the petition on: (1) the intimate relationship between the work of the instrument mechanics and the production process, that is, the high degree of functional integration; [39] (2) the twenty-five year history of bargaining, including the fact that the record demonstrated that the incumbent union had provided adequate representation for the craftsmen; [40] and (3) the importance of labor

---

[37] *Id.* at 397.

[38] *Id.* at 398.

[39] *Id.*

[40] *Id.* at 399.

relations stability in an industry vital to the country's national defense.[41]

Member Fanning's dissent, as did the majority opinion, reviewed section 9(b)(2) and its legislative history. However, he disagreed both with the standards adopted by the majority and the application of those standards. He concluded that Congress intended the Board to accord identical treatment to both the severance and the initial organization of craft units,[42] and he minimized the importance of a history of plantwide bargaining.[43] In addition, he found that section 9(b)(2) created a presumption in favor of craft representation in a severance petition.[44]

Member Fanning then proposed a different set of standards to be used in deciding craft severance cases. First, with respect to the relevance of a successful history of collective bargaining, he agreed that severance should be denied where there is a showing that the interests of the craft and industrial employees have been merged, or, alternatively, that the pattern of representation in the rest of the industry has been one of plantwide rather than craft representation.[45] However, he then qualified this rule by stating that he would

> nevertheless, permit such separate representation where it is necessary to free a small group of skilled craftsmen from a bargaining structure in which, because of their minority position, their legitimate special interests have been subordinated to the interests of the majority of unskilled employees.[46]

Thus, in his view a stable history of collective bargaining is of only minor importance in determining the propriety of a requested craft severance.

Second, with respect to functional integration Member Fanning disagreed with the majority of the Board. He noted that although the presence of a highly integrated production system would not "necessarily" destroy the right of skilled employees to seek representation in a separate unit it would, in fact, tend to dissipate the

---

[41] *Id.* at 398.

[42] *Id.* at 402.

[43] *Id.* at 403.

[44] *Id.*

[45] *Id.*

[46] *Id.*

separate identity of craft employees.[47] It would appear that while he would not disregard the nature of the particular production process, he would require a higher degree of integration before denying severance than would the majority.

Finally, Member Fanning concurred in the remaining "standards" adopted by the majority. He observed that the majority included the *American Potash* standards within the *Mallinckrodt* test—that the employees constitute true craftsmen, and that the petitioning union be a "traditional representative" of such employees—and that these standards would weigh in favor of severance though no longer conclusively.[48] In addition, he agreed that consideration should be given to any attempts made by the craft employees to maintain their separate identity despite their inclusion in the broader unit, including consideration of the past opportunities, if any, which have been afforded them to obtain separate representation.[49]

Applying these standards to the facts in *Mallinckrodt*, Member Fanning found that the three grounds set forth in the majority's opinion were not sufficient to justify a dismissal of the petition. He rejected the argument that the integration of the employer's operations had merged the interests of the skilled and unskilled employees and had thus destroyed the separate identity of the craft.[50] He further contended that the majority's conclusion would be inconsistent with the *E. I. duPont de Nemours* case [51] decided that same day in which the majority granted a self-determination election despite an operation which allegedly was more highly integrated than that in *Mallinckrodt*.[52] With respect to the bargaining history and labor stability arguments, he indicated that an examination of the company's history revealed that in three prior instances separate units had been carved out from the production and maintenance unit, and that such multiunit bargaining had not been disruptive of labor stability.[53] Consequently, he concluded that section 9(b)(2) required

---

[47] *Id.*

[48] *Id.* at 403-404.

[49] *Id.* at 404.

[50] *Id.* at 406.

[51] E.I. duPont de Nemours & Co., 162 N.L.R.B. 413 (1966).

[52] 162 N.L.R.B. at 405-406.

[53] *Id.* at 405.

the Board under these circumstances to grant a self-determination election to the skilled craftsmen.[54]

While both opinions advance a policy of flexibility in order to compromise the diverse employee interests, the majority has implicitly demonstrated a partiality toward the more comprehensive unit (and, thus, industrial employees) whereas Member Fanning favors separate representation (and, thus, craft employees).

APPLICATION OF THE MALLINCKRODT DOCTRINE

In applying the principles established in *Mallinckrodt*, the NLRB has followed a discernible pattern; a majority of the Board has continually placed heavy reliance upon the existence of a long history of industry-wide or plantwide collective bargaining.[55] It is submitted that this reliance has caused the NLRB to grant or deny severance on the same "stable history of bargaining" criterion utilized in *American Can*.[56] Member Fanning's persistent opposition to this trend has engendered a series of four to one splits which commenced with *Holmberg, Inc.*,[57] decided on the same day as *Mallinckrodt*.

Professing to apply the new *Mallinckrodt* standards, the majority in *Holmberg* based its denial of severance upon two findings: first, that the craft group shared a substantial community of interests with the other employees [58] and, second, that the twenty-four year history of stable bargaining demonstrated that the craft group had been adequately represented.[59] Member Fanning attacked the finding of a community of interests by marshalling several facts indicating the weakness of that common bond.

---

[54] *Id.* at 407.

[55] *See, e.g.,* McCord Corp., 169 N.L.R.B. No. 7, 67 L.R.R.M. 1082 (1968); Aerojet-General Corp., 163 N.L.R.B. No. 23, 64 L.R.R.M. 1427 (1967); American Bosch Arma Corp., 163 N.L.R.B. No. 23, 64 L.R.R.M. 1403 (1967), wherein the requested severances of toolroom employees were all denied. *See also* Allied Chem. Corp., 165 N.L.R.B. No. 23, 65 L.R.R.M. 1285 (1967), wherein the Board in a four to one decision (Member Fanning dissenting) denied severance to a unit of carpenters; and Jordan Marsh Co., 174 N.L.R.B. No. 187, 70 L.R.R.M. 1445 (1969), wherein severance was denied to a unit of bakers.

[56] *See generally* Note, *Unit Determination and the Problem of Craft Severance,* 19 Western Reserve Law Review 326 (1968).

[57] 162 N.L.R.B. 407 (1966).

[58] *Id.* at 409.

[59] *Id.* at 410.

He noted that the petitioning employees worked in a separate location under separate supervision and spent 80 percent of their time performing skilled functions.[60] He stressed the differences in wage rates and contractual provisions and accused the majority of ignoring these factors while giving undue weight to those working conditions and benefits which were similar for both the craft group and other employees.[61] Having refuted the finding of a community of interests, he concluded that "an examination of [the *Mallinckrodt*] standards and their application to the facts herein reveal that, in fact, conclusive weight is being given to the broader bargaining history." [62]

This pattern was repeated with little variation in the subsequent cases of *Lear-Siegler, Inc.*[63] and *Mobil Oil Corp.*[64] In *Mobil*, Member Fanning found the majority's denial of severance inconsistent with an objective application of *Mallinckrodt* to the facts, and determined that the majority's emphasis on functional integration and a long and stable bargaining history had betrayed its lack of objectivity.[65] He noted that the majority's continued emphasis on functional integration would effectively deny to any employees engaged in a supporting function the right to separate representation, and that the effect would be to virtually eliminate bargaining by plant "subdivision," despite the mandate of section 9(b)(2).[66] The majority responded to this charge by specifically disclaiming any implication that it was establishing a presumption against the appropriateness of plant subdivision units,[67]

---

[60] *Id.* at 411.

[61] *Id.* at 412.

[62] *Id.*

[63] 170 N.L.R.B. No. 114, 67 L.R.R.M. 1522 (1968).

[64] 169 N.L.R.B. No. 35, 67 L.R.R.M. 1154 (1968). See also cases cited at note 55 *supra*.

[65] 169 N.L.R.B. No. 35 at 11, 67 L.R.R.M. at 1157.

[66] *Id.* at 10 n.13, 67 L.R.R.M. at 1157 n.13.

In Dundee Cement Co., 170 N.L.R.B. No. 66, 67 L.R.R.M. 1409 (1966), Member Fanning again made reference to his colleagues' disregard of § 9(b) of the Act:

> If [§ 9(b)] . . . is now to be ignored on initial organization, there is ample precedent to suggest it is even less likely to be adhered to by this Board in the disposition of subsequent representation issues.

Id. at 15, 67 L.R.R.M. at 1414.

[67] 169 N.L.R.B. No. 35 at 7, 67 L.R.R.M. at 1156.

and cited two cases in which severance had been awarded to such units.[68]

In his dissent in *Mobil,* Member Fanning further denounced the presumption that the mere presence of a history of industry or plantwide bargaining is indicative of adequate representation and stable industrial relations. He questioned whether those groups traditionally granted separate representation would now be required to show overt protest actions against the larger unit in order to qualify for separate representation.[69] Instead of the adequacy of representation being determined by Board fiat, he advocated that the craft group be permitted to express by vote its reaction to representation by the larger unit,[70] thus eliminating consideration of the bargaining history. It appears he would order an election wherever at least one of the six *Mallinckrodt* tests would favor severance. Such a clear abdication of the Board's responsibility to determine the appropriate unit would result in many of the same problems which existed under the *American Potash* rule.

As the Board continued to apply the principles enunciated in *Mallinckrodt,* the importance of the bargaining history factor became more apparent, and in *Radio Corp. of America*[71] the petitioning group attempted to circumvent that factor. The Board dismissed a petition for severance citing as one ground the long history of stable bargaining.[72] The petitioner had attempted to overcome this point by arguing that since the broader unit had contained both guards and non-guards—a situation prohibited by section 9(b)(3) of the Act—the overall production and maintenance unit was inappropriate.[73] Accordingly, it was advanced, there was really no history of bargaining which the Board could consider in applying the principles of *Mallinckrodt.*[74] The panel, however, rejected this argument, holding that it was unnecessary to pass upon the appropriateness of the existing unit. The Board reasoned:

---

[68] *See* Buddy L Corp., 167 N.L.R.B. 808 (1967); Mesta Mach. Co., 167 N.L.R.B. No. 10, 66 L.R.R.M. 1007 (1967).

[69] 169 N.L.R.B. No. 35 at 10-11, 67 L.R.R.M. at 1157.

[70] *Id.* at 11, 67 L.R.R.M. at 1157.

[71] 173 N.L.R.B. No. 72, 69 L.R.R.M. 1368 (1968).

[72] *Id.* at 13, 69 L.R.R.M. at 1372.

[73] *Id.*

[74] *Id.*

One of the factors that *Mallinckrodt* requires us to consider is the history of collective bargaining, with emphasis on whether the existing patterns of bargaining are productive of stability in labor relations. In considering the bargaining history, we are not determining the appropriateness of the existing unit, as that question is not in issue. . . . Rather, we are merely passing upon a petition to grant a craft unit and, in doing so, we are considering the history of amicable bargaining in the larger unit as a factor showing stability in the present situation, as opposed to what the labor relations outlook might be if severance were granted.[75]

The Board's position would appear to be defensible; again, accepting labor relations stability as a primary objective in determining a craft severance case, the existing unit should be examined only to determine its effect on the total labor relations environment.

The opinions of the NLRB in those cases where craft representation has been denied profess to observe the principles and policies of *Mallinckrodt*. However, those decisions consistently raise doubt as to whether these principles and policies are being applied in an objective fashion. Even those cases where the Board has granted separate representation do not signify a departure from the Board's subjective application of the six *Mallinckrodt* tests. Those cases since *Mallinckrodt* in which a craft unit has been deemed appropriate by the Board may be divided into two categories: first, those which involve the initial organization of a craft unit not previously represented in collective bargaining, and to which a more liberal rule has been applied and, second, those in which the craft employees were members of a broader unit but were not actually represented by that unit.

E. I. duPont de Nemours & Co.[76] was the first of the cases involving initial organization. When compared with its companion case, *Holmberg, duPont* demonstrates that separate representation in the context of initial organization is more readily permitted than severance from an existing broad unit because gen-

---

[75] *Id.* at 13-14, 69 L.R.R.M. at 1373. It was also noted that the Act only prohibits the Board from finding a mixed unit of guards and non-guards, but does not prevent the parties from consenting to such a unit. *Id.*

[76] 162 N.L.R.B. 413 (1966). *See also* Mesta Mach. Co., 167 N.L.R.B. No. 10, 66 L.R.R.M. 1007 (1967); Fremont Hotel, Inc., 168 N.L.R.B. No. 23, 66 L.R.R.M. 1250 (1967); Myers Drum Co., 165 N.L.R.B. (1967), where the Board, in granting separate self-determination elections, placed great emphasis upon the fact that the requested employees had been previously unrepresented.

erally it is less disruptive of industrial harmony. In *duPont* the Board found a high degree of functional integration: the employer's operation consisted of a continuous flow process; the craft employees spent more than 90 percent of their time in production areas, and their work was coordinated with that of the production operators.[77] Notwithstanding these findings, the majority concluded that this functional integration, where there were no "other considerations of . . . overriding force,"[78] had not resulted in a merger of the separate community of interests:

> [Functional integration] is not in and of itself sufficient to preclude the formation of a separate craft bargaining unit, unless it results in such a fusion of functions, skills, and working conditions between those in the asserted craft group and others outside it as to obliterate any meaningful lines of separate craft identity.[79]

In a concurring opinion Member Fanning reiterated his accusation that in this initial organization case, as in severance cases, conclusive weight was being given to the bargaining history factor. He agreed with the majority "except to the extent that it relies on the absence of bargaining history on a more comprehensive basis as a reason for finding that the [craft employees] constitute a unit appropriate for purposes of collective bargaining within the meaning of Section 9(b) of the Act."[80] The similarity of the facts in *duPont* and *Mallinckrodt* makes it difficult to reconcile the disparate results. The fact that the craft unit was approved in *duPont*—which is distinguishable from *Mallinckrodt* only in the total absence of prior bargaining history—lends considerable support to the opinion expressed by Member Fanning.

Although the case of *Anheuser-Busch, Inc.*[81] is frequently considered to represent the granting of a severance petition, it is in fact a case involving initial organization. Notwithstanding several factors which weighed heavily against separate representation, the NLRB granted the separate unit emphasizing that there

---

[77] 162 N.L.R.B. at 416-417.

[78] *Id.* at 419. It appears that the only "consideration" which the Board would have deemed of "overriding force" was a history of collective bargaining. *Id.* at 418.

[79] *Id.* at 419.

[80] *Id.* at 421.

[81] 170 N.L.R.B. No. 5, 67 L.R.R.M. 1376 (1968).

was no relevant history of collective bargaining because the electrical maintenance department had been established subsequent to the last collective bargaining agreement, and the electricians had not participated in that agreement.[82] Thus, the Board stated that it viewed "the situation . . . as the initial establishment of a unit rather than a case of severance from a traditional unit."[83] A comparison of this case with the earlier *Square D Co.*[84] case indicates that the Board gave conclusive weight to the bargaining history factor in *Anheuser-Busch*. Separate representation was denied in *Square D* on facts indistinguishable from those in *Anheuser-Busch* except for a thirteen-year bargaining history.

Another case which has been considered a severance case but which more closely resembles initial organization is *Safeway Stores, Inc.*[85] There, a unit of bakers was severed from a larger unit of retail clerks. The Board noted that, although the craft group had been fully represented by the broader unit, the employer in 1963 had reorganized the bakery department by assigning to the bakers new responsibilities which were typical of the skilled bakers' trade.[86] The Board also found that the proposed craft unit had a separate community of interest by emphasizing (1) the different working hours,[87] (2) the separate and distinct lines of seniority,[88] and (3) the lack of interchangeability of employees between the bakery and the rest of the store.[89] The Board concluded that "the bargaining history of the [baker's] inclusion in the broader unit [did] not militate against their severance, *particularly in view of the recent changes in the employer's method of baking, and the changed job requirements.*"[90] It appears that, absent the drastic job reorganization, the Board

---

[82] *Id.* at 4, 67 L.R.R.M. at 1377.

[83] *Id.* The Board further noted that "while not controlling in a non-severance situation, the *Mallinckrodt* tests are useful" in initial organization cases. *Id.*

[84] 169 N.L.R.B. No. 140, 67 L.R.R.M. 1336 (1968).

[85] 178 N.L.R.B. No. 64, 72 L.R.R.M. 1133 (1969).

[86] *Id.* at 4, 72 L.R.R.M. at 1134.

[87] *Id.* at 5, 72 L.R.R.M. at 1135.

[88] *Id.*

[89] *Id.* at 4-5, 72 L.R.R.M. at 1135.

[90] *Id.* at 6, 72 L.R.R.M. at 1135 (emphasis supplied).

would have denied severance relying upon the bargaining history factor.[91]

Two additional facts were offered in order to rationalize the Board's apparent change in policy. First, a consideration of conditions in the rest of the "industry" demonstrated that other retail supermarkets in the geographical area had entered into contracts with the petitioning union covering in-store bakers, and that affiliates of the petitioning union represented bakers in other Safeway stores located elsewhere.[92] Second, an examination of conditions within the local unit revealed that labor relations stability had not been disrupted by separate representation for meat cutters in the same stores.[93]

It is submitted that the rationale advanced in *Safeway* would not be applied by the Board to industries unlike the retail grocery business. In manufacturing industries the fragmentation of bargaining units produces the corresponding likelihood of a "double strike" situation, where the separate craft unit, because of the skill of its members and the essential nature of their work, has the economic power to shut down the entire production operation. It is suggested that such power would not accrue to the unit of bakers severed in *Safeway*. Thus, severance might be conducive to immediate industrial peace without causing future economic harm to the employer.

The second category includes cases in which actual severance from an existing broader unit was permitted principally because the craft employees were not in fact represented by that unit. In *Jay Kay Metal Specialties Corp.*,[94] the Board noted that, although the craft group previously had been included in an overall production and maintenance unit, the collective bargaining agreements had permitted the employer to negotiate individually with the craft employees regarding job classifications, wage rates, and other conditions of employment. It was found that in fact such individual negotiations had occurred.[95] Thus, the Board

---

[91] *Cf.* Buckeye Village Market, Inc., 175 N.L.R.B. No. 46, 70 L.R.R.M. 1529 (1969), where a 22-month bargaining history was considered "substantial, if not controlling, in determining the appropriate unit." *Id.* at 5, 70 L.R.R.M. at 1531.

[92] 178 N.L.R.B. No. 64 at 5-6, 72 L.R.R.M. at 1135.

[93] *Id.*

[94] 163 N.L.R.B. 719 (1967)

[95] *Id.* at 720-721.

concluded that the craftsmen had maintained their separate community of interest.[96]

In *Buddy L Corp.*[97] severance was granted where the history of bargaining demonstrated that, although the craft group was ostensibly a part of the broader unit, it had not participated for the previous four years in any collective bargaining negotiations.[98] In fact, the craft employees had dealt directly with management concerning grievances rather than utilizing the contractual grievance procedure.[99] This separate community of interests was reinforced by findings that the employees constituted a true craft group,[100] that their work was functionally distinct from production work,[101] and that the petitioning union was a traditional representative of such employees.[102] The history of industry and plant bargaining was considered, but the evidence was found to be inconclusive; thus, because it could not be determined that severance would disturb the stability of industry labor relations, it was felt that "to deny separate representation where to do so advances the cause of stability little, if at all, might also carry the seeds of instability." [103]

THE NATIONAL TUBE INDUSTRIES AFTER MALLINCKRODT

During the period when the Board adhered closely to the *National Tube* doctrine, the NLRB created what became known as the four "favored industries," principally because of their immunity from the rule of *American Potash*. However, with the adoption of the *Mallinckrodt* principles, the Board stated that in future craft severance cases it would show no preference for or against severance, that all relevant factors would be considered, and that all industries would be treated equally. Since that time the Board has had occasion to reexamine only two of the four

---

[96] *Id.* at 721.

[97] 167 N.L.R.B. 808 (1967).

[98] *Id.* at 5, 66 L.R.R.M. at 1151.

[99] *Id.*

[100] *Id.* at 2, 66 L.R.R.M. at 1150.

[101] *Id.* at 4, 66 L.R.R.M. at 1151.

[102] *Id.* at 3, 66 L.R.R.M. at 1150-1151.

[103] *Id.* at 6, 66 L.R.R.M. at 1151-1152.

favored industries, lumber and aluminum. A review of those cases indicates that the vestiges of earlier special treatment still persist, and that the Board has still placed heavy reliance upon the industry history of bargaining.

All three of the petitions for separate representation which have arisen in the lumber industry have been dismissed by the Board. In *Timber Products Co.*,[104] the Board noted that the "integration of operations" theory of *National Tube* and *Weyerhaeuser Timber* had been relegated by *Mallinckrodt* to being "but one relevant factor in determining the appropriateness or inappropriateness of a proposed unit, regardless of the industry involved." [105] The denial of separate representation in *Timber Products* appears to rest principally upon the finding that the requested employees did not constitute a true craft group but were merely "specialized workmen." [106] However, the Board noted that, although there was no history of bargaining at Timber Products' plant, the pattern of bargaining in the lumber industry has been on a plantwide rather than a craft basis, and has been conducive to labor relations stability.[107] The implication is clear that even had the employees been deemed a true craft group, their case would not have been viewed as other initial organization cases. Rather, because in the majority's view functional integration is common ot all lumber industry operations, the industry pattern of bargaining would probably control. In his dissent Member Fanning rightly commented that "the result reached by the majority herein is dictated more by consideration of the history of bargaining in this industry than by a consideration of whether these employees qualify as craftsmen under our recent *Mallinckrodt* and *duPont* decisions." [108] He pointed out that the craft qualifications of the electricians found here to be mere specialists were comparable to those of the electricians in *duPont* who had been granted a self-determination election.[109]

Apparently, the majority were aware of this inherent inconsistency as they felt compelled to offer assurances that the dis-

---

[104] 164 N.L.R.B. No. 109, 65 L.R.R.M. 1189 (1967).

[105] 164 N.L.R.B. No. 109 at 9, 65 L.R.R.M. at 1189-1190.

[106] *Id.* at 10, 65 L.R.R.M. at 1190.

[107] *Id.* at 9, 65 L.R.R.M. at 1189-1190.

[108] *Id.* at 17, 65 L.R.R.M. at 1193.

[109] *Id.* at 12, 65 L.R.R.M. at 1191.

missal of this petition should not be construed as foreclosing separate representation in the initial establishment of "appropriate" craft units in the lumber industry.[110] These assurances were an attempt to respond to Member Fanning's criticism:

> [V]iewing this denial of a craft unit on initial organization in conjunction with the recent *Mallinckrodt* decision, with its emphasis on prior bargaining history whenever severance is requested, it seems quite unlikely that a unit of maintenance electricians has any possibility of being found appropriate at this plant at any future time. This type of craft employee, foreclosed generally "in lumber" from separate representation during the 18-year sway of *Weyerhaeuser*, is still foreclosed despite the apparent demise of *Weyerhaeuser*.[111]

In the second lumber industry case, *Potlatch Forests, Inc.*,[112] a Board panel dismissed a petition for separate representation, again finding that the employees were specialists and not craftsmen. The Board found that the multiplant bargaining agreement did not apply to the new plant where the requested employees worked. Thus, the panel implicitly conceded that this was a case of initial organization, but, unlike *Timber Products*, relied entirely upon the finding that the employees were specialists. The panel did not allude to the industry pattern of bargaining, but their failure to do so should not be interpreted as a change in policy, for it appears that the craft qualifications of the employees in *Potlatch* were considerably weaker than those of the employees in *Timber Products*. Thus, it was unnecessary for the Board to place reliance upon the industry pattern of bargaining in order to support dismissal of the petition.

In *United States Plywood-Champion Papers, Inc.*,[113] the most recent of the three lumber industry cases, the "specialist" approach was inapplicable as the employees did not claim to constitute a craft unit but, rather, sought severance as a departmental unit.[114] Dismissal was based in part upon a merger of community of interests brought about by a history of common supervision, functional integration, similarity of work, and trans-

---

[110] *Id.* at 11 n.16, 65 L.R.R.M. at 1190 n.16.

[111] *Id.* at 16, 65 L.R.R.M. at 1192-1193.

[112] 165 N.L.R.B. No. 89, 65 L.R.R.M. 1454 (1967).

[113] 174 N.L.R.B. No. 48, 70 L.R.R.M. 1163 (1969).

[114] *Id.* at 2, 70 L.R.R.M. at 1163.

ferability of employees among departments.[115] As in *Timber Products*, the industry history of bargaining appears to have been controlling even though there was found to be no relevant plantwide history of bargaining because bargaining had been suspended during the preceding seven years.[116] The majority noted

> that the employer is engaged at least in substantial part in the basic lumber industry. This industry has historically bargained on a plant-wide basis, which has been conducive to a substantial degree of stability in labor relations, and this background was a substantial reason for the rule announced in *Weyerhaeuser Co.* We no longer adhere to the *Weyerhaeuser* doctrine, but determine the appropriateness of units in this industry based on the same factors as any other type of enterprise. However, the integrated nature of the operations as well as the industry bargaining pattern and stability which were the underlying reasons for the *Weyerhaeuser* decision remain valid factors to be considered and weighed in making unit findings, even though they were not sufficient in and of themselves to preclude consideration of other relevant factors.[117]

The decisions in *Timber Products, Potlatch Forests,* and *United States Plywood-Champion* raise doubt as to the Board's application of the principles established in *Mallinckrodt.* The *National Tube* doctrine created a pattern of integrated unit collective bargaining in the lumber industry. *Mallinckrodt* specifically rejected that doctrine. The NLRB, however, despite its pronouncements to the contrary has continued to rely upon this "established pattern of bargaining" to deny both the severance and the initial organization of craft units in the lumber industry.

Only one case has arisen in the aluminum industry since the adoption of the *Mallinckrodt* standards. In *Alcan Aluminum Corp.*[118] the Board dismissed a request for a unit of maintenance

---

[115] *Id.* at 12, 70 L.R.R.M. at 1166-1167.

[116] *Id.* at 10, 70 L.R.R.M. at 1166.

[117] *Id.* at 10-11, 70 L.R.R.M. at 1166.
Two members dissented on the basis that the facts were indistinguishable from those presented in the earlier case of Crown Simpson Pulp Co., 163 N.L.R.B. No. 109, 64 L.R.R.M. 1409 (1967), where a self-determination election had been granted to the maintenance department employees of a pulp mill operation. 174 N.L.R.B. No.48 at 17-18, 70 L.R.R.M. at 1168.

[118] 178 N.L.R.B. No. 55, 72 L.R.R.M. 1097 (1969).

employees and granted one for an overall production and maintenance unit.[119] In so ruling the majority presented a detailed
factual analysis to substantiate its finding that the employer's
operations were highly integrated.[120] As in two of the lumber
cases, reference was made to the fact that while *Mallinckrodt*
overruled *National Tube*, the integrated nature of the employer's
operations and the pattern of bargaining in the industry were
still relevant considerations in making unit determinations.[121]

In his dissent Member Fanning commented that the majority's
decision left craft and maintenance employees in the aluminum
industry in the same position as before *Mallinckrodt*:

> [The *Mallinckrodt*] decision in significant part dealt with a prom-
> ised end to plantwide unit guarantees in four basic industries. My
> colleagues subscribed to this principle, but they have now effec-
> tively negated application of it in the aluminum industry, just as
> their *Timber Products* decision . . . did in the lumber industry.[122]

CONCLUDING REMARKS

The decision of the NLRB in *Mallinckrodt* was an admirable
attempt to achieve an optimal compromise solution to the craft
unit dilemma. The pronouncements therein represented the successful culmination of a history of unsuccessful craft unit policies. The principles established by the Board in *Mallinckrodt*
are to be commended. However, subsequent application of those
principles reveals that, in reality, the standards set forth in
Mallinckrodt have been used not to *reach* a conclusion, but rather
to *support* one. For example, in the lumber industry cases, the
Board placed heavy reliance upon the high degree of functional
integration. But in the *duPont* case, where there was an equal
degree of integration, it "reasoned" that this factor was "not in
and of itself sufficient to preclude the formation of a separate
craft unit." [123] Such legerdemain makes irresistible the conclusion
that "in actual operation the decision to deny or grant separate

---

[119] *Id.* at 11, 72 L.R.R.M. at 1101.

[120] *Id.* at 1-10, 72 L.R.R.M. at 1098-1101.

[121] *Id.* at 10, 72 L.R.R.M. at 1101.

[122] *Id.* at 13, 72 L.R.R.M. at 1102.

[123] 162 N.L.R.B. at 419.

representation has frequently been used as the criterion to determine which factors will be utilized and in what manner." [124]
Member Fanning's recurring criticism that his colleagues have consistently given conclusive weight to the bargaining history factor also has merit. The Board's craft unit determinations substantiate this accusation. Of approximately forty craft severance cases brought before the Board, only a few were won by the petitioning union,[125] and those cannot be considered typical craft severance cases for reasons explained earlier.[126]

Member Fanning's accusations, however, represent an attack merely upon the penumbra of the NLRB's craft severance policies. The crux of the issue involves a choice between craft unionism and industrial unionism. More specifically, the Board majority has weighed the diverse interests of the skilled and unskilled employees along with the interdependency of the bargaining power relationship and has concluded that the few must sacrifice for the good of all.

Despite this favoritism, there is still much to be said in behalf of the NLRB's craft unit determinations. Should the Board adopt a policy of freely granting separate representation to craft employees, it may well be sowing the seeds of labor relations instability. The members are clearly aware that a lenient policy toward severance of craft employees from the larger comprehensive unit may undermine the bargaining position of the majority of the firm's employees. The recent experience of a large paper manufacturer is illustrative of the disruption which unit fragmentation may create. The company's production employees were represented by an industrial union while the boiler room employees constituted a separate unit represented by a different union. The collective bargaining agreement for the larger unit expired on August 8. After several days of negotiation and a brief strike, a new agreement was reached. On August 16 the agreement with the boiler room employees expired and their representative insisted upon higher benefits than had been given to the production workers. The company now found itself between

---

[124] Cohen, *Two Years Under Mallinckrodt: A Review of the Board's Latest Craft Unit Policy,* 20 Labor Law Journal 195, 214 (1969).

[125] It should be noted that a Board panel did grant one of three severance petitions in National Cash Register, 168 N.L.R.B. No. 130, 67 L.R.R.M. 1041 (1967).

[126] *See also* Mason & Hanger—Silas Mason Co., 180 N.L.R.B. No. 63, 73 L.R.R.M. 1010 (1969).

Scylla and Charybdis. To accede to the union's demands would induce resentment and disharmony among the production workers. However, to stand fast would invite a strike and possible disruption of the entire production process. Thus, a minority of employees successfully forced both the employer and the full complement of production workers into a position from which *only* the minority could benefit.

Although the NLRB's craft severance decisions have merited Member Fanning's criticisms, the policy alternative he advocates is pregnant with the seeds of industrial unrest. His opinions indicate an attempt—despite protestations to the contrary—to apply a rigid rule which would in nearly all cases lead to fragmentation of the bargaining units. One need only examine the industrial relations problems of the railway, maritime, newspaper, and construction industries to appreciate the unwholesome consequences of such fragmentation. Multiunion bargaining in these industries has nourished inter-union rivalries, disrupted the free flow of commerce, and necessitated extensive government intervention in the collective bargaining process. Congress surely did not intend to foster such a chaotic and unstable relationship.

CHAPTER IV

Unit Modification: Development and Use of the Unit Clarification Petition

The issues involved in bargaining unit cases do not cease with the initial unit determination. The employer-employee relationship is dynamic and, as such, must continually change to meet the needs of society. Consequently, the National Labor Relations Board has held that unit determinations, made at the first step in the collective bargaining process, are not immutable. The procedure for resolving disputes over the delineation of an existing unit is through the unit clarification and amendment of certification petitions.

An examination of the devolpment and traditional uses of the unit clarification petition will reveal that this procedure has provided an expedient means for settling existing unit disputes. The National Labor Relations Board, however, has recently attempted to extend the applicability of the petition. In January 1968, in a case involving Libby-Owens-Ford [1] three members of the NLRB, over the bitter dissent of two of their colleagues, converted the unit clarification procedure into a mechanism which permits unions to expand the scope of multiplant bargaining, regardless of employer opposition and without adequate examination of the employees' alternate desires. This Board action is now beginning to generate a series of union attempts to gain expanded bargaining units that they have been unable to secure through collective bargaining.

This chapter will examine the history, role, and use of the unit clarification procedure and contrast this role and use with the NLRB's decision in *Libbey-Owens-Ford*. The final section will

This is a revised version of an article originally published in *University of Pennsylvania Law Review*, Vol. 117, No. 8 (June 1969). Copyright 1969 University of Pennsylvania. Reprinted by permission.

[1] Libbey-Owens-Ford Glass Co., 169 N.L.R.B. No. 2 (1968).

review the subsequent applications of this precedent-setting decision and their potential effects upon the free system of collective bargaining.

HISTORY OF THE UNIT CLARIFICATION PETITION

The dynamics of any employment relationship dictate that the adjudication of this relationship must be provided with a certain degree of flexibility. The Congress of the United States recognized this need in the National Labor Relations Act. Section 10(d) of that Act provides:

> Until the record in a case shall have been filed in a court, as hereinafter provided, the Board may at any time upon reasonable notice and in such manner as it shall deem proper, modify or set aside, in whole or in part, any finding or order made or issued by it.

Pursuant to the power granted in section 10(d), and the authority granted in section 9 of the Act, the NLRB enacted rule 102.60(b) of its Rules and Regulations.[2] It is therein provided that "[a] petition for clarification of an existing bargaining unit or a petition for amendment of certification, in the absence of a question concerning representation, may be filed by a labor organization or by an employer." [3]

The wording of Rule 102.60(b) would appear to imply that the unit clarification (UC) petition and the amendment of certification (AC) petition may be used interchangeably. A cursory examination of the relevant cases would seem to lead to the same conclusion. There are, however, certain differences which have evolved. From its origination the amendment of certification petition was intended to be used only by a labor organization which had obtained representation rights through a Board certification procedure. The petition form itself indicates this by requiring the case number in which certification was granted.

---

[2] NLRB determinations in representation proceedings are not considered final orders within § 10 of the Act. Accordingly, such determinations are subject to judicial review only when they are incidental to a review of an unfair labor order. Because of this, § 10(d), which is applicable to unfair labor practice proceedings, can be considered as implicitly approving the concomitant power associated with § 9 of the Act. *See* Carey v. Westinghouse Elec. Co., 375 U.S. 261 (1964) in which the Supreme Court gave tacit approval to the Board's enactment of the Rule.

[3] *See also* 29 C.F.R. § 101.17 (1969).

By comparison, the unit clarification petition has had a some-what inconsistent history. Prior to 1957, the NLRB had not questioned the propriety of an uncertified union using the UC petition. In the case of *Bell Telephone Co.*,[4] however, the company challenged the right of the labor organization—to whom the company had granted voluntary recognition—to use the clarification procedure. The Board ruled that where the union had never been certified, where the union's majority status was not in issue, and where neither party wanted an election because they desired only a determination of the status of certain disputed employees, it had no statutory powers to make such a determination. The decision in *Bell Telephone* concluded that no "legal power" can be derived from the Act with regard to an uncertified union because its status as employee representative did not evolve through a specific Board determination as provided in the statute.[5]

The Board's 1957 decision in *Bell Telephone* effectively denied the benefits of Rule 102.60(b) to any uncertified union. If a dispute arose over the inclusion or exclusion of certain employees in the bargaining unit, the uncertified labor organization was compelled either to seek a Board certification or to seek a settlement with the employer. The latter alternative, although promoted by the NLRA, could prove difficult because of a lack of consistent guidelines in previous Board decisions which could serve as the basis for agreement. Choosing the former alternative would give rise to two potentially serious problems. First, a "question of representation" would have to be found to exist, and second, if such a determination were made, other labor organizations would be free to compete for the right to exclusive representation of the employees in the bargaining unit. It thus becomes apparent that the decision in *Bell Telephone* tended to reduce the value of the unit clarification procedure to unions.

The decision in *Bell Telephone* remained in effect until 1964, when the Board decided the case of *Brotherhood of Locomotive Firemen & Enginemen.*[6] In that case a union represented employees in an uncertified unit composed of certain office personnel. The employer filed a unit clarification petition requesting a de-

---

[4] 118 N.L.R.B. 371 (1957).

[5] *See* Brotherhood of Locomotive Firemen & Enginemen, 145 N.L.R.B. 1521, 1523 n.4 (1964), in which the Board summarized the rationale for the decision reached in the *Bell Telephone* case.

[6] 145 N.L.R.B. 1521 (1964).

termination of the status of certain "supervisory personnel."
The union argued that on the basis of *Bell Telephone* the Board
cannot clarify an uncertified unit. In granting the employer's
petition, the NLRB stated that

> Upon careful reexamination and reconsideration of the decision in
> *Bell Telephone* we conclude that there is ample statutory support
> for the Board's authority to determine the status of the Grand
> Lodge employees at issue even though the Grand Lodge Office is
> a unit which, formally, has never been found appropriate by the
> Board.[7]

The result of the decision was to allow both certified and uncertified labor organizations to seek clarification of existing bargaining units. The amendment of certification petition, however,
remains for use only by a previously Board certified union. Although there exists this overlapping area between the two petitions, in practice the amendment of certification petition is generally used when a certified union is involved while the unit
clarification petition is generally used by an uncertified labor organization. There does remain, however, another distinction between the two Board procedures.

In the case of *Harrington Bottling Co.*,[8] the International
Brotherhood of Teamsters filed a unit clarification petition. The
petitioner, which had been the recognized collective bargaining
representative of the employees of Central Wholesale, Inc., sought
to substitute a purchaser of the company, Harrington Bottling
Company, in lieu of Central as the employer doing the recognizing. The employer, Harrington, opposed the petition "on the
grounds that at the time of the purchase it had another plant in
Butte, Montana, covered by a contract with another union, which
contract it claims is applicable to the purchased plant." [9] Patrick
Walker, Regional Director for Region 19, dismissed the UC petition without reaching the substantive arguments. Mr. Walker
first explained that "the Board has made it possible to transfer
'Board certifications' from a seller to a purchaser by means of a
procedure for amending outstanding certifications (the AC petition)." After discussing the overruling of the *Bell Telephone*
case, the Regional Director concluded:

---

[7] *Id.* at 1523.

[8] N.L.R.B. Case No. 19-UC-46 (September 24, 1968).

[9] *Id.* at 1.

[the NLRB] did not, however, specify that its unit clarification procedure would do for noncertified units what its certification amendment procedure would do for certifications or would grant recognition where recognition had not been extended.[10]

The effect of the Regional Director's decision in *Harrington,* if followed, is to preclude the use of the UC petition to substitute a purchasing employer's name in the existing collective bargaining agreement. Although the AC petition may be used to accomplish this, an uncertified labor organization is, of course, prohibited from using it. Since such a union would have to file a certification of representative (RC) petition, it would be confronted with all the problems commensurate with a representation campaign. In dismissing the clarification petition in the *Harrington* case, the regional director specifically concluded that his decision did not preclude the petitioner from filing a timely representation petition.[11]

Referring again to rule 102.60(b), it can be seen that neither the unit clarification nor the amendment of certification petition may be used where a "question concerning representation" exists. The Board has consistently held that where a question of representation is present, the petition for clarification must be dismissed and that the proper procedure is a petition seeking an election pursuant to section 9(c) of the Act.[12] The reason for the Board's rule that the unit clarification and amendment of certification petition may only be used in the absence of a question concerning representation is easily discernible. Section 9(c)(1) of the Act provides for a specific procedure where the Board determines that a question of representation does exist.[13] Absent such a determination neither the employer nor the union may file a representation petition.[14]

---

[10] *Id.* at 2.

[11] Coca-Cola Bottling Co., 133 N.L.R.B. 762 (1961). Although the union had filed a representation petition, the Board elected to treat it as a motion for clarification.

[12] *See* News Syndicate Co., 164 N.L.R.B. No. 69 (1967); Howmet Corp., 162 N.L.R.B. No. 143 (1967); Standard Oil Co., 146 N.L.R.B. 1189 (1964); General Elec. Co., 144 N.L.R.B. 88 (1963); Dayton Power & Light Co., 137 N.L.R.B. 337 (1962).

[13] *See* American Stores Co., 130 N.L.R.B. 678 (1961).

[14] The "certification of representative" petition and the "representation" petition both constitute the proper procedure for requesting a § 9(c)(1) election. The distinction is that the former is used by a labor organization while the latter is filed by the petitioning employer.

It is certainly obvious that a ruling concerning the presence or absence of a question relating to representation may well be determinative of the propriety of a particular procedure.[15] But the Act does not contain any comprehensive definition of what in fact constitutes such a question, although certain sections do provide some indication of the legislative intent. Section 9(c) (1) (A) (i), for example, provides for the filing of a petition by a labor organization which alleges that a substantial number of employees desire collective bargaining while their employer declines to recognize their representative. Based on this mandate, the Board has concluded that where the employer declines to recognize a union asserting representative status, *inter alia,* there is a question concerning representation.[16]

The question then is whether the inverse situation holds true. Does the absence of an employer's declination or refusal to recognize the petitioning union require a per se ruling that no question of representation exists? This issue was raised in the case of *General Box Co.*[17] The employer there resisted the union's representation petition on the grounds that it recognized the petitioner, and therefore no question of representation existed. The labor organization argued that because certified bargaining agents are given advantages and benefits which recognized unions do not enjoy, there exists a representation question.

The Board concluded that "an employer's recognition of a union which asserts representative status does not, in and of itself, negate the existence of a question concerning representations."[18] The Board then determined that, in this case, there were sufficient facts to constitute a representation question. First, the petitioner asserted a majority standing; second, it expressed a desire to secure a certificate; and finally, it filed a formal petition asking for an election.[19]

---

[15] While a question concerning representation must be present to maintain a representation petition, the Board will, sua sponte, convert the petition to a unit clarification petition when necessary. *See* Coca-Cola Bottling Co., 133 N.L.R.B. 762 (1961).

[16] "The Board initially considers in [representation] proceedings whether or not a question concerning representation has arisen, and generally finds that it is the case if the employer has refused to recognize a union seeking to bargain collectively for employees in a given unit." 10 NLRB Annual Report 16 (1945).

[17] 82 N.L.R.B. 678 (1949).

[18] *Id.* at 682.

[19] *Id.* at 682-683.

One need not be an expert in labor law to realize that the facts found to be sufficient in that case are common in every case in which a petition is filed under section 9(c)(1). Moreover, the Board's third statement is circular. The Board reasons that in order to file a representation petition, a question concerning representation must exist. The mere filing of such a petition, however, tends to create a representation question. Thus, despite the employer's voluntary recognition, an uncertified union may successfully file a petition under section 9(c)(1). The deterrent to a union filing such a petition is that it allows outside organizations to compete for bargaining rights. On the other hand, a representation proceeding affords the employees the greatest freedom of choice, which is not true of the unit clarification petition. Moreover, as will be pointed out below, the unit clarification procedure can be used to extend union power at the expense of both the employees and the employer without full recognition of the rights of either of the latter.

TRADITIONAL USES OF THE UNIT CLARIFICATION PETITION

Unit clarification has been used in two general areas: cases involving a new or uncertain job classification and cases in which the petitioning party alleges that expanded operations constitute an accretion to the existing bargaining unit. The Board itself has stated that:

> Clarification of a certification or amendment of a unit description may be in order where a new employee classification has been created, or an employer's operations have been expanded subsequent to a certification, and the employees involved are normal accretions to the certified unit.[20]

Dispute Over Job Classifications

Westinghouse Electric Corp.[21] illustrates the use of the unit clarification petition where the parties are in conflict over job classifications. The union's certification covered all employees with the exception of the specific exclusion of "manufacturing engineers." During the period of a collective bargaining agreement, Westinghouse employed certain personnel whom they clas-

---

[20] Standard Oil Co. (Ohio), 146 N.L.R.B. 1189, 1191 (1964).

[21] 142 N.L.R.B. 317 (1963). *See also* Boston Gas Co., 136 N.L.R.B. 219 (1962), which involves the identical problem.

sified as manufacturing engineers. In their unit clarification petition the labor organization alleged that despite the employer's classification the new employees were part of the bargining unit. The Board ruled that the disputed employees performed duties that were typical of manufacturing engineers. Since these employees historically were excluded from the bargaining unit, the Board dismissed the petition.

Another situation in which the clarification petition has been used extensively is that in which an employer transfers employees into and out of the bargaining unit. If management were given unfettered discretion to transfer employees out of an existing bargaining unit, the effectiveness of collective bargaining would, of course, be greatly diminished. Decreasing the size of the unit might sharply decrease the bargaining power of the union. On the other hand, restricting a firm's right to move employees could prove an imposing barrier to an efficient and economic allocation of resources. The clarification procedure provides a means for the Board to balance these conflicting interests. In reaching a decision concerning the merits of the unit clarification petition, the Board examines the nature of the new employment and the potential effects of the transfer.[22] A similar consideration has been used to resolve disputes concerning the status of summer employees.[23]

Where a firm's employees are organized in two or more bargaining units represented by different labor organizations, a movement of personnel between units may create union rivalry and disrupt the company's production. The NLRB was confronted with this problem in *Libby, McNeill & Libby*.[24] The Packinghouse Workers represented all packinghouse employees, while the United Steelworkers were certified to represent manufacturing employees located in an adjoining plant. For business reasons, the employer transferred depalletizing machiners from the manufacturing plant to the canning plant. The Steelworkers claimed a continuing right to represent the transferred employees, since the move did not change the true nature of the employment. Simultaneously, the Packinghouse Workers claimed representation rights because the new employees constituted an accretion to its bargaining unit. By accepting either argument

---

[22] *See, e.g.*, Formica Corp., 142 N.L.R.B. 433 (1963).

[23] B. J. Carney Co., 157 N.L.R.B. 1285 (1966).

[24] 159 N.L.R.B. 677 (1966).

the employer would have immediately subjected himself to an unfair labor practice charge based on section 8(a)(5) of the NLRA.[25] The Board resolved this tripartite conflict by an adjudication based on the clarification petitions filed by all parties.

In situations such as that in the *Libby* case, the employer finds himself in a precarious position. If, for example, the company were to have continued bargaining with the losing party over the transferred employees, the NLRB would have found it guilty of an unfair labor practice. Such a result is a high price to charge the employer for making what, even in retrospect, would have been a reasonable decision. An optimal solution would be to have the involved parties examine prior Board decisions and thereby determine who should properly represent the disputed employees. Such a solution would certainly yield large savings in both time and money. Furthermore, the parties would be able to reach a compromise without outside intervention —a legislative policy clearly endorsed by the Act. Unfortunately, inconsistencies in NLRB decisions could well prevent any successful implementation of this solution. Even the most astute students of industrial relations are strained to reconcile many Board decisions.[26] Since the parties are understandably reluctant to "gamble," they must resort to the most expedient Board procedure—the unit clarification petition.

Traditional Problems of Jurisdiction in Job Classification Disputes

A question raised in conjunction with job classification cases concerns the jurisdiction of the National Labor Relations Board. Jurisdiction depends upon the nature of the controversy. If the controversy is whether certain work should be performed by workers in one bargaining unit or those in another, then section 8(b)(4)(D) of the NLRA is applicable. This section provides that where there is controversy over work assignments, the Board may only act when there is a strike or the threat of a strike. On the other hand, where the controversy involves which

---

[25] Section 8(a)(5) of the National Labor Relations Act makes it an unfair labor practice for an employer to refuse to bargain collectively with the representatives of his employees, "subject to the provisions of Section 9(a)." This latter section states that the designated representative shall be the exclusive representative for all employees in the bargaining unit.

[26] For an illustration of inconsistent NLRB decisions, see Comment, 47 Boston University Law Review 139 (1967).

union should represent the employees doing a certain type of work, section 9 is applicable, and the unit clarification petition may be utilized.

This jurisdictional problem was confronted by the Supreme Court in *Carey* v. *Westinghouse Electric Corp.*[27] The International Union of Electrical, Radio and Machine Workers (IUE) was the exclusive representative for the production and maintenance employees at one of Westinghouse's plants. Another union, the Federation of Independent Westinghouse Salaried Unions, represented all salaried and technical workers at the same plant, excluding all plant and maintenance personnel. The IUE filed a grievance under the collective bargaining agreement alleging that certain employees now represented by the Federation were doing plant and maintenance work. Westinghouse contended that the controversy was a representation question and within the jurisdiction of the NLRB and refused to arbitrate. Subsequently, the IUE petitioned a New York supreme court for an injunction against the employer, which was subsequently denied.[28] On certiorari, the United States Supreme Court reversed the New York courts and granted IUE's request. After making the fine distinction between work assignment controversies and representation issues, the Court stated that "the Board clarifies certificates where a certified union seeks to represent additional employees; but it will not entertain a motion to clarify a certificate where the union merely seeks additional work for employees already within its unit." [29] The Court was also forced to decide whether the state court had jurisdiction. It concluded that a state court or an arbitrator may entertain jurisdiction regardless of the nature of the controversy—work assignment or representation—since there was no danger that they could usurp the power of the NLRB, when "[t]he superior authority of the Board may be invoked at any time." [30]

Justice Hugo Black, dissenting with Justice Clark, reasoned that requiring arbitration ex parte for the Federation is offensive to due process because the arbitrator's award—although not

---

[27] 375 U.S. 261 (1964).

[28] 15 App. Div. 2d 7, 221 N.Y.S.2d 303 (1961) (affirming and modifying unreported Special Term decision), *aff'd*, 11 N.Y.2d 452, 184 (N.E.2d 298, 230 N.Y.S.2d 703 (1962), *rev'd*, 375 U.S. 261 (1964).

[29] 375 U.S. at 268-269.

[30] *Id.* at 272.

binding on Board or court—is in the words of the majority "persuasive." Second, the employer could be sued under section 301 of the Taft-Hartley Act in either state or federal court for an alleged contract violation arising out of his failure to bargain with the right union. The employer must guess which of his employees he will be instructed to assign to the jobs by an arbitrator, the Board, or a court. Objecting to a penalty for predictive error, Justice Black commented:

> If he happens to guess wrong, he is liable to be mulcted in damages. . . . The Court's holding, thus subjecting an employer to damages when he has done nothing wrong, seems to me contrary to the National Labor Relations Act as well as to the principles of common everyday justice.[31]

As a result of the majority's decision in *Carey,* the IUE's grievance petition went to an arbitrator who decided to split the representation rights between the two labor organizations. Dissatisfied with this award, the employer filed a unit clarification petition before the Board, which granted exclusive representation rights to the Federation concluding that the arbitrator's award was ineffective because all of the parties involved were not represented in the proceeding, and also because there were two contracts involved. Thus, four years after the Supreme Court's decision the controversy in *Carey* was finally settled.[32]

McDonnell Co.,[33] a recent case in which the Board was again confronted with the conflict between a work assignment issue and a representation issue, further illustrates the adverse effects of the decision in *Carey.* The International Brotherhood of Electrical Workers (IBEW) represented the construction and maintenance employees, while the International Association of Machinists and Aerospace Workers represented production personnel. Both organizations claimed representation rights for certain "circuit analyzers." Early in 1965, the Machinists initiated and emerged victorious in arbitration proceedings from which the IBEW was excluded. Subsequently, the IBEW received an award in a separate arbitration proceeding in which the Machinists did not participate.

---

[31] 375 U.S. at 275.

[32] Westinghouse Elec. Corp., 162 N.L.R.B. 768 (1967).

[33] 163 N.L.R.B. No. 31 (1968) ; *see* ABC, 112 N.L.R.B. 605 (1956).

When the IBEW sued to enforce their arbitration award and to declare the earlier arbitrator's award null and void, the Machinists intervened and requested enforcement of the award favoring them. Victimized by this jurisdictional dispute, the employer filed a unit clarification petition, and the district court granted a stay of all proceedings pending disposition of the Board hearing.

Based on *Carey*, the majority of the Board reasoned that the dispute involved a representation and not a work assignment issue. The two dissenting members, who would have dismissed the clarification proceeding as involving a work assignment issue, also based their decision on *Carey*. It took almost four years, two arbitrators, a federal district court and the National Labor Relations Board to settle a simple bargaining unit clarification. Given the lack of NLRB guidelines, the unit clarification petition eventually proved to be the best solution.

The Accretion Issue

Cases in which there has been an increase in the level of employment compose another area in which the unit clarification procedure has traditionally been utilized. A typical increase might be caused by an expansion in the employer's labor force or by the acquisition of another plant through purchase or merger. In situations such as these the NLRB must determine whether the addition is an accretion to the existing bargaining unit or a new grouping of employees which requires a representation election under section 9(c)(1).

Such a determination is vital to the employer, the labor organization, and the employees. Where, for example, there is a mere addition of a department to a single store, a finding of a new unit would require an election that would harvest all the typical pressures of union elections. Management would also face the possibility of work stoppages and boycotts from more than one union, and the difficulty of bargaining with several unions representing employees with the same community of interests. On the other hand, a determination that an entirely distinct group of employees, which in reality has separate duties, functions, and interests, is an accretion to the existing unit would require the company to fit a new factual situation into an existing bargaining structure and to incorporate contract provisions based on policies that were developed without consideration of the later addition. Section 9(b) provides that where two groups of employees do not share a community of interests, separate elections must be provided in order to assure the employees "the fullest freedom in exercising the rights guaranteed by [the] Act." To do otherwise would deny employees the right, supposedly guaranteed by the Act, to choose whether they wish to be represented and, if so, by whom.

When determining whether the disputed employees constitute an accretion, the Board examines certain factors to ascertain whether a community of interests exists. Such factors include the history of the bargaining unit,[34] the geographic proximity or isolation of the new employees,[35] the functions, duties, and skills of the entire work force,[36] and the administrative territories or subdivisions of the employer.[37] In a recent case [38] that clearly illustrates the Board's use of these various factors, the International Brotherhood of Electrical Workers alleged in a unit clarification petition that certain salaried warehouse employees constituted an accretion to an existing unit. Before Westinghouse expanded its Hillside, New Jersey operations by moving a warehouse there from Newark, the labor organization was the exclusive bargaining representative for all salaried workers in the employer's Hillside manufacturing and repair department. Finding that the warehouse department was physically separate from the manufacturing and repair department, and that the supervision and functions of the employees were distinct, the Board ruled that the petition for clarification was an improper procedure for resolving the issue, and held that representation rights could only be gained through a section 9(c)(1) election.[39]

---

[34] Brockton Taunton Gas Co., 132 N.L.R.B. 940 (1961).

[35] Fox Co., 158 N.L.R.B. 320 (1966); Gas Serv. Co., 140 N.L.R.B. 445 (1963).

[36] Worthington Corp., 155 N.L.R.B. 222 (1965); Gas Serv. Co., 140 N.L.R.B. 445 (1963).

[37] Westinghouse Elec. Corp., 173 N.L.R.B. No. 51 (1968); Pacific States Steel Corp., 134 N.L.R.B. 1325 (1961).

[38] Westinghouse Elec. Corp., 173 N.L.R.B. No. 51 (1968). For a discussion of the NLRB's use of these factors, see Note, *The Board and Section 9(c)(5): Multi-Location and Single-Location Bargaining Units in the Insurance and Retail Industries*, 79 Harvard Law Review 811 (1966).

[39] Whenever a unit clarification procedure alleges an accretion to an existing unit, the Board must examine substantive arguments to determine the propriety of the procedure. If these substantive arguments are rejected, the petition is dismissed, but this is not a finding for the respondent.

An examination of a number of cases involving alleged accretions has shown that the NLRB has used these so-called "factors" inconsistently. Although each factor, taken by itself, can be the basis for a given result, if more weight is given to one factor than another, a different or inconsistent result may prevail. These inconsistencies have placed the employer in the unenviable position which Justice Black found objectionable in his dissent in *Carey*: that is, an employer who bargains with the wrong union commits an unfair labor practice and is liable for damages under section 301 of the Taft-Hartley Act, even if he has acted reasonably.[40] Such a holding certainly seems to contravene the policies of the NLRA and to violate any sense of justice and fairness.[41]

While providing some relief, the unit clarification procedure should not be considered the "optimal" solution, due to the fact that it requires the intervention of an external agency in contravention of the national policy of free collective bargaining. However, the recent decision of the Supreme Court in *Transportation-Communication Employees Union* v. *Union Pacific Railroad Co.*[42] provides the basis for a promising solution.

In 1952, the Union Pacific Railroad Company placed into operation a computer system which automatically performed the communications functions previously done by telegraphers represented by the Transportation-Communication Employees (T-C) Union. Operation of the computers was assigned to clerks represented by the Brotherhood of Railway Clerks. The T-C Union brought a claim to the National Railroad Adjustment Board that the computer work should be performed by the telegraphers. After the Brotherhood of Railway Clerks refused to participate, the Board found for the telegraphers. A petition for enforce-

---

[40] In the case of NLRB v. Spartans Indus., Inc., 406 F.2d 1002 (5th Cir. 1969), the Fifth Circuit Court of Appeals enforced a Labor Board order holding the employer guilty of an unfair labor practice on the grounds that the company had recognized one of two contesting unions as the proper bargaining agent for employees at a new store. At the outset of the dispute the employer remained neutral and refrained from transferring old employees to the new store. However, because of pressing economic considerations, it became necessary to recognize one of the unions. The NLRB ruled that despite the economic realities of the situation and the reasonableness of the employer's decision, the granting of recognition constituted a violation of the Taft-Hartley Act.

[41] A detailed discussion of the accretion doctrine is presented in Chapter V, *infra.*

[42] 385 U.S. 157 (1966).

ment of the Board's award was filed in the federal district court, which dismissed the case, as the Supreme Court later noted, "on the ground that the clerk's union was an indispensable party, and that the telegraphers, though given the opportunity, refused to make it a party." [43] The court of appeals affirmed this decision [44] and the Supreme Court granted certiorari.

In an opinion written by Justice Black, who dissented with Justice Clark in *Carey*, the Supreme Court affirmed the decisions of the lower courts and remanded the case to the Adjustment Board. Justice Black noted first that collective bargaining agreements, unlike ordinary contracts for the sale of goods or services, must be considered in conjunction with all other related collective bargaining agreements, as well as trade practice and custom. He then criticized the past practice of requiring two bilateral actions to resolve a trilateral problem. To correct this, the Court remanded the case to the Adjustment Board and directed it to give the Railway Clerks

> an opportunity to be heard, and, whether or not the clerks' union accepts this opportunity, to resolve this entire dispute upon consideration not only of the contracts between the railroad and the telegraphers, but "in light of . . . [contracts] between the railroad" and any other union "involved" in the overall dispute, and upon consideration of "evidence as to usage, practice and custom" pertinent to all these agreements. . . . The Board's order, based upon such thorough consideration after giving the clerk's union a chance to be heard, will then be enforceable by the courts.[45]

The effect of the ruling was to require the National Railroad Adjustment Board to resolve this trilateral dispute through a joinder process. The Board was required to consider the interests of all parties involved whether or not they participated.

Because the Court's decision in *Transportation-Communications Employees Union* was based on the Railway Labor Act, the decision would not necessarily be controlling in a case arising under the NLRA. However, an examination of the Court's opinion reveals an analysis couched in terms broad enough to be applied easily to all trilateral jurisdictional disputes. One proponent of this procedure has summarized it as follows:

---

[43] *Id.* at 159.

[44] Transportation-Commun. Union v. Union Pac. Ry., 349 F.2d 408 (10th Cir. 1965).

[45] 385 U.S. 157, 165-166 (1966) (citation omitted).

We may now anticipate the Court's ultimate sanctioning of an arbitral joinder procedure under which arbitrators (not courts) would be recognized to possess a first-instance procedural jurisdiction to deny the arbitrability of work-assignment grievances unless the grieving union shall also sanction inclusion in the hearing, as a 'party,' of any other union claimant. Refusal to join as a party in those circumstances, rejecting the correlative right thereafter to participate in designating another arbitrator before whom the issue may be heard on the merits, should foreclose the declining union from later reopening the issue before the Labor Board. Its day in court will have come and gone.[46]

Therefore, Justice Black's opinion provides a basis for resolving the problems created by *Carey* and by the NLRB's inconsistency. Unless it is followed in jurisdictional dispute cases arising under the NLRA, the employer must continue to utilize the unit clarification petition for relief.[47]

ABUSES OF THE UNIT CLARIFICATION PROCEDURE

In many cases labor unions have attempted to use the unit clarification petition to sidestep the freedom of choice guaranteed to all employees by the National Labor Relations Act. Although unions presumably represent the best interests of employees, in many situations they have interests divergent from those of the workers they represent. Thus, by requesting a particular bargaining unit, "the union may be seeking not so much to vindicate employee interests as to sweep additional employees into its jurisdiction or, simply, to prevent a rival union from organizing a group of employees which it wants for itself." [48] During initial organization campaigns the union will usually petition for a bargaining unit composed only of groups that it feels it can

---

[46] E. Jones, *A Sequel in the Evolution of the Trilateral Arbitration of Jurisdictional Labor Disputes—The Supreme Court's Gift to Embattled Employers*, 894-895 (University of California Institute of Industrial Relations Reprint No. 188, 1968).

[47] Another approach was recently provided by the Third Circuit Court of Appeals. Pursuant to a section 301 suit to compel arbitration, the defendant-employer moved to join the second union. The Court ruled upon this decision in *Transportation-Communications Employees Union* and Rule 19 of the Federal Rules of Civil Procedure to grant the defendant's motion. Window Glass Cutters League of America v. American St. Gobain Corp., 428 F.2d 353 (3rd Cir. 1970), *affirming* 47 F.R.D. 255 (W.D. Pa. 1969).

[48] Hall, *The Appropriate Bargaining Unit: Striking a Balance Between Stable Labor Relations and Employee Free Choice*, 18 Western Reserve Law Review 479, 485 (1967).

successfully organize. Although the Act specifically prohibits using extent of organization as a controlling factor in unit determinations,[49] many of the country's leading labor authorities seriously question the NLRB's adherence to this statutory mandate.[50]

Once it acquires representation rights the union will continue to strive to enhance the size of the unit. The search for additional dues-paying members is often made at the expense of both rival unions and employee freedom. The unit clarification petition provides a strong weapon in the union's arsenal. Although a section 9(c)(1) representation election protects the employee's freedom of choice, it allows rival unions to challenge the incumbent union's right to be the exclusive representative, whereas the unit clarification petition permits the union to increase the size of the bargaining unit without giving the employees an opportunity to change or eliminate representatives.

The line between the use and abuse of this generally desirable procedure can be maintained only by an impartial National Labor Relations Board. Until recently, the Labor Board has drawn the line with care. For example, in *Gould National Batteries, Inc.*,[51] the Board preserved the rights guaranteed to unrepresented employees by the NLRA [52] when it dismissed a unit clarification petition which sought to combine one unit of 276 unionized employees with two units comprised of 117 unrepresented workers.

Another situation in which the unit clarification petition may be abused is where a technical accretion has occurred, but the

---

[49] "In determining whether a unit is appropriate for the purpose specified in sub-section (b) the extent to which employees have organized shall not be controlling." 29 U.S.C. § 159(c)(5) (1964).

[50] One commentator has stated that

An examination of the cases that have dealt with contested bargaining unit questions supports the conclusion that the Board has a pronounced tendency to establish as appropriate whatever unit most reflects the extent of the union's organizational success, regardless of other considerations.

H. Rains, *Determination of the Appropriate Bargaining Unit by the NLRB: A Lack of Objectivity Perceived*, 8 Boston College Industrial and Commercial Law Review 175, 176 (1967).

[51] 157 N.L.R.B. 679 (1966). *See also* Kaiser Co., 59 N.L.R.B. 547 (1944), in which the union, which represented 2,000 employees, alleged that the 1,000 newly hired personnel represented an accretion to the existing unit. The Board denied the unit clarificaiton petition and ruled that the new employees were entitled to a representation election.

[52] 29 U.S.C. § 157 (1964).

union has long "slept on their rights." In one case, for example, the union had gained representation rights to all clerical employees.[53] Three years later a unit clarification petition was filed alleging that certain "coders" were an accretion to the existing unit. The Board held that because the disputed employees had been in existence since the original certification and the union had never requested representation rights, it waived its rights to gain representation by means of an accretion.[54] The proper procedure would be a section 9(c)(1) election.[55]

This so-called "waiver" or "estoppel doctrine" has been used infrequently, but effectively, to prevent a misuse of the unit clarification petition. In *Beaunit Fibers, Inc.*[56] the union's original certification covered all plant and maintenance personnel. In practice, however, bargaining was conducted on behalf of only those employees receiving hourly wages. In a unit clarification petition the union requested representation rights for the salaried plant and maintenance employees, but the Board held that the union's inaction constituted a waiver and dismissed the petition because a question of representation now existed.

The waiver doctrine is necessary to control the clarification procedure, but the determination of when it is applicable is a frustrating endeavor.[57] As with the equity doctrine of laches, some flexibility is necessary, but it would be reasonable for Congress to require the Board to set forth basic guidelines to which interested parties may look.[58]

Traditionally the unit clarification petition has served a useful and desirable function.[59] Where the parties dispute a certain job

---

[53] Remington Rand Div. of Sperry Rand, 132 N.L.R.B. 1093 (1961).

[54] *Id.*

[55] *See* Standard Oil Co., 146 N.L.R.B. 1189 (1964); General Elec. Co., 119 N.L.R.B. 1233 (1958).

[56] 153 N.L.R.B. 987 (1965); *cf.* FWD Corp., 131 N.L.R.B. 404 (1961), in which the employer and the union, throughout the 19-year bargaining history, had frequently changed the size of the unit. Finally the union petitioned for clarification of certain employees. The Board found that the unit represented by the petitioner was "too indeterminate" to permit resolving by motion for clarification the question of the disputed employees.

[57] *See* Westinghouse Elec. Corp., 173 N.L.R.B. No. 43 (1968).

[58] *See* Lufkin Foundry & Mach. Co., 174 N.L.R.B. No. 90, 70 L.R.R.M. 1262 (1969).

[59] Once it has been determined that the unit clarification is the proper procedure, the Board will issue an order designed to clarify the existing

classification, or where there is an alleged accretion to the existing bargaining unit, the clarification procedure has been valuable. It has provided the flexibility necessary in a dynamic employment relationship. But it is also clear that the unit clarification petition has the potential to distort and disrupt industrial relations. Used improperly, it could be a severe obstacle to the freedom of choice guaranteed to employees by the NLRA. The deciding factor is the impartiality and judgment exercised by the National Labor Relations Board. In the past, the limitations imposed on the use of the procedure have, to a large extent, been able to protect the rights of the employer, the labor organization and, most importantly, the employees. Recent developments, however, have given cause for great concern. As a veteran of the NLRB staff has stated: "The unit decisions consistently encourage the growth of unionism as such, *rather than protect the rights of employees.*" [60] The next section of this chapter examines these recent developments to determine the real extent of the truth of this comment.

NEW USE OF THE UNIT CLARIFICATION PROCEDURE

Since its inception the unit clarification petition has been used only where there has been some change in the employment pattern. The creation of a new job classification, the movement of personnel, or the acquisition of a new plant have all involved some change which would clearly affect the delineation of the existing bargaining unit. Where, however, there has been no change in the employment pattern, the Board has found no need to clarify the bargaining unit. Unfortunately the decision in *Libbey-Owens-Ford Glass Co.*[61] completely ignored these precedents.

ambiguity. The question then is when the order will take effect. Because disputed employees may be covered by a particular collective bargaining agreement, and because the NLRB cannot, under § 8(d) of the NLRA, in most circumstances, force the parties to change the terms of a current agreement, the Board's order might not be effective until the temination date of the contract. However, in Smith Steel Workers, 174 N.L.R.B. No. 41 (1969), the Board split on other issues, but unanimously felt that a unit clarification order takes effect immediately, because it does not change or modify a current collective bargaining agreement, but corrects such a contract.

[60] K. C. McGuiness, *The New Frontier NLRB* (Washington: Labor Policy Association, 1963), p. 97 (emphasis added).

[61] 169 N.L.R.B. No. 2 (1968). This decision was reaffirmed and the election results certified in Libbey-Owens-Ford Glass Co., 173 N.L.R.B. No. 187 (1968).

Libbey-Owens-Ford

There were ten company plants involved in *Libbey-Owens-Ford*, all of which were engaged in the production and fabrication of glass and glass products. Eight of these plants constituted one multiplant unit for which the United Glass and Ceramic Workers' Union was the certified representative.[62] The remaining two plants, one located at Brackenridge, Pennsylvania and the other at Lathrop, California, were each separate bargaining units. Both of these units were also represented by the Glass Workers. The multiplant unit has been in existence since 1939, the Brackenbridge unit since 1943, and the Lathrop unit since 1962. Although certified as the representative for the multiplant unit, the union had only received voluntary recognition by the employer for the two single-plant units. In 1961, before the Lathrop plant was in operation, the union requested inclusion of the employees at Lathrop in the multiplant unit. The company refused. Subsequently, a collective bargaining agreement recognized Lathrop as a separate bargaining unit. In 1965 multiplant negotiations the Glass Workers demanded the inclusion of both Brackenridge and Lathrop in the bargaining unit. But the employer again refused the requested expansion, leaving the three units covered by separate collective bargaining contracts.

The union, unable to obtain its objectives through the process of good faith bargaining, filed a unit clarification petition asking the NLRB to consolidate the three units into one multiplant bargaining unit. The petition did not allege a dispute over job classifications, an accretion, or any other change from the previously existing employment pattern. Voting three to two,[63] the Board granted the clarification, ordering elections to be held in the single plant units to determine if the employees favored consolidation. Hoping to enjoin the election, Libbey-Owens-Ford filed a motion for summary judgment in the Federal District Court for the District of Columbia. In granting the motion,[64] the Court concluded that: "[T]he National Labor Relations Board acted in excess of, and contrary to, the statutory author-

---

[62] Employees who were responsible for glass cutting operations were represented in a separate unit by the Window Glass Cutters League of America.

[63] Board Members McCulloch, Brown, and Zagoria were the majority, while Members Fanning and Jenkins dissented.

[64] Libbey-Owens-Ford Glass Co. v. McCulloch, 131 U.S. App. D.C. 190, 67 L.R.R.M. 2712 (1968).

ity conferred on it in the National Labor Relations Act." [65] The Board filed an appeal before the circuit court which, in a two-to-one decision, reversed the injunction on the grounds that the lower court lacked jurisdiction to entertain the motion.[66] The United States Supreme Court recently denied the employer's petition for certiorari.[67]

The NLRB decision in *Libbey-Owens-Ford Glass Co.* raises a number of important issues. The most prominent is whether the unit clarification can properly be used to consolidate existing bargaining units. The earliest Board decision involving this issue was *Chrysler Corp.*,[68] in which the United Automobile Workers filed a motion to consolidate three separate units. In granting the motion the Board relied on the fact that the parties treated the three units as one, that the terms of one contract applied to all units, and the extent of organization. Because the first two facts were not present in *Libbey-Owens-Ford*, and because the NLRB is barred from considering the extent of organization as a controlling factor, this early Board decision is clearly distinguishable from the instant case.

No prior NLRB decisions are directly on point, but a similar situation existed in *St. Regis*,[69] a case decided by the NLRB Regional Director for the Sixth Region. The Pulp and Sulphite Workers filed a motion for unit clarification in which they sought consolidation of several separate units. The regional director properly denied the motion, concluding that:

> While the International's Motion is styled as one for unit clarification, it is apparent from the foregoing *that there is no dispute between the parties as to unit composition or unit description which would require clarification*. Rather, the dispute between the parties centers about the scope of the unit and thereby places in issue the basic appropriateness of five individual units . . . , as opposed to a single multi-plant unit. The International, by its Motion, is in effect requesting that a determination be made of a question concerning representation in a unit which it claims to be appropriate. The Board, however, has consistently held that

---

[65] 131 U.S. App. D.C. 190, 67 L.R.R.M. at 2716.

[66] McCulloch v. Libbey-Owens-Ford Glass Co., 403 F.2d 916 (D.C. Cir. 1968).

[67] 393 U.S. 1016 (1969).

[68] 42 N.L.R.B. 1145 (1942) ; *see* Western Union Tel. Co., 61 N.L.R.B. 110 (1945) ; West Virginia Pulp & Paper Co., 53 N.L.R.B. 814 (1943).

[69] St. Regis Paper Co., No. 6-R-1193 (N.L.R.B. Director for 6th Region, 1967).

the policies of the Act and of the Board require that such matters be determined through the filing of a petition in a representation proceeding.[70]

The Board did not discuss the *St. Regis* case in the *Libbey-Owens-Ford* decision. In the NLRB's brief before the court of appeals, however, it was argued that these two cases were distinguishable due to the fact that the units in the *St. Regis* case were represented by the various locals and not by the International Union.[71] Admittedly, this is a valid factual distinction, but the regional director's reasoning was based on the fact that there was no dispute concerning unit composition or description which would require clarification—a fact that was common to both cases.[72]

From the preceding discussion of the traditional use of the unit clarification, it is apparent that the Board developed the procedure to clarify a unit description which, because of a change in the employment pattern, had become ambiguous and was disputed. In *Libbey-Owens-Ford* there was no change in the employment pattern and no ambiguity or dispute over unit description. Nevertheless, the Board still proceeded to "clarify" the units. In previous cases the Board strongly condemned such a misuse of the unit clarification petition. In *Bath Iron Works Corp.*,[73] for example, the company had two operating divisions, each separately represented by the same union. Subsequent to a merger of the divisions, the union filed a unit clarification petition requesting that the units be combined. The Board reasoned that:

> It is clear from the above that the changes in corporate reorganization have not effected such changes in the status of the employees as would require us to find that the two units have been merged. . . . For these reasons and because of the outstanding contracts, we conclude that the issues raised here are not properly to be resolved at this time in this type of proceeding.[74]

---

[70] *Id.* at 3-4 (emphasis added).

[71] Reply Brief for Appellant at 5, McCulloch v. Libbey-Owens-Ford Glass Co., 403 F.2d 916 (D.C. Cir. 1968).

[72] *St. Regis* is a weak precedent, having been decided by the regional director, rather than by the NLRB.

[73] 154 N.L.R.B. 1069 (1965).

[74] *Id.* at 1070-1071.

Considering the fact that there was no change in the status of the employees of the Libbey-Owens-Ford Glass Co. (there was not even the corporate reorganization which took place in *Bath Iron Works*) and that the outstanding contracts specifically recognized separate bargaining units, it is difficult to reconcile these cases. Instead of attempting to reconcile or distinguish them, the Board cited *Bath Iron Works* in support of their position.[75]

If we again examine the traditional application of the clarification procedure, another deviation from the precedent in *Libbey-Owens-Ford* becomes apparent. The Glass and Ceramic Workers gained certification of the multiplant unit in 1939, and voluntary recognition in the single-plant units in 1943 and 1962. During the organizational campaigns in the single-plant unit, the union had the right to request a single multiplant bargaining unit. Although the filing of a section 9(c)(1) representation petition would have properly given the NLRB jurisdiction to determine the appropriate bargaining unit, the Glass Workers "slept on their rights." On the basis of prior Board decisions, the waiver doctrine should have prevented this so-called clarification.

Another form of estoppel has been used to prevent an employer, who had specifically recognized certain employees in a contract coverage clause, from using the unit clarification to exclude them at a later time.[76] In *Libbey-Owens-Ford*, the bargaining units had separate and distinct contracts each containing a coverage clause applicable only to the respective unit. In other words, the union had specifically recognized and accepted the existence of three separate bargaining units. The majority opinion does not explain the reason that a union is able to escape from a contract that would estop the employer. It appears that the Board has disregarded precedent and ignored the intended and proper use of the clarification procedure. Whether or not it was wise to disregard precedent is, at best, questionable. It does seem, however, that the Board should have explained its action. Yet even a more basic question remains—does the Board have the statutory authority to use the unit clarification petition to consolidate units?

---

[75] Libbey-Owens-Ford Glass Co., 169 N.L.R.B. No. 2 (1968).

[76] *See* Sangamo Elec. Co., 112 N.L.R.B. 1310 (1955).

The Question of Authority

Counsel for Libbey-Owens-Ford argued that since it is admitted that no question of representation exists, the NLRB has no jurisdictional basis to determine the scope of the bargaining unit.[77] Hence, the Board has no statutory authority to reshape the unit by consolidation. The employer also argued that if section 9 is read as a whole, the word "case" in the provision in section 9(b)[78] means a case where a representation question exists. Lastly, the company argued that since subparagraph (5) of subsection (c) specifically limits the authority granted in section 9(b), it is apparent that unit determinations are restricted to cases arising under section 9(c). Therefore, section 9(c)(1) limits the Board's authority to designate appropriate units to cases in which a question of representation exists.

Answering these arguments, the General Counsel for the Board stated that "the Act provides the Board with implied authority to entertain this kind of petition notwithstanding the absence of a question of representation . . . ."[79] He reasoned that since section 9(b) does not specifically limit unit determinations to cases involving a representation question, the Board has implied authority to decide purely unit disputes, "since changed circumstances can create unit disputes without at the same time raising new questions of representation."[80] Therefore, there must be a procedure to handle such situations. Unfortunately, the General Counsel neglected to illustrate any "changed circumstances" which would warrant Board intervention.

Unwilling to accept the employer's arguments, the majority of the NLRB stated:

> We find no merit in the Employer's position that the union was required to resort to a representation proceeding to resolve the issue. . . . .

---

[77] Brief for Employer for Rehearing and Oral Argument at 6-9, Libbey-Owens-Ford Glass Co., 169 N.L.R.B. No. 2 (1968).

[78] The Board shall decide in each case whether, in order to assure to employees the fullest freedom in exercising the rights guaranteed by this Act, the unit appropriate for the purposes of collective bargaining shall be the employer unit, craft unit, plant unit or subdivision thereof . . . .
29 U.S.C. § 159(b) (1964).

[79] Brief for Appellant at 12, McCulloch v. Libbey-Owens-Ford Glass Co., 403 F.2d 916 (D.C. Cir. 1968).

[80] *Id.*

If the overall 10-plant unit sought and the existing single-plant units are all presumptively appropriate, it is not a difficult matter for the Board to make available to the employees in each of the hitherto separately represented plants an opportunity to express their preferences in a secret ballot election between continued representation in their one-plant units, or addition to the multi-plant unit. And the current contracts for those separate plants interpose no bar to such separate self-determination elections because the purpose of this proceeding is not to affect existing contracts, *but to mark out the appropriate unit for future bargaining.* . . .

We conclude from the above review of outstanding principles and the arguments herein that the Petitioner has adopted a procedure which would appear to encompass its desired relief. We are unable to perceive any reason why a further delay should be required where, as here, no question of the presumptive propriety of the employer-wide unit exists and *only the technical problems of bargaining history and employer opposition have prevented its establishment.*[81]

The reasoning of the majority circumvents the arguments presented by the employer, and the dissenting members are quick to point this out.

[The majority] ignore the fact that the void they undertake to fill—"to mark out the appropriate unit for future bargaining" without affecting existing contracts and, obviously, without reference to a representation issue—is a statutory void. Authorization for this type of election is completely lacking under the Act. Representation is not in issue in this case. Unit scope is.[82]

Furthermore, the dissenters concluded, employer opposition is not a mere "technical problem," [83] but, rather, it is a factor to be considered seriously and the existence of such opposition does not "justify rationalizing the existence of the requisite authority for solution by the employees." [84]

The decision in *Libbey-Owens-Ford* reveals another conflict between the Board members concerning the existence of a requisite statutory authority. In granting the Union's clarification petition, the Board ordered a secret ballot election be held in the two single-plant units. They reasoned that the statute contains no

---

[81] Libbey-Owens-Ford Glass Co., 169 NLRB No. 2, 67 L.R.R.M. 1096, 1098 (1968) (emphasis supplied).

[82] 169 N.L.R.B. No. 2, 67 L.R.R.M. at 1099.

[83] 169 N.L.R.B. No. 2, 67 L.R.R.M. at 1100.

[84] *Id.*

prohibition against giving "some weight to employee preference." [85] On the contrary, they argued, Congress approved the use of such self-determination elections [86] as evidenced by the section 9(b) requirement to offer professional and craft employees the right to such elections. The dissenters, however, took the view that "there simply is no present statutory authority for permitting employees to decide, in a representational vacuum, which contract unit they wish." [87] They first based their view on the fact that self-determination elections have only been used in connection with the selection of a bargaining representative which arises in a section 9(c)(1) representation proceeding. Second, they stated that the 1947 (Taft-Hartley) amendments to the Act, which allowed self-determination elections by professional and craft employees, were actually *limitations* imposed by Congress on the Board's power to define units. These congressional limitations are further exemplified by section 9(e)(1) which requires a secret ballot election to determine whether a labor organization's authority to negotiate a union shop agreement should be rescinded. [88] The dissent concluded that "these statutory realities are ignored by the majority." [89] This is the same position taken by the dissent in the appellate court.

The Board's decision in *Libbey-Owens-Ford* is disturbing not only because it contravenes congressional intent, but also because it limits, rather than expands, both the freedom of association and the adherence to free collective bargaining which the Act espouses. The United Glass Workers' interest in the larger unit stems from the natural desire of unions to insulate their position against rival unions. By means of the unit clarification petition, the NLRB helped the Glass Workers repel the Teamsters, who had already made overtures to the employees in the Lathrop, California, plant and who may well have found a place on the ballot in a representative election. Thus, not only did the Board's novel procedure favor one union over another, but it effectively

---

[85] 169 N.L.R.B. No. 2, 67 L.R.R.M. at 1098.

[86] *See* Globe Mach. & Stamping Co., 3 N.L.R.B. 294 (1937).

[87] 169 N.L.R.B. No. 2, 67 L.R.R.M. at 1099.

[88] In addition to the election authorized by § 9(c)(1) and § 9(e)(1), § 209 of the Taft-Hartley Act allows such an election in national emergency disputes to determine whether the employees wish to accept the final offer of settlement made by the employer.

[89] 169 N.L.R.B. No. 2, 67 L.R.R.M. at 1099.

denied the employees their full rights to choose their representatives.

Moreover, far from giving the employees the "fullest freedom" (as the majority of the Board averred), this decision limited not only the freedom of the employees in the two single-unit plants, but those found in the multiunit plants as well. It is logical to assume that the 8,237 employees in the multiplant unit would be as greatly affected by the consolidation as the 835 employees in the two single-plant units, since an enlarged bargaining unit would increase the problem of changing bargaining representatives in future years. Yet the 8,237 employees had no voice in the election which determined whether two plants should be added to their bargaining unit.

This case involves yet another disturbing problem—the disruption and destruction of free collective bargaining. Beginning with the enactment of the Wagner Act of 1935,[90] Congress emphasized that the interests of the nation were best served by a system of free collective bargaining. An examination of the statutes and of the expressions of legislative intent [91] which accompany them indicate a congressional purpose of minimizing government regulation. Under a system of free collective bargaining, government regulation must be aimed at facilitating the agreement-making process. "Thus, the determination of the appropriate bargaining unit . . . must be confined to encouraging settlement without outside intervention." [92]

The majority's decision in *Libbey-Owens-Ford* shows a disregard of our free collective bargaining system. In the 1961 multiplant contract negotiations, the union requested inclusion of the Lathrop, California plant (which did not begin operations until 1962) in the multiplant unit. The company refused the request, but, in turn, had to concede to other union demands. Subsequently, a separate contract which covered only the Lathrop plant was negotiated and was in effect at the time of the Board decision. During the next multiplant negotiations in 1965 the union

---

[90] Act of July 5, 1935, ch. 372, §§ 1-16, 49 Stat. 449-57, *as amended* 29 U.S.C. §§ 151-66 (1964).

[91] McCulloch v. Libbey-Owens-Ford Glass Co., 403 F.2d 916 (D.C. Cir. 1968).

[92] P. Abodeely, *Compulsory Arbitration and the NLRB*, Labor Relations and Public Policy Series, Report No. 1 (Philadelphia: Industrial Research Unit, Wharton School of Finance and Commerce, University of Pennsylvania, 1968), p. 6.

again requested inclusion of the Lathrop plant and added an additional request for the Brackenridge plant as well. The employer, again at the cost of conceding to other union demands, refused the consolidation. Finally, the union persuaded a majority of the NLRB to give them what they were unable to obtain through good faith collective bargaining.

The dissenters accurately concluded that the majority opinion in *Libbey-Owens-Ford* contravenes the basic policy of the National Labor Relations Act. Section 1 of the Act provides that the policy of the United States is "to eliminate the causes of certain substantial obstructions to the free flow of commerce and to mitigate and eliminate these obstructions . . . by protecting the exercise by workers of full freedom of association, self-organization, and designation of representatives of their own choosing . . . ." The effect of the majority's decision in *Libbey-Owens-Ford* was to provide the union with the economic power simultaneously to shut down two additional plants of the company by striking and, thus, to obstruct additionally the free flow of commerce. Moreover, the enlargement of the bargaining unit increased the scope of negotiations and with it the scope of potential dispute. By the constitution and by-laws of the United Glass Workers, any one wage committeeman can prevent acceptance of a collective bargaining agreement.[93] The consolidation of the units not only increased the size of the wage committee, but also provided each committee member with the power to impede, if not prevent, a settlement. This is scarcely appropriate for the furtherance of industrial peace.

The concept of collective bargaining—"of two powers seeking their respective goals in a free and open market" [94]—is a workable solution which depends on minimal external intervention. In October of 1968, Libbey-Owens-Ford began new multiplant negotiations with the union. The consolidation of units was again requested and the employer, wanting the union to concede on other demands, offered to merge the Lathrop plant. This offer, and the union's decision to accept it, were directed by the economic realities of the market place—realities that were ignored by the Board's decision in *Libbey-Owens-Ford*.

---

[93] Brief for the Employer at 32, PPG Industries, Inc., N.L.R.B. Case No. 6-UC-8 (December 9, 1966).

[94] P. Abodeely, *supra* note 92, at 6.

Aftermath of Libbey-Owens-Ford

The National Labor Relations Board decision in the *Libbey-Owens-Ford Glass Co.* case has provided the unions with an immensely powerful economic weapon. After using the threat of consolidation during collective bargaining to force the employer to make concessions, the union can petition the Board to merge the units. But the impact of the decision is also felt as early as the union's organizational campaigns.

> For example, a union decides to organize two plants of an employer. It is apparent to the organizer that the union has a better chance of winning at plant "A" than at plant "B". It therefore petitions for a single unit at plant "A" and after winning the election is certified on a single unit basis. Later when chances of success at plant "B" seems brighter, it petitions for an election at plant "B" on a single unit basis. It wins the election and is certified, again on a single-plant unit basis. It then petitions for clarification of the unit to include both plants. The process can continue *ad infinitum* as the union continues to "nibble away" at the employer. Such a procedure does not lead to industrial stability—it leads to chaos, confusion, and conflict.[95]

Labor organizations, aware of the potential of the *Libbey-Owens-Ford* decision, have not hesitated to use it. The United Glass and Ceramic Workers, after its success against Libbey-Owens-Ford, filed a unit clarification petition against PPG Industries, Inc.[96] The petition sought to consolidate three single plant units with one multiplant unit. As in the earlier case, the union had attempted to obtain consolidation in every multiplant contract negotiation in the period from 1954-1966.[97] The com-

---

[95] Brief for Employer at 48, PPG Industries, Inc., N.L.R.B. Case No. 6-UC-8 (December 9, 1966).

[96] PPG Industries, Inc., N.L.R.B. Case No. 6-UC-8 (December 9, 1966). On May 22, 1968, the regional director transferred the case to the Board without rendering an opinion.

[97] During the March 1969 multiplant negotiations, the union again demanded consolidation of the three single-plant units with the multiplant unit. When the company refused this demand, the union then requested a 30 day differential between the termination date of the four bargaining contracts. After considerable negotiation, termination dates with a differential were agreed upon. In the memorandum of agreement, the company promised that if, prior to February 16, 1972, the court issued a final decision ordering consolidation and if the employees at each plant voted in an election to join the multiplant unit, all contracts would terminate on February 16, 1972. In return, it was agreed that should the NLRB render a decision unfavorable to the company, the union will take such action as may be necessary

pany, at the expense of conceding to other union demands, refused the requested expansion. Having failed to obtain its demands in the collective bargaining process, the union sought help
from the NLRB.

Once again, the Board members split three to two; but this
time the majority dismissed the union's petition.[98] The swing
vote was provided by Member Zagoria, who concurred with the
decision but not the reasoning of Members Fanning and Jenkins.
The latter two members reemphasized the arguments presented
in their dissenting opinion in *Libbey-Owens-Ford*. Member Zagoria, however, found the cases to be distinguishable:

> In that proceeding [*L-O-F*] the ultimate unit sought by the Peti-
> tioner was employer-wide and, as such, was presumptively appro-
> priate. In the present situation, the unit sought comprises only
> part of the Employer's glass operations and in no event could it
> extend to the entirety of such operations.[99]

Accordingly, he concluded, the unit sought could not be appropriate on any basis other than by mutual agreement of the parties.

Chairman McCulloch and Member Brown dissented, contending
that for the reasons stated in the earlier case the union's request
should be granted. They objected to Member Zagoria's decision
on the ground that here, as in *Libbey-Owens-Ford*, the resulting
unit would consist of all employees doing the same kind of work
and represented by the same bargaining agent. The fact that
other employees working in the glass division were either not represented or represented by a union other than the petitioner was
considered to be of no significance. To the dissenters, the majority's opinion precluded the merger of separate bargaining units
in all cases except with the consent of the employer.

Members Fanning and Jenkins disagreed with their colleagues
interpretation of their opinion. They pointedly commented that:

> Contrary to our dissenting colleagues' assertion, we are not
> holding that a merger of separate bargaining units can only occur
> with the consent of the employer. We believe, however, that when
> *the normal tests of administrative coherence, geographical cohe-*

---

to make it possible for the company to appeal to the courts.   *See* Memorandum of Agreement Between PPG Industries, Inc. and United Glass and
Ceramic Workers of North America, AFL-CIO, Canadian Labour Congress,
at 1, March 26, 1969.

[98] PPG Industries, Inc., 180 N.L.R.B. No. 58, 73 L.R.R.M. 1001 (1969).

[99] 180 N.L.R.B. No. 58, 73 L.R.R.M. at 1005.

siveness, bargaining history or mutual consent are not met, there must be some showing that, nevertheless, the single plant units belong in the overall unit by virtue of such factors as common terms and conditions of employment, substantial uniformity of wage systems and fringe benefits, substantial integration of operations, interchange of employees across unit lines and the like. Such a showing has not been made in this case.[100]

The decision in *PPG* did little to end the conflict between the Board members. In *Cities Service Oil Co.*,[101] Chairman McCulloch again dissented from the decision reached by Members Fanning and Jenkins. The Oil, Chemical and Atomic Workers had requested the Board to combine three separate, unrepresented plants with the existing twenty-plant unit. The majority of the panel dismissed the petition because none of the factors set forth in *PPG* were present. Chairman McCulloch, on the other hand, would have allowed the employees to vote for inclusion in the multiplant unit. The dissenter did agree with his colleagues that each of the three plants constituted a separate appropriate unit and that elections could properly be held at each of the plants.

The United Glass and Ceramic Workers, undaunted by its defeat in PPG Industries and encouraged by the retirement of Member Zagoria, attempted to use the unit clarification petition against Rohm and Haas Company.[102] The petition requested the Board to combine into one multiplant unit three separate units all represented by the Glass Workers. Alternatively, the union sought elections in each of the units to ascertain the employees preference for inclusion in one multiplant unit. The employer argued for a dismissal, relying on *PPG* and the fact that here, unlike in the earlier cases, there existed no history of any multiplant bargaining.

In an unanimous decision, the NLRB panel dismissed the union's petition. Members Fanning and Jenkins pointed out that since 1949, the petitioner had made numerous proposals in contract negotiations requesting joint bargaining for the various units. Beginning in 1966 and continuing to date, the union had engaged in "coalition bargaining" with the employer. The other labor organization involved in the coalition was the Oil, Chemical,

---

[100] 180 N.L.R.B. No. 58, 73 L.R.R.M. at 1004 (emphasis supplied).

[101] 182 N.L.R.B. No. 6 (1970). The issues in this case arose on a representation petition and not on a unit clarification petition.

[102] Rohm & Haas Co., 183 N.L.R.B. No. 20, 74 L.R.R.M. 1257 (1970).

and Atomic Workers, the union which sought to combine bargaining units in the *Cities Service* case. All during this time, the company consistently rejected multiplant bargaining.

Referring to their decision in *PPG*, the members concluded that the unit configuration requested by the union was inappropriate on any basis except agreement of the parties. They commented that:

> [the] array of units which the Petitioner would have us merge is not identifiable as an employer administrative division, as geographically related, or as related by a history of bargaining. As we explained in *PPG Industries, Inc., supra*, where, as here, these tests are not met, there must be some showing that the separate units belong 'in the overall unit' by virtue of such factors as common terms and conditions of employment, substantial uniformity of wage systems and fringe benefits, substantial integration of operations, interchange of employees across unit lines, and the like. Such a showing has not been made in this case.[103]

Regarding the requested elections, Members Fanning and Jenkins once again asserted that the NLRB lacked statutory authority to conduct elections under these circumstances.[104]

Member McCulloch [105] issued a separate, concurring opinion. Contending that the instant case was factually distinguishable from both *Libbey-Owens-Ford* and *PPG Industries*, he commented:

> In each of those cases, there was an established multiplant unit long adhered to by the parties in the conduct of their labor relations, and the elections directed therein could only have resulted in increasing the scope of the already existing multiplant unit into a larger appropriate multiplant bargaining unit. In this case, on the other hand, the parties have bargained solely on the basis of units of plantwide or narrower scope. Thus there is no history or pattern of multiplant bargaining, and the multiplant unit which the Petitioner seeks herein to have created, over the Employer's objections, would not be appropriate under the traditional objective standards applied by the Board.[106]

In thus dismissing the union's petition, Member McCulloch placed sole and controlling weight upon one unit factor—the history of bargaining. Unlike his colleagues, he neglected to con-

---

[103] *Id.* at 4, 74 L.R.R.M. at 1258.

[104] See text accompanying note 77, *supra*.

[105] In June of 1970, President Nixon appointed Edward Miller as the new NLRB chairman.

[106] 183 N.L.R.B. at 6, 74 L.R.R.M. at 1258.

sider such factors as common terms and conditions of employment, uniformity of wages and fringe benefits, integration of operations, and interchange of employees. While couching his decision in terms of an appropriate bargaining unit determination, Member McCulloch failed to give consideration to all the unit factors created and used by the NLRB.[107]

The latest case involving the "new use" of the unit clarification procedure was *Firestone Tire & Rubber Co.*[108] The importance of the case resided in the fact that the new NLRB chairman, Edward Miller, was to participate in the decision. Not unexpectedly, Members Fanning and Jenkins voted for dismissal of the union's petition while Members McCulloch and Brown would have granted the requested consolidation. Chairman Miller was thus presented with the deciding vote.

The new chairman voted for dismissal, but unfortunately, his decision never reached the substantive issues. Chairman Miller offered the following analysis and conclusion:

> The Union filed its petition herein less than a year after the Board had certified it as the representative of the Employer's Akron firemen, and without, so far as appears, having first made a genuine effort to negotiate a separate collective bargaining contract covering the employee unit for which it was certified. The principle is now deeply rooted in our law that "a bargaining relationship once rightfully established must be permitted to exist and function for a reasonable period in which it can be given a fair chance to succeed." *Franks Bros.* v. *N.L.R.B.*, 321 U.S. 702, 725. The Board has long recognized that consideration of claims questioning the continued viability of a Board certification within a year after issuance, not only does violence to that principle but also disrupts the orderly and stable labor relations that a certification is designed to promote. Accordingly, the Board has established and consistently applied a rule requiring the dismissal of any representation petition filed during the certification year. See *Centr-O-Cast & Engineering Co.*, 100 NLRB 1507. It is true that the petition in this case does not concern the representative status of the certified Union, but only the unit in which bargaining is to be conducted. But, in the opinion of Chairman Miller, the Board action sought by this clarification petition would be no less disruptive of the orderly and stable labor relations envisioned by a certification than would the action sought by a representation

---

[107] American Cyanamid Co., No. 2-UC-34 (1970) involved another unit clarification proceeding in which there was no history of multiplant bargaining. The union's petition was dismissed by the Regional Director for Region 8.

[108] 185 N.L.R.B. No. 11, 74 L.R.R.M. 1761 (1970).

petition. This petition should, therefore, at a minimum, be governed by the same principles and be subject to the same rules with regard to timely filing. He would therefore dismiss the petition herein as having been untimely filed.[109]

It was specifically noted that the Chairman's opinion in no way intimated any view on the propriety of using the unit clarification procedure to consolidate existing bargaining units.[110] It would thus appear that the final resolution of the conflict must await future Board and court decisions.

CONCLUDING REMARKS

The unit clarification petition was developed as an instrument of flexibility which was demanded by the dynamics of the employment relationship and the goals of the NLRA. Where there is a disputed job classification or an allegation of an accretion, the clarification procedure provides an expedient and valuable means of resolution. But even where changes existed in the employment pattern, limitations and controls on the procedure were found to be necessary. Decisions like *General Box Co.*[111] and doctrines such as estoppel prevented the unit clarification petition from being misused by either or both parties. The early decisions of the Board showed an awareness of the potentially destructive effects of a procedure which might deny the employees their freedom of choice. The decision in *Libbey-Owens-Ford* ignores this without providing an explanation for such an abrupt reversal of policy.

It is difficult to imagine that a consolidation of previously existing, separate bargaining units was envisioned as a function of the clarification petition. Such a use constitutes a drastic and unwarranted change from the intended and traditional uses of the unit clarification petition. Moreover, "clarifying" units by consolidating them ignores the controls and limitations on the procedure which have always been recognized as necessary to prevent abuses. By substituting NLRB fiat for collective bargaining, and by denying both employees and employers their rights under the Act, the *Libbey-Owens-Ford* decision contravenes public policy. In

---

[109] 185 N.L.R.B. No. 11, 74 L.R.R.M. at 1762 (footnotes omitted).

[110] 185 N.L.R.B. No. 11, 74 L.R.R.M. at 1762 n.6.

[111] 82 N.L.R.B. 678 (1949).

his bitter dissent, Judge Tamm of the United States Court of Appeals for the District of Columbia Circuit critically remarked:

> The case illustrates the consistent tendency of administrative agencies to assume and exercise by accretion powers not granted to them specifically or by necessary implication. Undoubtedly, in most instances, this grasping for non-authorized powers is motivated by a sincere desire to perform more effective and efficient functions. I believe that the courts must insist, however, that the administrative agencies confine their operations specifically to those fields of activity which are bounded by the statutes which create their authority and authorize their operations. If additional power or functions are essential to a proper discharge of an agency's responsibilities, those powers or functions should not be self-created but should be sought from the Congress.[112]

---

[112] McCulloch v. Libbey-Owens-Ford Glass Co., 403 F.2d 916, 918 (D.C. Cir. 1968) (dissenting opinion).

CHAPTER V

The Effect of Reorganization, Merger, or Acquisition on the Appropriate Bargaining Unit

The fastest growing and most critical area of NLRB unit determinations involves post-bargaining situations. As one Board regional director recently commented, "However critical is the Board's determination of the appropriate unit in initial organization, its decisions in the post-bargaining situations seem to me even more critical, both in representation and unfair labor practice cases." [1]

The market forces set into motion by a reorganization, merger, or acquisition probably have the greatest effects upon an existing bargaining unit. An NLRB determination that a particular corporate structural change results in anaccretion to the existing unit or a new grouping of employees is of vital importance to the involved parties. For example, in the case of an addition of a department to a single store, a finding of a new bargaining unit requiring a separate representation election could subject the parties to all the pressures attendant upon union elections. Such a holding may well enhance the possibility of work stoppages and boycotts from more than one union,[2] as well as the difficulty of bargaining with several unions involving single-store employees having similar problems requiring common solution. On the other hand, a determination that an entirely new store or plant situated geographically, socially, and economically in an isolated location is an accretion to the existing bargaining unit would require the parties to hammer a new factual situation into an existing bar-

---

Another version of this chapter will appear in *George Washington Law Review*, Vol. 39 (March 1971).

[1] B. Samoff, *Law School Education in NLRB Representation Cases*, 21 Labor Law Journal 691, 703 (1970).

[2] For a full discussion of the issue of strikes and boycotts, see R. Dereshinsky, *Common Situs Picketing and the NLRB*, Industrial Research Unit, Preliminary Research Paper No. 6, University of Pennsylvania, 1970.

gaining structure and adapt thereto contract provisions resulting from policy considerations which never envisioned the later addition.[3] In each of these situations, the Board is confronted with the congressional mandate of assuring employees "the fullest freedom in exercising the rights guaranteed by this Act." The consequences of these divergent and sometimes conflicting interests have been to force the National Labor Relations Board to become involved in a delicate balancing process. The decisions to be examined in this article are the results of that process.

In order to facilitate an examination of the problem, this chapter is divided into three basic sections. The first consists of a brief summary and analysis of the effects of a corporate reorganization upon the appropriate bargaining unit. The second section compares NLRB cases in which an accretion is found to exist or, on the other hand, a new unit is established thus requiring a representation election. The final section considers the rights and obligations of a successor employer, an issue which, due to a recent Board decision,[4] has become controversial in the area of labor relations.

CORPORATE REORGANIZATION

The determination of the appropriate unit for purposes of collective bargaining is, by its very nature, an exercise in political science.[5] As such, unit cases necessarily involve a balancing of divergent and sometimes conflicting interests. In order to facilitate this process, as well as to introduce consistency in unit decisions, the NLRB has developed certain "factors" to be applied to the various situations. Ostensibly, these factors include a common community of interests, geographic proximity or isolation, the employer's administrative or territorial divisions, functional integration or separation, the degree of employee interchange and the bargaining history of the unit. Other than holding that no one factor should be given controlling weight, the Board has never attempted to define the relative importance of each con-

---

[3] Use of the unit clarification procedure in accretion situations is discussed in Chapter IV, *infra*.

[4] William J. Burns Int'l Detective Agency, Inc., 182 N.L.R.B. No. 50, 74 L.R.R.M. 1098 (1970).

[5] Note, *The Board and Section 9(c)(5): Multi-Location and Single-Location Bargaining Units in the Insurance and Retail Industries*, 79 Harvard Law Review 811 (1966).

sideration.[6] An examination of the various unit decisions, however, reveals that the NLRB has traditionally placed heavy reliance upon the bargaining history factor.[7]

The relevance to unit delineations of the bargaining history factor may be founded on a number of considerations. First, where there has existed successful and harmonious collective bargaining, there is strong, empirical evidence of a workable relationship. That the continuance of a harmonious relationship is congressional policy is indeed gainsay. That a successful bargaining history is indicative of this is undeniable. Second, the very existence of a history of bargaining creates a community of interests among employees, even where such a community might not have existed at the commencement of the bargaining relationship. The existence of a common seniority system, pension plan, and other conditions of employment create an intermingling of employee interests and needs. A disregard of this relationship could create serious industrial relations problems.[8]

The application of the bargaining history factor, and its alleged ability to demonstrate industrial stability, is useful only where there is to be a continuation of the historical employment pattern. Where a corporate structural reorganization has been sufficiently significant so as to change the employment pattern, the factor loses its applicability. In the absence of compelling circumstances, the NLRB is reluctant to modify a prior unit determination or a contract unit established as a result of collective bargaining.[9] Neither the existence of a prior Board decision nor the presence of a long history of successful collective bargaining, however, precludes the modification of a unit to adjust to changed circumstances.[10] Indeed, as early as 1950, the Board reasoned that the bargaining history factor is not determinative of a unit issue where, since the prior certification, a sufficiently significant

---

[6] These factors and the relevant cases are discussed in Chapter II, *supra.*

[7] Cohen, "Two Years under Mallinckrodt: A Review of the Board's Latest Craft Unit Policy," 20 Labor Law Journal 195 (1969).

[8] A third rationale for the NLRB's use of the bargaining history factor is based upon the potential problems arising from inter-union rivalries. The application of the factor in unit determinations, especially those involving the craft severance issue, allegedly offers protection to the incumbent union. See Chapter II, *supra.*

[9] Murray Co., 107 N.L.R.B. 1571 (1954).

[10] Baltimore Transit Co., 92 N.L.R.B. 688 (1950).

change in the employer's organization has occurred so as to dictate a different result.[11]

As noted above, the bargaining unit decisions of the NLRB involve an interest balancing process. Situations involving a corporate reorganization are certainly illustrative of the rule. On one hand, a long and successful history of collective bargaining mandates a continuation of the existing unit configuration. On the other, changed circumstances may require a new unit delineation. In conducting this balancing process, the Board members have generally agreed that the "changed circumstances" must be considered to be "substantial changes." [12] As in many other labor issues, the NLRB has failed—intentionally or otherwise—to define what is meant by substantial. While this provides the Board with a high degree of flexibility, it may lead to an appreciable lack of consistency. It would not seem unreasonable to require the Board to set forth guidelines by which the parties may judge the propriety of their actions.

Suppose, for example, that an employer is confronted by a union demand to meet for purposes of negotiating a new collective bargaining agreement. The employer refuses, contending that an earlier corporate reorganization (or an immediately pending one) has so disturbed the employment pattern as to cause the existing unit to become inappropriate. Pursuant to the NLRA, the union files an unfair labor practice charge alleging an illegal refusal to bargain. The Board's decision in the case hinges upon the appropriateness of the unit. That is, the correctness of the employer's judgment, regardless of its reasonableness or justification, will determine the employer's guilt or innocence of the unfair labor practice. Penalizing an employer on the basis of a predictive error is indeed objectionable.[13]

Frito-Lay Inc.[14] is a case illustrative of a corporate reorganization and its effect on an existing bargaining unit. In April of 1968, a Board regional director approved a unit of employees employed in Area 4 of Region II of the company's western divi-

---

[11] Kroger Co., 88 N.L.R.B. 243 (1950); *accord*, Federal Elec. Corp., 162 N.L.R.B. 512 (1966).

[12] Richmond Greyhound Lines, Inc., 65 N.L.R.B. 234 (1946); Globe Oil & Refining Co., 63 N.L.R.B. 958 (1945).

[13] See Justice Black's comment on this situation, Chapter IV text at footnote 31, *supra*.

[14] 177 N.L.R.B. No. 85, 71 L.R.R.M. 1442 (1969).

sion in its western zone. At that time, the administrative organization of the Frito-Lay consisted of zones which were made up of divisions that were divided into regions. The regions were split into areas which were composed of districts. The regional director, certifying a unit coextensive with an area, relied on the fact that each area manager had considerable autonomy. Subsequent to a union-won representation election, Frito-Lay refused to meet for negotiations and the union filed a charge of refusal to bargain. The company defended on the sole ground that organizational changes rendered the bargaining unit inappropriate.

Unfortunately for the employer, the trial examiner found that the existing unit had not been sufficiently modified so as to become inappropriate. Despite the elimination of the area manager position, the examiner found no "significant" changes:

> Clearly "the evidence . . . does not establish a change in either operation, operation scope or composition of the unit." Nor does it . . . show such changes in the managerial and supervisory setup as would significantly affect the employees in the unit.[15]

On appeal to the NLRB, Chairman McCulloch and Members Fanning and Brown, disagreeing with the examiner's decision, discussed the refusal-to-bargain charge of the union. The members commented that a *prima facie* violation of section 8(a)(5) is established once the General Counsel has shown the existence of the union certification and the subsequent request and refusal to bargain by the employer. "The burden then shifts to the [employer] to establish that the circumstances upon which the underlying unit was found appropriate no longer exist and that the unit is therefore no longer appropriate."[16] In the instant case, the Board panel relied primarily upon two factors to find that the employer successfully rebutted the *prima facie* case. First, the nationwide corporate reorganization, undertaken on the recommendation of a management consultant firm, was instituted for legitimate business reasons and without intent to evade the company's labor obligations. Second, while admitting that there was no significant change in individual job content, the Board found that the elimination of the area manager position destroyed the "essential" unifying factor of the original unit.

---

[15] *Id.*

[16] 177 N.L.R.B. No. 85, 71 L.R.R.M. at 1444.

Without taking a position as to the legitimacy of either the trial examiner's or Board's decision,[17] it should be noted that the employer is subjected to penalization for predictive error. In determining the employer's innocence or guilt of the alleged unfair labor practice, the Board failed to consider the reasonableness of the company's position with regard to the appropriateness of the unit. The employer is forced, at the expense of an unfair labor practice charge, to guess as to the appropriateness of the collective bargaining unit. The absence of NLRB guidelines in the making of this decision does indeed work a severe hardship. Moreover, should the employer be fortunate enough to "guess" as to the appropriateness of the unit, he may still be subjected to liability because the Board may find another unit configuration to be appropriate, albeit less appropriate than the one chosen by the employer.[18]

Jurisdictional Work Disputes

An area closely related to the problems of corporate reorganization involves the so-called jurisdictional work disputes. Where a firm's employees are organized in two or more bargaining units represented by different labor organizations (or different locals of the same union), a corporate reorganization resulting in a movement of personnel between units may create union rivalry and disrupt the company's production. Here again, the NLRB must conduct a balancing process between conflicting interests. Restricting or prohibiting a company's right to move employees could prove an imposing barrier to an efficient and economic allocation of resources. Alternatively, if management were given unfettered discretion to transfer employees out of an existing unit, the effectiveness of collective bargaining would be greatly diminished.

The procedure generally utilized by the Board in jurisdictional work dispute cases is the unit clarification or amendment of certification petitions. Pursuant to the authority granted in section 9 and 10(d) of the National Labor Relations Act, the Board promulgated rule 102.60(b) of its Rules and Regulations. It is provided therein that "[a] petition for clarification of an exist-

---

[17] LTV Aerospace Corp., 170 N.L.R.B. No. 40, 67 L.R.R.M. 1471 (1968) where the Board found the employer's reorganization did not justify a change in bargaining units.

[18] Black & Decker Mfg. Co., 147 N.L.R.B. 825, 828 (1964).

ing bargaining unit or a petition for amendment for certification, in the absence of a question concerning representation, may be filed by a labor organization or by an employer." [19] It should be noted that when the Board determines that a "question concerning representation" exists, the proper procedure is a section 9(c)(1) representation election. Where, however, the modification of the existing employment pattern is insufficient to raise a question of representation, the proper procedure to clarify bargaining unit issues is pursuant to rule 102.60(b).[20]

The problems involved in a jurisdictional work dispute and the vital role of the unit clarification petitions were recently illustrated in the case of *Joseph Cory Warehouse, Inc.*[21] The dispute between two locals of the International Brotherhood of Teamsters came about as a result of corporate mergers and consolidations of operations beginning in 1959, when Cory's operations were consolidated in Brooklyn. At that time, the Teamsters Joint Council ruled that Local 138 would represent all inside employees and Local 814 would represent outside employees (drivers and helpers). Shortly thereafter, the company opened a warehouse in Jersey City, New Jersey, which it staffed with Local 138 members. Drivers and helpers who were subsequently transferred to the Jersey City location became members of Local 138.

In 1964, Cory closed its Brooklyn warehouse except for ten employees—members of Local 814—who remained behind to service Cory's account with the Detroit Furniture Company. In 1967, another warehouse was opened in Elizabeth, New Jersey and all employees became members of Local 138. In March of 1969, the company lost the Detroit Furniture account and the ten employees transferred to Elizabeth, apparently with the understanding that they would join Local 138. Because of a lower wage scale and the fear of losing seniority, the ten Local 814 members refused to join Local 138. The parties subsequently agreed to submit the dispute to the Joint Council. Prior to any decision, the employer regained the Detroit Furniture account

---

[19] *See also* 29 C.F.R. § 101.17 (1969).

[20] While a question concerning representation must be present to maintain a representation petition, the Board will, sua sponte, convert the petition to a unit clarification or amendment of certification petition when necessary. *See* Coca-Cola Bottling Co., 133 N.L.R.B. 762 (1961) and Chapter IV, *supra*.

[21] 184 N.L.R.B. No. 73, 74 L.R.R.M. 1545 (1970).

and signed a collective bargaining agreement with Local 138. Thereafter, the Teamsters Joint Council ruled that the ten employees would remain members of Local 814 and would service the Detroit account exclusively. Unable to integrate its operations, Cory found itself confronted with situations where a partially loaded truck with non-Detroit furniture would be followed by one carrying Detroit furniture for the same customer.

On the basis of a unit clarification petition, the NLRB ruled that this situation involved an inappropriate bargaining unit. The Board members reasoned that the company's consolidations and mergers resulted in a situation where members of both locals performed the same work at the same location, were paid from the same office, delivered to the same customers and, but for different working hours, would have had the same supervision. "In short, except for the fact that Local 814 members have historically handled Detroit Furniture goods, there is no rational basis for maintaining such a separate unit." [22] Accordingly, the Board "clarified" the existing units so as to include all employees under the sole representation of Local 138.

The complicated factual situation in *Cory* and the NLRB's use of the unit clarification procedure are illustrative of the problems created by the dynamics of the employment relationship. Unions need to maintain job control, just as management must preserve the right to manage. These needs, forever present, were brought to the surface by the corporate reorganization. The procedures established in rule 102.60(b) provide the mechanism by which the Board attempts to balance these basic, conflicting needs. The success or failure of the NLRB has been the subject of much debate. Notwithstanding the legitimacy of either side, it is painfully clear that there currently exists a significant absence of consistent guidelines by which the parties may direct their actions.

Expanding or Contracting Units

An issue tangential to the appropriate bargaining unit determination concerns the effects of a fluctuating work force upon the propriety of a representation election. Pursuant to section 9(c)(1) of the NLRA, the Board is required to conduct a secret ballot election if "a question of representation affecting com-

---

[22] 184 N.L.R.B. No. 73, 74 L.R.R.M. at 1546.

merce" is found to exist.[23] In the case of an expanding or contracting work force, the degree of fluctuation must be examined to determine the presence or absence of the requisite question. Depending upon the result, the Board will either dismiss or entertain the election petition. If it is entertained, the election may be granted immediately or it may be postponed to some future date.

The various cases involving a fluctuating work force reveal a strong hesitation on the part of the Board to dismiss or even to postpone a representation election. The members appear to be aware of the fact that the employees' right to collective bargaining arises only when a union seeks or enjoys exclusive recognition. An election petition will be dismissed only when the Board find that the holding of an election would constitute an exercise in futility. For example, in the case of an expanding unit, a finding that the employer had hired less than one-half of its intended work force and that the new hires would have different job classifications was sufficient to warrant a dismissal.[24]

Alternatively, to grant an election where there is to be a substantial fluctuation in the work force would constitute a deprivation of the employees' statutory guarantees and a possible disruption to the "free flow of commerce." The NLRA guarantees employees the fullest freedom in exercising their section 7 right of joining a labor organization or refraining therefrom. In the case of an expanding unit, a premature election would deprive future employees of the choice of joining or not joining a union. Moreover, since section 9(c)(3) precludes the Board from holding more than one valid election in each year, these future employees would be denied their rights for a considerable period of time. In the case of a contracting unit, a premature election would have the effect of binding the employees to a particular representative—or to no representative—selected by employees

---

[23] The absence of a question concerning representation does not affect the granting of an election involving lawful organizational or recognition picketing by a noncertified union. Section 8(b)(7)(c)—added to the NLRA by the Labor Management Reporting and Disclosure Act of 1959—provides that in the presence of such picketing "the Board shall forthwith, without regard to the provisions of section 9(c)(1) . . . or the absence of a showing of a substantial interest on the part of the labor organization, direct an election in such unit as the Board finds to be appropriate. . . ." Accordingly, the effects of a fluctuating work force are inconsequential in these expedited election processes.

[24] Governale & Drew, Inc., 106 N.L.R.B. 1317 (1953); General Elec. Co., 106 N.L.R.B. 364 (1953).

who will be leaving, or already have left, the bargaining unit. Such a result could hardly be considered a preservation of the congressional policy of promoting employee freedom of choice. Finally, a premature election in any type of fluctuating work force potentially could bind the employer to an employment relationship which could prove to be economically inefficient at the company's full level of employment. The parties would be required to force a new factual situation into an existing bargaining structure created without regard to policy considerations envisioning the subsequent changes.

Despite these issues, the NLRB is generally reluctant to dismiss a representation petition. The more frequently utilized compromise between the conflicting interests is to entertain the petition but to postpone the election to some future time.[25] In the case of an expanding unit, an immediate election will be granted only when " (a) a 'substantial and representative' number of the anticipated full complement of employees in the appropriate bargaining unit is already employed in the plant, and (b) the employees who are currently employed are working in most of the proposed job classifications which the employer had planned to fill." [26]

In the recent case of *Uniroyal Merchandising Co.*,[27] the Regional Director for the Fifth Region was presented with an opportunity to apply these Board created standards. The Retail Clerks had filed a representation petition seeking an election in a unit comprised of all the employer's stores located in the Baltimore, Maryland area. The employer moved to dismiss the petition alleging the planned expansion of the unit. Disagreeing with the employer, the regional director reasoned:

> Since all new employees will be hired in existing identical job classifications which the parties stipulated should be included in the unit, a new hearing is not warranted and this petition will not be dismissed as urged by the Employer, but rather the election will be held in abeyance.[28]

---

[25] Regardless of the date of the election, the Board will require the petitioner to prove the requisite showing of interest and question concerning representation.

[26] 2 CCH Labor Law Reports, ¶ 2715 at 7119.

[27] Uniroyal Merchandising Co., N.L.R.B. Case No. 5-RC-6688 (March 14, 1969). Reported in *Retail Labor Report*, No. 1030 (March 28, 1969).

[28] *Id.*

Turning next to the union's request for an immediate election, the regional director found that the employer had "more than speculative" plans to increase the bargaining unit from three to seven stores thus raising the employee level from 13 clerks to 45 to 53 clerks. These facts, it was reasoned, required a delay in the election until "it is determined by the undersigned that a substantial and representative employee complement has been employed . . . ." [29]

The postponement of an election in the case of a contracting unit depends on somewhat different considerations. A mere reduction in the size of the bargaining unit is generally held to be insufficient grounds for postponing an election. In addition to a decrease in the employment level, the Board will consider: "(1) whether the personnel reduction is accompanied by material changes in the employer's operations . . . and (2) whether the employer's plans for a reduction or shutdown are definite and steps have been taken to execute the plans. . . ." [30] Thus, in *Electric Sprayit Co.*,[31] the NLRB found that a 70 percent reduction in the employer's personnel combined with a complete change in operations and processes due to a reconversion were sufficient to warrant a redetermination of representatives.

The NLRB's standards in fluctuating work force cases are generally capable of reaching an effective compromise between employer, employee and union interests. The relatively few cases dealing with the issue, however, reveal an excessively heavy favoritism towards granting an immediate secret ballot election. This favoritism may be rationalized by the fact that employees, in the absence of a representation election, are deprived of the benefits of collective bargaining. For collective bargaining to be an efficient institution in the industrial setting however, the dynamics of the employment relationship must be considered. A premature election potentially can deprive *all* employees of their freedom of choice, as well as forcing the union and the employer to bargain under unstable conditions.

THE ACCRETION ISSUE

Section 1 of the National Labor Relations Act provides that the national policy is "to eliminate the causes of certain sub-

---

[29] *Id.*

[30] 2 CCH Labor Law Reports, ¶ 2715 at 7119 (1968).

[31] 67 N.L.R.B. 780 (1946).

stantial obstructions to the free flow of commerce . . . by protecting the exercise by workers of full freedom of association, self-organization, and designation of representatives of their own choosing. . . ." While the mandate is clear, its application is shrouded with difficulties caused by the sometimes conflicting policy of promoting industrial stability. For example, when a department is added to a single store or plant, does our national labor policy favor a new representation election or merely an accretion to the existing bargaining unit? Undoubtedly, the holding of a section 9(c)(1) election would promote the highest degree of employee freedom of association. The new personnel would be allowed to choose between the existing union and a new union, or no union. Such a solution, however, may well contain the seeds of industrial instability. Separate bargaining units consisting of employees having similar wages, hours and working conditions could potentially lead to union rivalry and employee unrest. Moreover, there is a significantly increased possibility of work stoppages and boycotts leading to "substantial obstructions to the free flow of commerce."

The NLRB, attempting to compromise these conflicting national policies, has developed the doctrine of accretion. When there has been an increase in the employment level, whether due to merger, acquisition or straight expansion, the Board will decide whether the new employees constitute an accretion to the existing bargaining unit. In such a case, the employees automatically become members of the unit and are thereafter entitled to the rights and responsible for the obligations accompanying that membership. Absent the finding of an accretion, and where the new employees constitute an appropriate unit, the proper procedure is a section 9(c)(1) representation election. Pursuant to the contract bar rules developed by the Board, the election can be held only in the new unit. Absent consent by the parties, the units cannot thereafter be merged.[32]

---

[32] In *General Elec. Co.*, the Board split three to two on the issue of merging bargaining units absent the consent of both parties. Chairman Miller, joined by Members Fanning and Jenkins, ruled that the new division—a consolidation of two existing divisions—was entitled to a section 9(c)(1) election to decide which of two unions, if either, would gain representation rights. Concurring Members McCulloch and Brown agreed that a new election should be held but should the United Electrical Workers win, the bargaining unit should be added to the UE's existing multiplant unit. 185 N.L.R.B. No. 4, 74 L.R.R.M. 1710 (1970).

The factors which the NLRB will examine in determining the existence, or absence, of an accretion are illustrated by the case of *Super Markets General Corp.*[33] The company and the Retail Clerks International Association had entered into a collective bargaining agreement covering the employer's Danbury, Connecticut store. The contract provided for coverage of any new store opened in the geographical area corresponding to the union's jurisdiction. Shortly thereafter, the company opened a store in Bridgeport and required each new employee to designate the union as his collective bargaining representative. Charged with a violation of sections 8(a)(1)(2) and (3), the employer contended that the new store constituted an accretion to the existing Danbury unit. Disagreeing with this contention, the NLRB provided the following detailed analysis to show the inapplicability of the accretion doctrine:

> The facts herein demonstrate, and we find, that the Bridgeport store is a separate economic unit and not an accretion to the certified Danbury store unit, particularly as (1) the Danbury and Bridgeport stores do not comprise an administrative division of the Company's operations; (2) they are separately located and serve different markets; (3) they have separate managers who can effectively recommend hire and discharge; (4) they maintain separate bank accounts, separate payrolls, and separate seniority lists; (5) they have separate advertising and do some separate purchasing of food items; (6) there are differences in employees' classifications between the two stores; (7) Bridgeport employees were recruited locally and live in the Bridgeport area, and (8) since the initial opening period, there has been only a minimal number of transfers to the Bridgeport store. Moreover, there is on bargaining history in the two-store unit.[34]

The stringent application of the factors developed pursuant to the doctrine is indicative of the Board's reluctance to find an accretion. The NLRB's philosophy, and the one generally supported by the courts, appears to prefer the holding of a new representation election. The recent decision of the Fifth Circuit Court of Appeals in *Spartans Industries Inc.* v. *NLRB*[35] is illustrative of this philosophy. The employer and the Retail Clerks International were parties to a collective bargaining agreement covering employees in a two-store unit, with both stores located

---

[33] 170 N.L.R.B. No. 61, 67 L.R.R.M. 1498 (1968).

[34] 170 N.L.R.B. No. 61, 67 L.R.R.M. at 1499.

[35] 406 F.2d 1002 (5th Cir. 1969), *enf'g* 169 N.L.R.B. No. 47, 67 L.R.R.M. 1258 (1968).

in San Antonio, Texas. The agreement contained the following "after acquired" clause:

> the application of the terms and provisions of this Agreement shall embrace all present and future retail establishments of the Employer situated within the San Antonio, Texas metropolitan area. . . .[36]

At the same time, due to the acquisition of a competing retail food store, the company had a contract with the Amalgamated Clothing Workers covering one store also located in San Antonio. This agreement also contained an "after acquired" clause.

Attempting to expand its operations, Spartan opened a fourth store in the San Antonio area and staffed it with new personnel. Confronted by representation demands by both unions, the company initially adhered to a strict position of neutrality. Subsequently, for reasons not expressed, Spartan recognized the Retail Clerks and allowed them to come into the store. Pursuant to a suit filed by the Clothing Workers, the NLRB held the employer to be in violation of sections 8(a)(1) and (2).

The Fifth Circuit Court of Appeals, affirming the Board's decision, first noted the delicate balance between the accretion doctrine and the preservation of employee freedom. Quoting from the Ninth Circuit, the Court commented:

> Questions (of the propriety of accretion) arise only when the new group remains identifiable . . . . In these situations, the Board will examine the entire picture before permitting the new employees to be swallowed up by the bargaining representative of the employer's other employees without expressing their wishes in the matter.[37]

Turning to the application of the accretion doctrine, the Court reaffirmed the Board-created factors as being capable of protecting employee freedom while recognizing the need for industrial stability. The Court stated:

> To determine the applicability of the accretion doctrine, the Board considers the history of collective bargaining; the extent of centralized and local managerial control over labor relations and store policies; the geographic proximity of the stores to each other; the frequency of the interchange of employees between the stores, and whether any union is seeking a more limited or broader unit than

---

[36] 406 F.2d at 1004.

[37] *Id* at 1005. Citing NLRB v. Food Employees Council, 399 F.2d 501 (9th Cir. 1968).

the unit proposed. . . . In the case of *Pullman Industries, Inc.,* 159 NLRB 580 (1966), the Board established the additional consideration that the accredited unit should not numerically overshadow the pre-existing unit.[38]

Applying these considerations to the facts in the case, the Court found that the Board was justified in holding the accretion to be improper.

The Doctrine Applied

As the NLRB continued to develop and refine the accretion doctrine, it soon became evident that the situations affected by the doctrine would likewise increase. The employer generally favored the finding of an accretion over the holding of a representation election. The former allowed a continuation of an established relationship without further adding to the potential of work stoppages. A new election, on the other hand, would involve a time-consuming and costly process. The employer could well find himself confronted with new demands as to wages, hours and working conditions, as well as the possibility of union rivalry and increased work stoppages. Incumbent unions also were well aware of the advantages of the accretion doctrine. In addition to increasing the ranks of dues-paying members, the accreted employees may significantly enhance the economic bargaining power enjoyed by the union. A representation election, with its concomitant costs, provides the opportunity for a rival union to gain entrance into the company, lessens the incumbent's bargaining power and sets the stage for competitive rivalry.

Despite the self-serving interests of the employer and the incumbent union, the accretion doctrine does serve a vital role in comprising conflicting needs. The dynamics of the corporate setting inevitably lead to changes in the employment pattern. The resulting effects of these changes upon the appropriate bargaining unit are determined, in part, by the applicability of the accretion doctrine.

In *Kennecott Copper Corp.,*[39] for example, the company was confronted by a highly perplexing situation. The United Steelworkers represented employees who were classified as "production truck loaders," while the International Association of Machinists had representation rights for the "front end loaders." In Sep-

---

[38] 406 F.2d at 1005.

[39] 176 N.L.R.B. No. 13, 71 L.R.R.M. 1188 (1969).

tember of 1968, the employer established the new job classification of "lime quarry equipment operator" at its lime quarry operation. The new job, in effect, combined the duties previously performed by the truck loaders and front end loaders. Each of the two unions claimed representation rights. The Steelworkers filed a petition before the NLRB requesting a clarification which would find that the new job constituted production work and should therefore be an accretion to the Steelworkers' production and maintenance unit. The Machinists requested a dismissal of the petition and, in the alternative, argued that if the dismissal were denied, the new job classification should be accreted to its unit.

A Board panel, consisting of Members Brown, Jenkins, and Zagoria, first denied the intervenor's motion for dismissal. The members disagreed with the Machinists' contention that the petition involved a question of representation and/or a work assignment dispute. It was reasoned that "These arguments overlook the fact that the issue here is one of accretion—the addition of a newly-created job—to an existing collective bargaining unit." [40] Furthermore, with regard to a then pending grievance, the members contended that a delay would be ineffectual since the Steelworkers were not a party to the grievance and could therefore not be bound by its outcome. [41] Turning to the accretion issue, the panel applied—in what appears to be a proper fashion—the standard factors and concluded that the lime quarry operation position constituted an accretion to the Steelworkers' unit.

The application of the accretion doctrine in the *Kennecott* case eventually provided the basis upon which a harmonious resolution to the conflict was founded. It should be noted, however, that this resolution was not arrived at until May of 1969, some nine months after the appearance of the problem. Because of a lack of definitive guidelines and consistent NLRB decisions, the parties were unable, or at best unwilling, to settle the dispute internally. Congressional policy enunciated in the 1947 Taft-Hartley Amendments clearly intended to minimize governmental interference in the collective bargaining process. The NLRB—at

---

[40] 176 N.L.R.B. No. 13, 71 L.R.R.M. at 1189 n.2.

[41] For a discussion of this trilateral arbitration problem, see Jones, "A Sequel in the Evolution of the Trilateral Arbitration of Jurisdictional Labor Disputes—the Supreme Court's Gift to Embattled Employers," University of California Institute of Industrial Relations, Reprint No. 188 (1968).

least subsequent to the advent of the Kennedy Board [42]—has indicated what appears to be a diametrically opposed policy. Board decisions should provide the basis for private resolutions. That they have done so is, at best, questionable.

Safeway Stores, Inc.,[43] a 1969 case, is illustrative of the "close" decisions with which the parties must contend. In a three to two decision, a majority of the Board held the accretion doctrine to be inapplicable and, accordingly, granted a self-determination election to the employer's electronic data processing division employees. These employees had the option of voting for the intervening union, thus joining an existing clerical employees bargaining unit; for the petitioning union, thus staying as a separate unit; or for no union. Dissenting Members Brown and Jenkins applied the relevant factors and found an accretion to the intervenor's existing unit. They commented:

> Such factors relied upon by the majority as the equipment used by the EDP employees and their separate work area and higher salaries do not, on balance, as they did not in the *Goodyear Tire and Rubber Company* case, 168 NLRB No. 25, vest the employees in question with the requisite separate community of interest.[44]

In the *Goodyear* case [45] to which the dissenting members referred, a Board panel, on facts very similar to those in *Safeway*, denied the union's petition to hold an election for clerical employees. Again disregarding the legitimacy of either decision, the significant problem lies in the lack of consistency combined with the absence of articulated reasons for distinguishing the cases.

In yet another 1969 case, the problem of finding relevant guidelines was again made obvious. In *Warehouse Markets, Inc.*,[46] the employer owned and operated a number of retail grocery stores, all located in St. Anthony Village, Minnesota. The Retail Clerks International represented the firm's employees in a multistore unit. Subsequent to the opening of a new store, the employer petitioned for a representation election. Alleging the applicability

---

[42] K. C. McGuiness, *The New Frontier NLRB* (Washington: Labor Policy Ass'n, 1963).

[43] 174 N.L.R.B. No. 189, 70 L.R.R.M. 1438 (1969).

[44] 174 N.L.R.B. No. 189, 70 L.R.R.M. at 1441 n.7.

[45] 168 N.L.R.B. No. 25, 66 L.R.R.M. 1254 (1967).

[46] 174 N.L.R.B. No. 70, 70 L.R.R.M. 1192 (1969).

of the accretion doctrine, the union contended that the contract bar rules prevented the holding of a new election.

In a three to two decision, the employer's representation petition was granted. In holding the new store not to be an accretion, the majority members relied on infrequent employee interchanges; infrequent interchange of inventory and equipment; the new store manager's responsibility for placing merchandise orders, stacking shelves, and running the day-to-day operations, and the manager's right to hire. At the same time, the two dissenting members would have ruled in favor of an accretion relying on the following factors: all employees were interviewed by a roving supervisor, to whom the new store manager was responsible; all food was advertised under one label; all stores operated under a uniform pricing policy; all employees were provided with uniform pay and fringe benefits; and all accounting and payroll procedures were centrally administered. In further support of their position, the dissenters pointed out that the parties had previously submitted the issue to arbitration, which resulted in an award holding the new store to be an accretion and thus covered by the multistore contract.[47]

The NLRB admittedly is confronted with conflicting industrial relations policies. The Board is directed to preserve employee freedom of association while, at the same time, it is committed to the promotion of industrial harmony and stability. The resolution of these sometimes conflicting mandates necessarily involves a delicate balancing process. Such a process leaves no room for rigid rules applied in a mechanistic fashion. Flexibility becomes an absolute necessity, but flexibility to the point of inconsistency cannot, and should not, be tolerated. Although legitimate factual differences may give rise to different results, they cannot be used to justify an absence of clearly written opinions indicating the significance of these differences and the relative importance of the various factors. The lack of guidelines to which the parties

---

[47] There currently exists much conflict over the evidentiary value to be accorded an arbitrator's award. With regard to the accretion doctrine, one arbitrator recently commented:

Although it is clear that the Board cannot be deprived of its statutory authority of unit determination, it seems equally clear that both judicial authority and the Board itself recognize the advantage of accommodation in these matters to the arbitral process so long as the deliberations of the arbitrator evidence fealty to national labor policies.

Monogram Industries, Inc., decision of Arbitrator Thomas T. Roberts, December 1969. Reported in *Daily Labor Report* No. 242 (December 16, 1969).

may refer has been the cause of a significant number of unfair labor practices.

In the case of *Sunset House*,[48] an NLRB panel found both the employer and the incumbent union to be in violation of the Act. The employer operated a number of retail stores located in Southern California, the employees of which were represented in a multistore unit by the Retail Clerks International. Subsequent to the opening of a new store in San Francisco, the union requested, and the company granted, recognition rights to the new employees. Alleging the applicability of the accretion doctrine, the parties pointed to the high degree of functional integration, the history of multistore bargaining, and the strong community of interests. Without specifically disagreeing with these contentions, the Board panel found violations of sections 8(a)(2) and (3) and 8(b)(2). The accretion doctrine, the members reasoned, was inapplicable because of the 350-mile distance between the San Francisco store and the Southern California group of stores and the ramifications flowing from the geographical separation.[49] Because of their inability to guess which factor the Board would emphasize, the employer and union were ordered to cease and desist from interfering with employee rights and to "jointly and severally" reimburse all employees for dues and fees extracted from them.

An analysis of various NLRB unit decisions reveals a lack of consistency in the application of the various unit factors.[50] By manipulating the relative degree of importance of each factor, the Board is legitimately able to reach seemingly inconsistent results. For example, although the bargaining history factor has traditionally been accorded substantial weight, in the 1969 case of *Melbet Jewelry Co.*,[51] two members of a Board panel disregarded the factor and held both the employer and the union to be in violation of the Act. The majority disagreed with the parties' reliance on the accretion doctrine because the new store manager was in charge of day-to-day operations, possessed the power to hire and train new employees, and acted as the first step in the grievance procedure. Dissenting Member Brown contended that the relevant bargaining history—both of the employer

---

here involved and of the surrounding community—had been on a multistore basis. This history, he reasoned, was highly indicative of industrial harmony. Despite the soundness of Member Brown's arguments and regardless of the reasonableness of the employer's actions, the Board majority ordered the discontinuance of the "unlawful" conduct and the reimbursement of all dues and fees.

The unfairness of the NLRB's remedy in this type of case was recently attacked by a dissenting judge of the Ninth Circuit Court of Appeals. The case, *Sheraton-Kauai Corp.* v. *NLRB*,[52] involved an existing multiplant unit with a collective bargaining agreement containing a standard "after acquired" clause. Pursuant to this clause, the corporation granted recognition rights to the incumbent union for all employees of its newly acquired hotel. Ruling the single hotel to be an appropriate unit, the NLRB held the parties in violation of sections 8(a)(1) and (2) and 8(b)(1)(A) and (2).

In its appeal to the Ninth Circuit Court, the company did not dispute the Board's finding that the local unit would be appropriate. It was contended, however, that when, as here, the more inclusive multilocation unit is also an appropriate one, the addition of employees at a new location to that unit cannot be considered an unfair labor practice, especially in the absence of a claim by a rival union that it represents the employees. Disagreeing with this contention, the Court commented that where the single location unit is an appropriate one, the employees should be given a secret ballot election. In thus affirming the Board's decision, the Court ordered the company and the union to reimburse all employees.

Circuit Judge Jertberg, the lone dissenter, disagreed with the imposition of the remedy. He contended that in the circumstances of this case, where there could be no doubt as to the reasonableness of the parties' actions, the prescribed remedy was "oppressive and punitive." Furthermore, it should be noted that if the majority's decision is carried to its logical end, the accretion doctrine would become inapplicable in all cases where the new acquisition was an appropriate unit. Such a result undoubtedly would destroy the compromise solutions offered by the doctrine. The employer would be confronted with the onerous burden of having to determine the appropriateness of the unit

---

[52] 429 F.2d 1352 (9th Cir. 1970).

before deciding whether or not to abide by his contractual promises. Should he guess wrong, he is liable for damages.

SUCCESSOR EMPLOYER POLICY

The dynamics of the business world require that an enterprise continually grow. Undoubtedly, one of the most significant means of accomplishing this growth is through the acquisition—whether by purchase or statutory merger—of an existing firm. Prior to 1964, the industrial relations aspects of such an acquisition were generally considered insignificant in that corporation-contract law held the successor employer to be free from the collective bargaining agreement of his predecessor.[53] The Supreme Court, however, in the 1964 case of *John Wiley & Sons, Inc. v. Livingston*,[54] held that an unconsenting successor employer could be bound to arbitrate the status of the old contract if there was a substantial continuity of the enterprise after the transfer of ownership. On May 7, 1970, the National Labor Relations Board went far beyond the Supreme Court's holding in *Wiley*. In a series of four landmark cases,[55] the NLRB ruled that a successor employer and a predecessor union could be held to all the terms and conditions of the collective bargaining agreement negotiated between the union and the predecessor company. In subsequent cases, the Board endeavored to define the exact extent of this burdensome obligation.

To facilitate an anlysis of these NLRB decisions, it will be necessary to return briefly to *Wiley* and to the later cases applying that ruling. An examination of the NLRB's four landmark decisions will be followed by a review of the subsequent cases and an analysis of their implications. It is proposed that such an approach will raise serious doubts as to the legality and wisdom of the Board's position. Did the NLRB preserve labor stability, as the majority alleged, or, in fact, did it plant the seeds of greater instability?

---

[53] 15 Fletcher, "Private Corporations," Secs. 7117, 7121-22, 7125 (1961).

[54] 376 U.S. 543 (1964).

[55] William J. Burns Int'l Detective Agency, Inc., 182 N.L.R.B. No. 50, 74 L.R.R.M. 1098 (1970); Kota Div. of Dura Corp., 182 N.L.R.B. No. 51, 74 L.R.R.M. 1104 (1970); Travelodge Corp., 182 N.L.R.B. No. 52, 74 L.R.R.M. 1105 (1970); Hackney Iron & Steel Co., 182 N.L.R.B. No. 53, 74 L.R.R.M. 1102 (1970).

The Wiley Case

John Wiley & Sons was a publishing firm with an annual business of $9 million and a complement of some 300 nonunion employees. Interscience Publishers, Incorporated, also a publisher, had an annual business of about $1 million with about eighty employees, forty of whom were represented by the Retail, Wholesale and Department Store Union. The existing collective bargaining agreement contained no provision dealing with its survival or termination in the event that Interscience should enter into a merger agreement. In October of 1961, while the agreement was in existence, Wiley and Interscience merged. It was not, however, until January of 1962 that the functional merger actually took place and the Interscience employees moved into plants operated by Wiley. Basing jurisdiction on section 301 of the Labor Management Relations Act, the union brought suit in the federal district court to compel arbitration on the issues of seniority, pension contributions, job security, severance pay, and vacation pay. The Supreme Court [56] affirmed the decision of the Second Circuit Court of Appeals,[57] reversing the district court's refusal to order arbitration.[58]

Mr. Justice Harlan, writing for a unanimous Court, first confronted the issue of the lack of privity of contract. Defining collective bargaining agreements as a "generalized code," the Court held the normal rules of contract to be inapplicable and thus Wiley, even as a non-signer, could be compelled to the contractual duty to arbitrate. This duty, the Court continued, could be justified on the basis of the national labor policy favoring arbitration. The true rationale for the decision, however, can be found in Justice Harlan's comment that "the rightful prerogative of owners independently to rearrange their businesses and even eliminate themselves as employers be balanced by some protection to the employees from a sudden change in the employment relationship." [59]

The Supreme Court's decision in *Wiley* was not without limitations. Although the Court may have held, consistent with section 301, that the duty to arbitrate extends to all successor employers, it chose, rather, to issue the following limitation:

---

[56] 376 U.S. 543 (1964).

[57] 313 F.2d 52 (2d Cir. 1963).

[58] 203 F. Supp. 171 (S.D.N.Y. 1962).

[59] 376 U.S. at 549.

> We do not hold that in every case in which the ownership or corporate structure of an enterprise is changed the duty to arbitrate survives. . . . There may be cases in which the lack of any substantial continuity of identity in the business enterprise before and after a change would make a duty to arbitrate something imposed from without. . . .[60]

Analyzing the "continuity of identity" limitation, one commentator has criticized the Court for failing to specify the period of time being considered.[61] As noted earlier, the corporate merger was legally consummated in October of 1961. However, it was not until January of the next year that the functional merger took place. In the interim, the Interscience operation continued in the same location with the same employees. Undoubtedly, there existed substantial continuity in the identity of the business enterprise. Subsequent to the functional merger all of the Interscience employees were relocated into Wiley plants, thus causing the former corporation to lose its separate identity. Despite this seemingly important factual difference, the Court's decision contains references to both periods in finding a continuity of identity. "Thus the principle," concluded the commentator, "is established as continuity of identity of the business enterprise, but is applied as continuity of operation as evidenced by the transfer of employees."[62] A careful reading of the facts in *Wiley* does indeed support this proposition. Nevertheless, the subsequent Board and court decisions were soon to reveal that this difference between the stated and applied principles would not present any significant problems.

Application of the Wiley Doctrine

Shortly after the Supreme Court handed down its decision, two circuit courts of appeals were provided with an opportunity to apply the ruling in *Wiley*. Both cases, *Wackenhut Corp.*[63] in the Ninth Circuit and *Reliance Universal*[64] in the Third Circuit, in-

---

[60] *Id.* at 551.

[61] S. Bernstein, "Labor Problems on Acquisitions and Sale of Assets," Proceedings of New York University Twenty-Second Annual Conference on Labor 81 (1970).

[62] *Id.* at 86.

[63] Wackenhut Corp. v. United Plant Guard Workers, 332 F.2d 954 (9th Cir. 1964).

[64] United Steel Workers v. Reliance Universal, Inc., 335 F.2d 891 (3rd Cir. 1964).

volved a purchase situation as opposed to a merger, as in *Wiley.* Both courts agreed, however, that "the legal and equitable considerations involved in imposing a predecessor's obligations upon an independent successor are no different in a merger case than in a sale of business case." [65] Furthermore, in each case the business was sold intact, the bargaining unit was substantially unchanged and the purchaser conducted the operation as a separate identity. Accordingly, neither court was confronted with the issue of the continuing identity of the business enterprise.

The circuit courts' decisions, however, did differ, at least superficially. In *Wackenhut*, the Ninth Circuit interpreted *Wiley* to stand for the proposition that where there existed a substantial similarity in operations and a continuity of identity in the business enterprise, the new employer is bound by the *entire* collective bargaining agreement and "is bound thereunder to arbitrate the union grievances. . . ." [66] The Third Circuit Court's decision in *Reliance* rejected the Ninth Circuit's interpretation of *Wiley.* The Court noted that the Supreme Court specifically avoided imposing the entire agreement upon the new employer. The Third Circuit thus interpreted *Wiley* as requiring arbitration provided that the "arbitrator may properly give weight to any change of circumstances created by the transfer of ownership which may make adherence to any term or terms of that agreement inequitable." [67]

Despite the Third Circuit Court's rejection of *Wackenhut*, it would appear that the decisions do not substantially differ in terms of application. The court in *Reliance* acknowledged that the collective bargaining agreement remained the "basic charter of labor relations" but that the arbitrator was also free to consider any changed circumstances. Under *Wackenhut*, although the contract is said to survive the change of ownership, the arbitrator would still be free to examine any changed circumstances. The result of the arbitration under either decision would, in all probability, be the same.

Another decision in the *Wiley* line of cases was *Monroe Sander Corp.*[68] This case, coming out of the Second Circuit Court of

---

[65] *Id.* at 893.

[66] 332 F.2d at 958.

[67] 335 F.2d at 895.

[68] Monroe Sander Corp. v. Livingston, 377 F.2d 6 (2d Cir. 1967).

Appeals, confronted an issue which, although present in *Wiley*, was apparently overlooked. The Supreme Court, in ordering the purchaser to arbitrate with the predecessor union, failed to consider the effects of this arbitration upon Wiley's unrepresented employees. This problem was the basis for the dissenting opinion in *Monroe*.

Monroe Sander, a wholly owned subsidiary of American Petro-Chemical, was a paint plant whose employees were represented by a labor organization. In an effort to modernize, the parent company purchased the assets of Lacquer, a nonunion paint plant, and decided to close out Monroe. The union brought suit to compel arbitration, especially with regard to replacing Lacquer employees with Monroe employees. The majority of the Court of Appeals ordered Monroe and American Petro-Chemical to submit to arbitration. Judge Lumbard dissented from the majority's decision insofar as it required arbitration regarding the replacement of Lacquer's employees by Monroe's employees. He reasoned that because Lacquer's employees were unrepresented by any labor organization, they would be foreclosed from any effective representation at the arbitration proceeding. With regard to *Wiley*, Judge Lumbard attempted to distinguish the cases on the grounds that "Most cases following *Wiley*, like *Wiley* itself, involved successor employers at the same plant." [69]

In light of the Supreme Court's decision in *Wiley* and the interpretation provided by the various courts of appeals, it would seem that Judge Lumbard's attempt at distinguishing the cases is, at best, tenuous. More directly, it would appear that the Supreme Court failed to consider the effects upon Wiley's employees of arbitrating seniority and job security for Interscience's employees. In fact, in the final arbitration award issued in the *Wiley* case, discussed below, Arbitrator Benjamin Roberts offered the following comment:

> The unusual circumstance in the instant case was the absorption of the predecessor-employer's employees into the successor-employer's enterprise as a minority group within the enlarged unit *that was not represented by any union*.[70]

---

[69] *Id.* at 15.

[70] *In re* Interscience Encyclopedia, Inc., opinion and award of Arbitrator Benjamin C. Roberts, AAA Case No. L-45577-NY-L-138-65 (August 7, 1970), Reported in *Daily Labor Report* No. 173 (September 4, 1970) (emphasis supplied).

The Wiley Doctrine Extended

The National Labor Relations Board, interpreting the principles established in *Wiley*, expanded the obligations imposed upon successor employers. In *Overnite Transportation Co.*,[71] the purchasing employer sought to apply the wages and benefits prevailing at its other operations to the employees of the newly acquired business. Holding this to be an unfair labor practice, the Board ruled that it was illegal for a successor employer to unilaterally change terms and conditions of employment fixed by a predecessor's union contract unless and until good-faith negotiations for a new agreement with the predecessor's union reached an impasse. This decision was subsequently affirmed by the Court of Appeals for the Fourth Circuit.[72] Two years later, the Fifth Circuit Court of Appeals, in *NLRB v. Valleydale Packers*,[73] offered its approval of the Board's holding in *Overnite*.

The next tenet which the NLRB sought to impose upon a successor employer evolved in *Perma Vinyl Corp.*[74] The United States Pipe and Foundry Company purchased the assets of Perma Vinyl and continued to operate the plant as a separate entity. Prior to the completion of this acquisition, Perma Vinyl had been charged with discrimination in discharging four employees. Although the trial examiner had not rendered a decision at the time of the acquisition, U. S. Pipe did have actual knowledge of the pending litigation. Subsequently, the examiner, who was later affirmed by the Board, found the company to have been in violation of the Act.[75] U. S. Pipe was then served notice to show cause why it should not be required to remedy its predecessor's violation. The trial examiner, relying on Board precedent,[76] dismissed the complaint and held the successor company not bound by its predecessor's obligations. On review, the NLRB relied on *Wiley* to reverse the trial examiner and to hold the bona fide purchaser of a business liable for the seller's unfair labor practices. Because of the novelty of the decision, the Board ordered

---

[71] 157 N.L.R.B. 1185 (1966).

[72] Overnite Trans. Co. v. NLRB, 372 F.2d 765 (4th Cir. 1967), *cert. denied*, 389 U.S. 838 (1967).

[73] 402 F.2d 768 (5th Cir. 1968).

[74] 164 N.L.R.B. 968 (1967).

[75] 151 N.L.R.B. 1679 (1965).

[76] Symns Grocer Co., 109 N.L.R.B. 346 (1954).

reinstatement but without back pay. In subsequent cases, however, successor employers were held responsible for back pay as well as reinstatement.[77]

An interesting interpretation of *Perma Vinyl* was proposed in a recent trial examiner's decision. In *Southland Manufacturing Corp.*,[78] the primary issue was whether Propper International was a "successor" employer and thus obligated to remedy the unfair labor practice of its predecessor. The trial examiner first contended that the basis for the Board's decision in *Perma Vinyl* was the need to "balance the equities involved." Thus, he reasoned, in the setting of an unfair labor practice, successor employer means more than a substantial continuity of identity of the business enterprise. In addition to the usual "elements of continuity," *Perma Vinyl* requires a balancing of the equities between the new employer and the employees who were discriminated against.

Adopting this interpretation of *Perma Vinyl* and applying it to the facts of the case, the trial examiner offered the following analysis:

> All the material circumstances in the case, most important of which was the complete extinction of the Southland business in the 2½ years before Propper began his business, negate the General Counsel's and the Union's claim that Propper became Southland's successor under the *Perma Vinyl* doctrine. Certainly, Propper did not take over Southland's business as a going concern. Nor did he take over Southland's staff. Instead, he began his own business, recruited his own staff almost entirely through the Department of Labor, bought his initial equipment not from Southland, but on the Small Business Administration's foreclosure, and made his own lease with PRIDCO. Moreover, he took no customers from Southland but developed his own business until, apparently meriting confidence through his own performance, he has been able to procure the government contracts that Southland had lost because of its stubborn, foolish persistence in its unlawful course of conduct. Finally, although we may sympathize with Southland's strikers and the Union's attempt to remedy the wrongs done to them by Southland, *we cannot overlook the "equities" in the situation which would make any imposition of Southland's remedial obligations upon Propper not only "unfair" to Propper who had nothing to do with Southland's unlawful conduct and should there-*

---

[77] Emerson Elec. Co., 176 N.L.R.B. No. 98, 71 L.R.R.M. 1297 (1969); Texas Eastman Co., 175 N.L.R.B. No. 105, 71 L.R.R.M. 1098 (1969).

[78] NLRB-TXD No. 397-69 (July 22, 1969). Reported in *Daily Labor Report* No. 141 (July 23, 1969).

fore be accorded the fullest possible lawful "entrepreneurial free-dom" of operating his own business efficiently, but also to Propper's employees, the Small Business Administration, and PRIDCO.[79]

Accordingly, he concluded, balancing the equities leads to the re-sult that Propper was not a "successor" employer and was not obligated to remedy Southland's unfair labor practices. An NLRB panel consisting of Chairman Miller and Members Fan-ning and Jenkins subsequently affirmed the trial examiner's de-cision.[80]

Using the distinct advantage of hindsight, it becomes apparent that the NLRB's decisions in *Overnite* and *Perma Vinyl* were merely steps leading to the Board's recent landmark decisions. These early cases took the Supreme Court's decision in *Wiley* and expanded the successor employer's obligation to the predeces-sor union. Despite heavy criticism of this expansion,[81] the NLRB has now obligated the successor to abide by all the terms and conditions negotiated by the predecessor company and its union. Before examining these decisions, a number of other issues caused by the *Wiley* case should first be reviewed.

Continuity of Employment

As noted above, the Supreme Court limited the obligation to arbitrate to those situations in which there existed a "substan-tial continuity of identity in the business enterprise." This re-striction would appear to constitute the outer limits of the Court's power to impose arbitration on a nonconsenting successor since the list is used to establish that the collective bargaining agree-ment is at least "reasonably related" to the purchaser.[82] A radi-cal alteration of the business enterprise caused by the transfer of ownership would, under existing law, prohibit the arbitrability of the new employment status. The Supreme Court envisioned that the arbitrator, at most, would modify the existing contract to comply with the new situation. Where there existed a sub-

---

[79] *Id.* (emphasis supplied).

[80] Southland Mfg. Corp., 186 N.L.R.B. No. 111 (1970).

[81] Comment, *Successor Employer's Obligation to Remedy Unfair Labor Practices,* 8 Columbia Law Review 1602 (1968).

[82] Note, *The Successor Employer's Duty to Arbitrate: A Reconsideration of John Wiley & Sons, Inc. v. Livingston,* 82 Harvard Law Review 418 (1968).

stantial alteration, the arbitrator would be forced to write an entirely new agreement, a result certainly prohibited by law.

Despite the importance of the continuity of enterprise limitation, the Supreme Court did not establish standards or set forth specific factors to determine the existence of a substantial continuity. Subsequent court and Board decisions seized upon the various factual settings in *Wiley* and considered these to be dispositions of the issue. One commentator has noted that many of these later decisions failed to relate the factors to the contractual basis underlying the decision in *Wiley:* "[U]nder *Wiley*, a particular sign of enterprise continuity is significant only because it indicates that the prior contract is potentially suitable to govern the subsequent employment setting." [83]

Analyzing *Wiley* and the subsequent cases does reveal certain frequently utilized criteria in determining successorship. Probably the most critical of these is the number of predecessor employees retained or rehired by the successor employer. In fact, in *Wiley*, the Supreme Court stated that "continuity of operation across the change in ownership is adequately evidenced by the wholesale transfer of Interscience employees to the Wiley plant, apparently without difficulty." [84] In subsequent cases, the courts relied upon a retention of "substantially all" or a "majority" of the predecessor employees to find the necessary continuity of identity. [85]

Since the advent of *Wiley*, there has been considerable debate as to the validity of using continuity of employment to establish continuity of identity of the employing enterprise. Leaving aside the intricacies of the various discussions, it is generally agreed that retention of the predecessor employees is a positive indicator of continuity, but that nonretention is indicative of a lack of continuity only where the reason for the refusal to hire is made clear. [86] One commentator has noted that

> When the reason for failure to retain the predecessor's employees cannot be attributed to an improper motive, continuity is not found and the duty to continue bargaining is not imposed. The

---

[83] *Id.* at 429-430.

[84] 376 U.S. at 551.

[85] United Steelworkers v. Reliance Universal, Inc., 335 F.2d 891 (3rd Cir. 1969); Hotel Employees v. Joden, Inc., 262 F. Supp. 390 (D. Mass. 1966).

[86] Note, *The Successor Employer's Duty to Arbitrate, supra* note 82.

ultimate reason is that the union no longer represents a majority of the employees—or at least the successor may reasonably entertain a good faith doubt.[87]

When the nonretention of employees results from an attempt to circumvent the successor employer's obligations, the courts have generally disregarded the continuity of employment factor. For example, in *K. B. & J. Young's Super Markets, Inc.*,[88] the successor employer notified the predecessor's employees that they were to be discharged, effective as of the date of the sale. The operations were shut down for one day and then reopened. The Court of Appeals for the Ninth Circuit affirmed the NLRB's finding that there continued to exist a substantial continuity of the enterprise.[89] The successor employer, held to be in violation of sections 8(a)(3) and (5) of the Act, was ordered to reinstate the employees with back pay and to bargain with the union.

Another standard used frequently in determining successorship is the similarity of the employment setting. Such factors as manner of operations, similarity of equipment and supervisory personnel, and the product lines and potential customers are analyzed to determine the degree of continuity of identity of the business enterprise. In certain cases, such as *Wackenhut* and *Reliance*, the issue is simplified by the fact that there was no significant change in the employing unit. The purchaser buys the business intact and continues to operate it as a separate entity. Other cases, however, involve the incorporation of the predecessor's employees into the successor's original plants. Such a mingling of employees, although not alone sufficient to preclude a continuity of identity, does create serious industrial relations problems. The imposition of the predecessor's collective bargaining agreement could cause industrial disharmony between the old and new employees. Furthermore, the presence of competing unions—a subject discussed below—raises problems as to representation rights and overlapping jurisdiction. One authority, attempting to solve this dilemma, proposed the following thesis:

> The imposition of a seller's labor contract upon a buyer and the seller's union, subject to arbitration of any provisions made inequitable by the change in ownership, is not unreasonable where

---

[87] Bernstein, *supra* note 61, at 98.

[88] 157 N.L.R.B. 271 (1966).

[89] K. B. & J. Young's Super Markets, Inc. v. NLRB, 377 F.2d 463 (9th Cir. 1967).

the buyer continues the acquired business substantially intact. However, where the acquired business is functionally absorbed into other operations of the buyer, then the interests of other employees become involved and no obligation under the seller's contract should be imposed on the buyer.[90]

Unfortunately, the NLRB has chosen to follow this proposal only to a limited extent. Where there exist competing union claims to representation rights, the degree of functional integration may affect, at least in part, the Boards final decision.[91]

Competing Union Claims

A problem attributable to *Wiley*, although not specifically found in it, is the presence of competing union claims. The legal conflict arises over the application of the accretion doctrine, as discussed above, and the successor employer's obligation under *Wiley*. This situation first appeared in *McGuire* v. *Humble Oil & Refining Co.*,[92] a 1966 decision of the Second Circuit Court of Appeals. The seller, which operated a coal and fuel oil business, had a collective bargaining agreement covering its drivers and mechanics. The purchaser, Humble Oil, also had a labor agreement covering its drivers and mechanics, but with a different union. Subsequent to the purchase, Humble offered employment to all of the seller's employees who could pass the physical exam. The thirteen employees hired were integrated with Humble's 250 drivers and 95 mechanics. Relying on *Wiley*, the predecessor union brought suit in the federal court to compel arbitration. Meanwhile, the NLRB, based on a unit clarification petition, ruled that the predecessor's employees constituted an accretion to the existing bargaining unit. The court refused to compel arbitration, reasoning that an opposite decision would require Humble to commit an unfair labor practice because of the presence of a majority union. The Court of Appeals relied on the presence of a competing union to reconcile its decision with the ruling in *Wiley*.

---

[90] Bernstein, *supra* note 61, at 84.

[91] The NLRB and the courts have generally agreed that the form of transfer does not affect the existence of a continuity of identity. Motor City Dodge Co., 185 N.L.R.B. No. 88 (1970).

[92] 355 F.2d 352 (2nd Cir. 1966), *cert. denied* 384 U.S. 988 (1966).

A year after the *McGuire* decision, the NLRB decided *Federal Electric Corp.*[93] Federal Electric had been under contract with the National Aeronautics and Space Administration to perform certain services, including operation of the logistics division. Data Duplicators, a small corporation, was responsible for all duplicating processes at the NASA operations. Federal's employees were represented by the Communication Workers of American (CWA), while the Office and Professional Employees Union (OPE) had representation rights for Data's employees. On the basis of competitive bids, NASA awarded the duplicating services operations to Federal. Prior to beginning this operation, Federal interviewed Data's employees and hired eleven of the predecessor's 28 employees for the new operation which had a total complement of 30 employees. Subsequently, the OPE demanded bargaining rights for the duplicating services and, upon the employer's refusal, brought a section 8(a)(5) action.

A panel of the NLRB unanimously reversed the trial examiner's decision which held the employer to be in violation of the Act. The Board offered a two-pronged analysis of the problem. First, with regard to the determination of the appropriate bargaining unit, the members found that

> the unit of Data's quick-copy employees formerly represented by OPE has ceased to exist as a separate unit, and, further, that the quick-copy employees do not constitute a separate appropriate unit but are an integral part of the certified departmental unit represented by CWA.[94]

Having found no separate appropriate unit, the panel next turned to the trial examiner's finding that Federal was a successor employer and thus obligated to bargain with OPE. Pointing to the significant change in the employment setting—methods of operation, compensation, etc.—and to the fact that only 11 of Data's 28 employees were hired for an operation requiring 30 employees, the Board reasoned that "it is clear that the absorption of the smaller Data operation into the larger one of the Respondent has resulted in a distinct change in the employer-employee relationship." [95] It was concluded that since there existed no successor relationship, OPE had no bargaining rights. Because the new

---

93 167 N.L.R.B. No. 63, 66 L.R.R.M. 1089 (1967).

94 167 N.L.R.B. No. 63, 66 L.R.R.M. at 1091.

95 *Id.*

operations constituted an accretion to the existing unit, CWA could bargain for the predecessor's employees.

The approach used in *Federal Electric* was in no way unique.[96] The considerations which the Board relied upon to find an accretion were also used to prove the absence of a successor relationship. The factors which were given varying degrees of weight included the size of the units, the character of the jobs and the degree of functional integration of operations, such as interchange of employees, common wage and benefit patterns and centralized managerial and labor relations control.[97] Although these considerations may have modified those used in *Wiley*, they did serve to avoid a direct conflict between the accretion and successorship doctrines.

A different solution to the problem of competing union claims was proposed in *Red Ball Motor Freight, Inc.*[98] This 1967 decision of the Fifth Circuit Court of Appeals involved a combination of two terminals—previously operated on separate units, each with its own union—into a single terminal. The parties agreed to submit to an NLRB-conducted election to determine which of the two unions would be given exclusive bargaining rights to the combined unit. Pending the election, one of the unions processed a grievance on behalf of its members through the Joint Grievance Committee established under the National Freight Agreement. When the employer refused to comply with the award, a suit was brought to compel enforcement. The Court of Appeals, referring to both *Wiley* and *McGuire*, reasoned that the pending election required Red Ball to maintain a position of neutrality. If the employer were to accept the arbitration award pursuant to its contract with the one union, this action could adversely affect the results of the representation election. Accordingly, the Court denied enforcement of the award.

When a consolidation results in an entirely new operation, the combination may cause the previously existing units to become inappropriate. The existing agreements would be temporarily abrogated by operation of law and an election would be held in the new unit to determine which of the previous unions would

---

[96] Simmons Co., 126 N.L.R.B. 656 (1960).

[97] Spelfogel, *Labor Liabilities in Purchases, Acquisitions and Mergers: The NLRB's Successor and Accretion Doctrines*, 21 Labor Law Journal 577, 580 (1970).

[98] Southern Conf. of Teamsters v. Red Ball Motor Freight, Inc., 374 F.2d 932 (5th Cir. 1967).

gain exclusive bargaining rights. Consistent with the decision in *Red Ball*, the employer may not deal with or recognize either union until one of them is certified for the new bargaining unit.

The recent case of *Home Furniture Co.*[99] reveals that there exists a third approach to the problem of conflicting union claims. Home and Bethlehem Furniture Company executed a contract whereby Home agreed to purchase Bethlehem's furniture plant in Red Lion, Pennsylvania. Six days after execution of the contract, Bethlehem and Allied Workers of America, the bargaining agent for the production and maintenance employees at Red Lion, agreed to a new two-year collective bargaining agreement. On settlement day, Home's vice president wrote to Allied advising it that Home adopted the current collective bargaining agreement between Allied and Bethlehem. Shortly thereafter, the Upholsterers' International Union, the bargaining agent for Home's employees at its two other furniture plants in the area, learned of these events and demanded recognition as exclusive bargaining agent at Red Lion. Home thereupon withdrew recognition from Allied and granted representation rights to the Upholsterers for all three of its plants.

On the basis of the charges filed by Allied, the trial examiner referred to Board precedent to find that an accretion to the existing unit had occurred. Nevertheless, he upheld the charges because of the recognition of Allied by Home and because of "the fact that a single-plant unit at Red Lion might have been held appropriate and the employees there might have preferred to be represented by Allied in a *Globe* type election. . . ."[100] Since Home's actions pre-empted the holding of this election, the examiner concluded that the employer violated his duty of neutrality and thus sections 8(a)(1) and (5) of the Act.

On appeal to the NLRB, the trial examiner's decision was adopted with modifications. The crucial issue in the Board's decision, as the Court of Appeals for the Third Circuit was later to note, was the finding that the Red Lion plant constituted a separate appropriate bargaining unit. The Board, in deciding this issue, provided the following analysis:

> In all the circumstances of this case, we find no merit in the contention of Home and Upholsterers that the employees of Red Lion were merged into or accreted to the bargaining unit of York em-

[99] 174 N.L.R.B. No. 113, 70 L.R.R.M. 1304 (1969).

[100] Home Furniture Co. v. NLRB, 419 F.2d 179, 181 (3rd Cir. 1969).

ployees represented by the Upholsterers. *The Red Lion employees constituted a separate appropriate unit while employed by Bethlehem and continued as such when Home became their employer.* Upon acquiring the plant, Home retained all the employees, recognized Allied as their bargaining representative, adopted the existing contract covering them, and continued to check off their dues in favor of Allied, as Bethlehem had done. At all times, it is clear, Allied was the bargaining agent for the Red Lion employees.[101]

Reviewing this analysis, the Court of Appeals found it to be "legally insufficient." In determining the appropriateness of a bargaining unit, the Court reasoned, the Board is required to consider, in addition to the history of bargaining, such factors as the geographical location, the extent of employee interchange, the degree of functional integration and the similarity of job skills. Having failed to do this, the case was remanded to the Board for further consideration.

Unlike its predecessors, the settlement in *Home Furniture* was grounded upon the determination of an appropriate bargaining unit. Utilizing the traditional factors developed in unit cases, the Board will determine whether the acquired operation is a separate unit or an accretion to the existing unit. A finding of an accretion requires that the successor employer's union be given exclusive bargaining rights, while the existence of separate units raises a question concerning representation which could be resolved best by the use of a self-determination election. This was the position adopted by the trial examiner in *Home Furniture.* The Board, however, refused to hold an election because of the unique fact that Home had specifically adopted the predecessor employer's contract.

The problems created by competing union claims in successorship cases are complex. The cases involving this issue seem to confuse rather than clarify this complexity. The NLRB's recent decision binding the successor employer to the predecessor's collective bargaining agreement undoubtedly will affect how these competing claims will be resolved. The nature of this resolution, however, must await future judicial and administrative decisions.

Wiley on Remand

The merger between John Wiley and Interscience occurred during October of 1961. Judicial action began in 1962, with the

---

[101] *Id.* at 181 (emphasis supplied by the Court).

Supreme Court's decision being handed down in 1964. The case was not finally settled until August 7, 1970, nine years after the problem arose. Considering the legal consequences of the *Wiley* decision and the time, money and energy spent in obtaining it, the final award of Arbitrator Benjamin C. Roberts seems ironic.[102]

After reviewing the facts and judicial history of the case, Arbitrator Roberts confronted the issue of procedural arbitrability. The employer contended that pursuant to Article XVI of the collective bargaining agreement, the union abandoned the grievance by failing to file notice with the employer within four weeks of its occurrence. The union countered by arguing that the pending merger, with its potential effect of eliminating the entire contract, served to modify the procedural limitations. Accepting this position, the arbitrator commented:

> In conclusion, the issues submitted for review are arbitrable despite the failure to conform with the prerequisite procedures in Article XVI. The Arbitrator finds that by their conduct the parties consented to deviate from these terms due to the peculiar nature of the dispute and implicitly agreed to deal with their differences at the top levels without restrictions in time and in disregard of escalation through the several steps of the grievance procedure. No inferences can be drawn from this finding that would detract from the contractual commitment of the parties to the provisions in Article XVI. By agreement the parties may modify the terms of their contract and they did so in this case for the particular disputes as stated in the submitted issues. Therefore they are arbitrable.[103]

The second issue, and the one upon which the final award ultimately depended, was the determination of the termination date of the Interscience agreement. The employer contended that the merger of October 2, 1961 terminated the contract. The arbitrator disagreed. Relying on *Wiley* and the other Board and court cases, he reasoned that the disappearance by merger of the corporate employer-party to the collective bargaining agreement did not terminate the rights that persisted by virtue of the Interscience agreement. The unconsenting successor was bound to its obligations until the contract termination date or "until there is

---

[102] *In re* Interscience Encyclopedia, Inc., opinion and award of Arbitrator Benjamin C. Roberts, AAA Case No. L-45577-NY-L-138-65 (August 7, 1970). Reported in *Daily Labor Report* No. 173 (September 4, 1970).

[103] *Id.*

a change of conditions that altered the separate identity within the new business enterprise, whichever occurred sooner." [104]

It is at this juncture that the arbitrator apparently diverged from the Supreme Court's opinion in *Wiley*. As noted above, the Court, in finding that there did exist a substantial continuity of identity, was not concerned with the fact that four months after the merger the total complement of employees were functionally integrated. The arbitrator, however, reasoned that this functional merger of employees was sufficient to destroy the separate identities. He offered the following, persuasive reasoning:

> In the present case, this conversion took place on January 12, 1962 when the former Interscience employees were moved to the Wiley quarters and co-mingled with the larger Wiley contingent. As expressed in the Wiley letter of October 2, 1961, the former Interscience clerical and shipping employees became a minority accretion to an identical unit of Wiley employees for which the Union was not the chosen bargaining representative. With the loss of the elements necessary for its viability, the collective agreement between the Company and the Union ceased to be enforceable. To have continued the contract and the Union's representational posture into the Wiley plant would have been contrary to the national labor policy referred to by the Court and as manifested in the majority representation principle inherent in the National Labor Relations Act. It also would have created a disparity in treatment among employees having a community of job interest and imposed an administrative problem that could be resolved only by imposing the minority terms upon the others.[105]

He thus concluded that the collective bargaining agreement terminated on January 12, 1962, the date of the functional integration.

The decision of the arbitrator, despite his contrary protestations, would appear to be irreconcilable with the opinion of the Supreme Court. The Court was obviously aware of the integration of the employees and considered this to be insignificant in compelling the successor to arbitrate certain claims. Before obligating Wiley, the Court found it necessary to determine that there existed a substantial continuity of identity. This it did, despite the merger of employees, and without regard to the effects of arbitration upon the purchaser's former employees.

The decision of the arbitrator, on the other hand, based the successor employer's obligations on whether or not the acquired

---

[104] *Id.*

[105] *Id.*

business was kept substantially intact. Furthermore, it was reasoned that "it would be inequitable and unreal to continue the Interscience Agreement provisions into the integrated Wiley group solely for the benefit of the former Interscience employees." [106] There would not be this inequality, however, when the former employees remained as a separate, indentifiable bargaining unit. It would appear that the arbitrator, like the NLRB, conditioned the purchaser's obligations upon an appropriate bargaining unit determination. The functional integration was sufficient to obliterate the separate units and thus terminate the predecessor's contract.

On August 7, 1970, the famous case of *Wiley* v. *Livingston* was finally brought to a conclusion. The arbitrator awarded a total of $338.00 to six former Interscience employees. An undistinguished ending for such an often debated decision. The issue of a successor employer's obligations to the predecessor's employees, however, is far from terminated. In May of 1970, the NLRB decided to impose even greater burdens on the successor employer.

THE NLRB'S SUCCESSOR DOCTRINE

Prior to the *Wiley* decision, the National Labor Relations Board was developing its own successor employer doctrine. The Board had ruled that where there was a substantial continuity in the "employing industry," the successor was obligated to *bargain* with the labor organization representing the predecessor's employees.[107] The determination of the successor employer relationship, as noted earlier, was based on the factors developed in bargaining unit cases. Specifically, the purchaser was obligated to recognize and bargain when the change in ownership did not destroy the appropriateness of the preexisting unit. Although extending the successor's obligations, the *Overnite* and *Perma Vinyl* decisions were likewise couched in terms of the appropriate bargaining unit. The recent decisions in *William J. Burns International Detective Agency* [108] and its progeny [109] were

---

106 *Id.*

107 Rohlik, Inc., 145 N.L.R.B. 1236 (1964); Johnson Ready Mix Co., 142 NLRB 437 (1963).

108 182 N.L.R.B. No. 50, 74 L.R.R.M. 1098 (1970).

109 See cases cited at note 55, *supra.*

the next major steps in the development of the NLRB's successor doctrine.

Burns International Detective Agency

Unlike *Wiley*, the *Burns* case did not involve an acquisition by one corporation of another. The change in employers was brought about by Burns' submission of a low bid, entitling it to perform the plant protection services for Lockheed Aircraft Company. These services previously were performed by the Wackenhut Corporation, whose employees were covered by a three year collective bargaining agreement negotiated by the United Plant Guard Workers. Prior to the takeover, Burns interviewed guards for employment who were at that time employed by Wackenhut. At the commencement of the service duties, Burns hired 27 guards formerly employed at Lockheed by Wackenhut and transferred an additional 15 of its own employees from other job sites.

The United Plant Guard Workers demanded that Burns recognize it as bargaining representative and honor the union's agreement with Wackenhut. The company refused and, in fact, recognized the American Federation of Guards as bargaining representative. The union consequently alleged, and the trial examiner agreed, that Burns violated the Act by failing to recognize and bargain with the Guard Workers and by recognizing the Federation. The trial examiner also found a violation of sections 8(a)(5) and (1) because of the successor's refusal to honor the terms of the Wackenhut agreement.

On appeal to the NLRB, a majority, over the dissent of Member Howard Jenkins, affirmed the decision of the trial examiner. Chairman McCulloch, joined by Members Fanning and Brown, first reaffirmed the Board's earlier decisions requiring a successor employer to recognize and bargain with the existing union. Turning to the central issue in the case, the members stated:

> The question before us thus narrows to whether the natoinal labor policy embodied in the Act requires the successor-employer to take over and honor a collective-bargaining agreement negotiated on behalf of the employing enterprise by the predecessor. We hold that, absent unusual circumstances, the Act imposes such an obligation.[110]

---

[110] 182 N.L.R.B. No. 50, 74 L.R.R.M. at 1098.

The imposition of this obligation was grounded on three issues. Section 8(d) of the NLRA provides that where there is a collective bargaining agreement in effect, "no party to such contract shall terminate or modify such contract," unless prescribed notices are served within certain time limits. That section further provides that the mutual obligation to bargain "does not compel either party to agree to a proposal or require the making of a concession." The majority, relying on section 8(d), reasoned that Congress recognized the paramount role in maintaining industrial peace played by the "parties' adherence to existing collective-bargaining agreements." The fact that Burns was not a party to the agreement was rationalized by the contention that the contract was "reasonably related" to the successor through its takeover of Wackenhut's Lockheed service functions contract and its hiring of Wackenhut employees. Dissenting Member Jenkins responded to this by commenting that

> Section 8(d) of the Act, in requiring "parties" to adhere to their agreements and give notice of termination well in advance, hardly supports the conclusion that the successor is bound by the agreement; for that section refers only to a "party" to the contract, the successor is not a party, and the issue before us is whether he should be treated as if he were a party.[111]

The majority did not, or were unable to, offer a response to their colleague's contention.

The Board's ruling that the existing agreement must continue in effect beyond the transfer of the business relied principally on *John Wiley & Sons* v. *Livingston*. After reviewing the Supreme Court's decision, the members emphasized the reliance on national labor policy as opposed to the common law doctrine of contracts. This national labor policy, it was reasoned, favored the continued existence of the collective bargaining agreement and thus allowed the Board to require the successor employer to adhere to all the terms of an agreement to which he was not a party.

Once again, Member Jenkins took issue with his colleagues, contending that the Supreme Court's decision was based on a policy favoring arbitration and the flexibility it offered. He concluded:

> Unlike my colleagues, who rely principally on *John Wiley and Sons* v. *Livingston* to require that the existing agreement must

---

[111] 182 N.L.R.B. No. 50, 74 L.R.R.M. at 1102.

> continue in effect beyond the transfer of the business, I see little
> in that case to support that conclusion. The employees' rights at
> issue there were of a very narrow range, such as seniority, vaca-
> tion pay, pension contributions and severance pay, rights which
> were fixed or already accrued by being, at least in part, earned
> through past performance of work, or "vested" as the Court re-
> ferred to them. The Court held only that the arbitration clause
> in the old agreement survived the merger as an available method
> of resolving issues concerning these "vested" rights. This hardly
> amounts to a holding that the entire old agreement must be im-
> posed on the new employment relation. *Indeed, the Court's ap-
> proval of arbitration and its inherent flexibility and adjustment to
> unforeseen circumstances might indicate that the old agreement
> should not be so imposed.*[112]

Further, it should be noted that the Board, in relying on *Wiley*,
neglected to utilize the traditional bargaining unit approach developed in earlier successor employer cases. The reason for this
may have been that the facts in *Burns* strongly favored the
finding of an accretion and not of separate units. If there had
been a functional integration of employees, the predecessor's
union would have lost its bargaining rights.

The majority's last contention was that stability in bargaining
relationships could best be achieved by imposing the predecessor's contract upon the successor employer. No inequity could be
perceived because the purchaser could make whatever adjust-
ments in the takeover of the business that were required by the
new obligations. The employees, on the other hand, could not
make a comparable adjustment. Accordingly, to protect the employees and to maintain industrial peace in this industry, the
successor must be bound to its predecessor's contract.

The promotion of bargaining stability and industrial peace is
commendable. Whether the Board's decision will achieve this
objective is doubtful. As Member Jenkins pointed out, the prac-
ticalities of the situation require a flexible, and not a mechanistic, approach. He reasoned that

> In such cases, our goal should be to permit the parties flexibility
> in working out their new arrangements if either desires to do so,
> rather than to impose the existing agreement when one side may
> be seriously dissatisfied with it. The new employer is not a party
> to the agreement, and the union did not join in shaping and exe-
> cuting it with his circumstances in mind. Thus, to impose the
> agreement on the new relation may in many cases prove a source

---

[112] *Id.*

of friction and disruption, rather than the stability for which my colleagues hope.[113]

With respect to the inequities which the majority was unable to discern, no consideration was given to the rights of the former employees of Burns. In addition to the 27 guards formerly employed by Wackenhut, the successor also utilized 15 of its employees transferred from other locations. Reasonably, it may be assumed that Burns integrated its work force, thus giving rise to similar working conditions, hours, supervisory personnel, etc. The Board did not consider the industrial relations consequences of splitting apart this appropriate bargaining unit. Having ignored the policy considerations behind the development of the accretion doctrine, the majority forced the parties into a bargaining relationship which was potentially unsuitable for the successor and its former employees. In the final arbitration award in the *Wiley* case, it was reasoned that "it would be inequitable and unreal to continue the Interscience Agreement provisions into the integrated Wiley group solely for the benefit of the former Interscience employees." [114] Surely, it is as unreal and inequitable to continue the Wackenhut agreement provisions in the integrated Burns group solely for the benefit of the former Wackenhut employees. The fact that this latter group of employees constituted a majority of the integrated unit may be used to distinguish the two cases. Nevertheless, the rights of Burns' employees and the degree of functional integration should have been considered by the majority in reaching a practical and equitable decision.

Companion Cases

The first of the companion cases, *Kota Division of Dura Corp.*,[115] presented the Board with the opposite side of the coin. After the takeover of the business enterprise by the successor employer, the predecessor's union requested bargaining for terms of a new collective bargaining agreement. The union contended that since the existing contract had no "successor or assigns" clause, the purchaser was obligated, on the unions' request, to

---

[113] *Id.*

[114] *In re* Interscience Encyclopedia, Inc. AAA Case No. L-45577-NY-L-138-65 (August 7, 1970).

[115] 182 N.L.R.B. No. 51, 74 L.R.R.M. 1104 (1970).

negotiate a new contract. Conversely, the employer reasoned that since there was no change in the acquired operation and because it specifically had assumed the old agreement, both parties were bound until the contract expiration date.[116] The Board majority, with Member Jenkins again dissenting, referred to its earlier decision and concluded that

> The *Burns* case involved the duty of a successor employer to honor the contractual obligations of its predecessor with the representative of its employees, whereas this case involves the obverse side of the coin, i.e., the right of the successor employee to insist upon the union's adherence to the contract negotiated with the predecessor employer. The legal policy considerations which impel our conclusion that the continuing vitality of a bargaining relationship and its contract obligations should be maintained in a successorship situation are, of course, the same in either case.[117]

Hackney Iron & Steel Co.[118] did not present any substantive variation from the Board's decision in *Burns*. Following an acquisition of assets, the successor employer refused to abide by the predecessor's collective bargaining agreement, or even to recognize or bargain with the labor union. In 1967, the NLRB found the employer to be in violation of sections 8(a)(5) and (1) and ordered it to recognize and bargain with the union.[119] The United States Court of Appeals for the District of Columbia subsequently sustained the Board's findings, but remanded on the issue of whether the employer was bound to comply with the existing collective bargaining agreement.[120] The Board majority, citing *Burns,* ordered the company to give retroactive effect to all clauses of the contract and to make the employees whole for all losses suffered.

The last of the companion cases, *Travelodge Corp.,*[121] was dis-

---

[116] The central issue in this case appears to have been the effects of the successor's assumption of the predecessor's collective bargaining agreement. The employer argued that only where a contract is assumed by the successor is the Board empowered to hold the contract binding upon both parties. To the contrary, the General Counsel contended, the agreement is binding only where both parties have so agreed. The trial examiner, relying in part on *Wiley,* agreed with the employer's position. *Id.*

[117] 182 N.L.R.B. No. 51, 74 L.R.R.M. at 1105.

[118] 182 N.L.R.B. No. 53, 74 L.R.R.M. 1102 (1970).

[119] 167 N.L.R.B. 613 (1967).

[120] 395 F.2d 639 (D.C. Cir. 1968).

[121] 182 N.L.R.B. No. 52, 74 L.R.R.M. 1105 (1970).

tinguishable from *Burns* in that the Board was unable to find the necessary "degree of continuity in the employing enterprise which would require that the Respondents honor the collective-bargaining agreement in issue." [122] Specifically, the four members noted that the contract had been executed for an eight year duration with a multiemployer group and that the successor had never sought nor been offered membership in the employer association. Furthermore, the original agreement had covered both motel and food employees. Subsequent to the change in ownership, the latter group was split off and operated independently. Lastly, the record offered insufficient indicia of a continuing identifiable bargaining unit. Without a showing of substantial continuity in the employing enterprise, the purchasing employer could not be held obligated to the predecessor's union.

Application of the Burns Decision

As in many other areas of law, the NLRB's precedent-setting decision in *Burns* appears to have generated its own followers. For example, in *S-H Food Service, Inc.*,[123] the successor employer raised the issue of what provisions, if any, of the predecessor's agreement could be exempted from the obligation imposed by *Burns*. In that case, the employer had recognized and bargained with the union and, in fact, had agreed to continue all but two of the contractual provisions. The insurance benefits were objectionable because of the high costs, and the dues checkoff was disallowed pending a showing of appropriate employee authorizations.

On appeal from the trial examiner's dismissal of the union's complaint, the employer contended that affirmation should be granted on the ground that the Board had not thus far held that failing to provide insurance benefits and to check off dues were proscribed, unilateral changes "when done by a successor." A Board panel, composed of Members Fanning, McCulloch, and Brown, disagreed with the employer. They reasoned:

> Now that the Board has decided in *Burns* that a successor must honor the contract of its predecessor, we think it would vitiate the meaning of that decision to except contractual provisions for hospital and insurance benefits as here. Benefits of this sort are in reality part of the wage package and although they constitute

---

[122] 182 N.L.R.B. No. 52, 74 L.R.R.M. at 1107.

[123] 183 N.L.R.B. No. 124, 74 L.R.R.M. 1418 (1970).

a separate bargainable issue whenever a new contract is being negotiated, we believe that they, like wages, must be continued for the remaining term of the predecessor's contract unless the successor and the bargaining representative can *mutually* agree to changes. Similarly, the checkoff provided in the contract is an important employer undertaking. . . . Accordingly we find that within the meaning of the *Burns* decision the checkoff provisions of a predecessor's contract should be preserved for the remaining life of the contract upon presentation to the successor of unrevoked voluntary authorizations from the employees.[124]

Thus, having found a violation of sections 8(a)(5) and(1), the Board ordered reinstatement of the insurance and checkoff provisions, plus reimbursement for any employee who had suffered an economic loss.

Ranch-Way, Inc.,[125] presented another opportunity for the NLRB to clarify the successor employer's obligations. The central issue in the case concerned the effects of the successor's good-faith doubt as to the continued existence of the union's majority status. The Board, reversing the trial examiner, considered the existence of the union's majority status and the employer's good-faith doubt to be irrelevant. The members held that "the normal presumption of union majority status which attaches during the term of a contract executed by the predecessor employer applies equally to its successor, and that the successor employer may not, during the life of the contract, assert a doubt as to its obligation to bargain with the incumbent union." [126]

This specific holding in *Ranch-Way* appears to be consistent with the majority view in *Burns*. The case, however, presents a serious problem. At the outset of the decision, the Board discussed and then found a "substantial continuity of identity in the employing industry." Setting forth the applicable standards, the members stated that

The key test in determining whether a change in the employing industry has occurred is whether it may reasonably be assumed that, as a result of transitional changes, the employees' desire concerning unionization have likely changed.[127]

---

[124] *Id.* at 3-4, 74 L.R.R.M. at 1419-1420 (emphasis supplied).

[125] 183 N.L.R.B. No. 116, 74 L.R.R.M. 1389 (1970).

[126] *Id.* at 3, 74 L.R.R.M. at 1392. The Board also noted in passing that the evidence relied upon by the trial examiner was insufficient, in its opinion, to rebut the presumption of the union's continued majority status.

[127] *Id.* at 3, 74 L.R.R.M. at 1391.

At the same time, it was held that the union's majority status and the employer's good-faith doubt were "irrelevant" to the decision. As a result, on one hand, the "key test" is the employees' desires, while, on the other hand, the employer is forbidden to question these desires. The purchasing employer finds himself in an unenviable position.[128]

Shortly after the decision in *Ranch-Way*, the NLRB modified its holding by developing a special rule to fit successorship in the construction industry. The case, *Davenport Insulation*,[129] involved the purchase of a contractor's residential construction division. The successor refused to recognize the union, arguing that the labor organization no longer enjoyed majority status. In opposition, the General Counsel contended that under *Burns* and *Ranch-Way*, it was unnecessary to show that the union continued to represent a majority of the employees. The trial examiner, dismissing the union's complaint, reasoned that to order bargaining where the union has lost its majority status would be contrary to the rationale of the successorship doctrine.

On appeal to an NLRB panel, Members McCulloch and Brown, over the dissent of Member Jenkins, affirmed the examiner's conclusion, but took a somewhat different approach. The Board, referring to section 8(f) of the NLRA,[130] noted that the current labor laws allow an employer in the construction industry to negotiate a valid collective bargaining agreement with a union which has not established its majority status.[131] A contract entered into pursuant to that section, however, does not give rise to the presumption of a continuing majority status; and thus, at

---

[128] *Accord*, Barrington Plaza & Tragniew, Inc., 185 N.L.R.B. No. 132 (1970).

[129] 184 N.L.R.B. No. 114, 74 L.R.R.M. 1726 (1970).

[130] Section 8(f) of the National Labor Relations Act provides, in part, that:

> It shall not be an unfair labor practice under subsections (a) and (b) of this section for an employer engaged primarily in the building and construction industry to make an agreement covering employees engaged (or who, upon their employment, will be engaged) in the building and construction industry with a labor organization of which building and construction employees are members (not established, maintained, or assisted by any action defined in subsection (a) of this section as an unfair labor practice) because (1) the majority status of such labor organization has not been established under the provisions of section 159 of this title prior to the making of such agreement . . . .

[131] *See* Bricklayers Local No. 3, 162 N.L.R.B. 476 (1966).

least to this extent, the current case is distinguishable from both
Burns and *Ranch-Way.* The Board then concluded:

> We hold, therefore, that where, as here, a contract with the prede-
> cessor employer has been entered into pursuant to Section 8(f),
> no duty is imposed upon the successor employer to honor its prede-
> cessor's bargaining obligation unless there is independent proof of
> the union's actual majority and of the successor employer's unlaw-
> ful refusal to bargain.[132]

By limiting its decision to contracts entered into pursuant to
section 8(f), the Board left unresolved the problems created in
Ranch-Way.

An issue recently presented to the NLRB concerned the obligations of a successor employer when the predecessor's agreement was applicable to a multiemployer bargaining unit. In the
case of *Solomon Johnsky,*[133] the trial examiner narrowed the
question to whether a collective bargaining agreement which covered a group of employees in a multistore, multiemployer unit
might be applied to a totally different bargaining unit—that is,
a single store of a new employer. Answering in the negative, the
examiner, without deciding successorship, held that the union
could not lawfully convert a multistore unit to a single store unit.
A Board panel of Chairman Miller and Members Fanning and
McCulloch disagreed, reasoning that under the *Burns* decision
the purchaser here was a successor employer and thus obligated
to honor the predecessor's contract. With regard to the multiemployer unit, the members contended that the separate unit was
also appropriate, that the contract recognized the separate identities of the various stores, and, finally, that there existed no administrative impediments to the application of the contract to
the new unit. Accordingly, the panel concluded, the existence of
the multiemployer unit did not alleviate the successor employer's
obligations as set forth in *Burns.*

A month later, in *Standard Plumbing & Heating Co.,*[134] the
Board reaffirmed its ruling that the existence of a multiemployer
unit would not affect the successor's obligation to honor the predecessor's contract. This latter case also involved an attempt by
the predecessor employer to untimely withdraw from the unit.
Noting that the successor had knowledge of the existing unfair

---

[132] 184 N.L.R.B. No. 114, 74 L.R.R.M. 1726 (1970).

[133] 184 N.L.R.B. No. 94, 74 L.R.R.M. 1610 (1970).

[134] 185 N.L.R.B. No. 63, 74 L.R.R.M. 1500 (1970).

labor practice, the Board ordered both employers to cease and desist the unlawful conduct.

Generally, the cases subsequent to the *Burns* decision have revealed imaginative, albeit unsuccessful, attempts to circumvent the successor employer's obligations as imposed by the NLRB.[135] The Board's holdings in these cases—whether good or bad—have been consistent with the philosophy espoused by the majority in *Burns.* Recently, General Dynamics Corporation and the New England Telephone Company requested the Board to apply this same philosophy to a somewhat different setting. The result was not wholly unexpected.

The issue presented to the Board in the *General Dynamics* [136] case was whether, when one union displaces another as bargaining agent for a group of employees, the "successor union" is bound by the "predecessor union's" unexpired contract. The case arose on a company objection to certain misrepresentations allegedly made by the Teamsters during an organizational campaign. Attempting to unseat the incumbent union, the Teamsters had informed the employees that if it won the election it, and it alone, would not be bound by the existing five-year contract. The union's campaign proved to be successful and the company filed objections. It was argued that the issue in *Burns* as to the obligation of a successor employer and the issue of a successor union were indistinguishable. Furthermore, the policy considerations drawn upon in *Burns* to require a successor to honor the predecessor's agreement—protection of the rights of employees, promotion of stability in labor relations and of industrial peace, and maintenance and adherence to labor contracts—were equally compelling to bind a successor union to its predecessor's agreement.[137]

An NLRB panel composed of Members Fanning, McCulloch and Jenkins disagreed and found the situations to be quite distinguishable. The Board noted that its 1953 decision in *American*

---

[135] *See* Emerald Maintenance, Inc., NLRB-TXD-620-70, Case No. 23-CA-3597 (1970).

[136] 184 N.L.R.B. No. 71, 74 L.R.R.M. 1522 (1970). Relying on its decision in *General Dynamics*, the Board refused to reconsider the petition of the New England Telephone Company. New England Tel. & Tel. Co., Case Nos. 1-RC-10718, 10719, 10720, 10721 (1970).

[137] Brief for the U.S. Chamber of Commerce in *General Dynamics.* Reported in *Daily Labor Report* No. 110 (June 8, 1970), at A-8.

Seating Co.[138] adopted the principle that a contract of unreasonable duration—generally considered to be more than three years
—would not bar full statutory collective bargaining following a
timely filed petition and certification of a new representative.
The representation made by the Teamsters was an accurate reflection of the operation of that principle. Furthermore, it was
reasoned, the *Burns* decision does not warrant a reconsideration
of *American Seating* because there exists no parallel between the
cases. The collective bargaining agreement involved in *Burns* was
not one of unreasonable duration. The Board commented:

> Whether a successor employer would be precluded from raising a
> question concerning representation if he acquired the business after
> three years had elapsed from the execution date of his predecessor's
> contract, or whether he would have the right to demand fresh
> bargaining if he acquired the business at such a time, are issues
> which have not yet been presented to us for decision. Those kinds
> of cases might, arguably at least, be considered as parallels to
> *American Seating* or to this case, but *this* case is *not,* in our judge-
> ment, parallel to those successorship cases which we have thus far
> decided.[139]

Based on the factual situation present in *General Dynamics,*
the NLRB's decision is accurate. It is consistent with precedent
and adheres to the contract bar rules.[140] Nevertheless, the philosophy and policies espoused by the Board in *Burns* lend strong
support to the company's position in *General Dynamics.* The optimum solution, it would appear, requires not an extension of
Burns, but rather its reversal.

Concluding Remarks

The problems involved in successorship cases can only be resolved by a delicate balancing of conflicting interests. At one
extreme, the NLRB might have refused to impose any obligations upon the successor employer—leaving the employees to
fend for themselves. Or, the Board might have chosen to follow
Wiley and the arbitration process. Alternatively, an adherence to
precedent would have resolved the conflict by requiring recogni-

---

[138] 106 N.L.R.B. 250 (1953).

[139] 184 N.L.R.B. No. 71, 74 L.R.R.M. 1522 (1970).

[140] The NLRB's application of the contract bar rules was further illus-
trated in two companion cases: Bluff City Transfer and Storage Co., 184
N.L.R.B. No. 83, 74 L.R.R.M. 1523 (1970) and Buckeye Cellulose Corp., 184
N.L.R.B. No. 84, 74 L.R.R.M. 1525 (1970).

tion and bargaining when there continued to exist an identity in the employing industry. The Board, however, chose none of these. Rather, it was found that the promotion of stability and the preservation of the labor agreement required the successor employer to honor all the terms and conditions of the predecessor's collective bargaining agreement. The Supreme Court's decision in *Wiley* was used only to the extent that it laid to rest the conceptual problems of privity.

The merits of the *Burns* decision have been, and I am sure will continue to be, extensively debated.[141] On one side, it is asserted that the new ruling offers predictability and ease of enforcement.[142] Of course, *a fortiori*, this would be true had the Board not imposed any obligations upon the successor. But then, the need to protect the predecessor's employees must also be considered; even though in *Kota Division* it was the employees' representative demanding bargaining. As to the preservation of the labor agreement, there are, once again, serious doubts. The collective bargaining agreement is merely the skeletal starting point of an employment relationship. It is the day-to-day interaction between the employer and his employees that give meaning and substance to that agreement. Furthermore, the heart of the collective bargaining process is consent—consent by both parties to live and work within an agreed upon set of conditions. The imposition of a contract upon a new employment setting is inconsistent with the traditional notions of a free system of collective bargaining.

The ultimate, practical consequences of these recent landmark decisions are probably more theoretical than real. It is highly unlikely that a corporation, contemplating the acquisition of a going concern, would fail to consider and plan for its future industrial relations problems. Unfortunately, small businesses will most likely be affected by the new successor employer obligations. When the extent of this effect is in doubt, one commentator quipped, "my advice to one contemplating the purchase of an organized plant is the same as the soundest birth control advice ever given—don't." [143]

---

[141] Spelfogel, *supra* note 97.

[142] Bernstein, *supra* note 61.

[143] *Id.* at 104.

CHAPTER VI

Bargaining Unit Determinations under Special Circumstances

In order to facilitate appropriate bargaining unit determinations, the NLRB has sought to categorize certain types of unit cases and to develop special rules applicable thereto. Situations involving professional employees and guards have been singled out by the National Labor Relations Act and accorded special treatment. Other situations—such as those dealing with confidential and clerical employees—have been provided with special principles developed by the Board. This chapter examines these special unit decisions and the statutory mandates set forth in section 9 of the NLRA.

CONFIDENTIAL AND CLERICAL EMPLOYEES

As long ago as 1944, the National Labor Relations Board recognized the need to exclude "confidential employees" from bargaining units composed of rank and file employees.[1] The Board had reasoned that

> Management should not be required to handle labor relations matters through employees who are represented by the union with which the company is required to deal and who in the normal performance of their duties may obtain advance information of the Company's position with regard to contract negotiations, the disposition of grievances, or other labor relations matters.[2]

Adhering to this policy, the Board has consistently denied requests to include confidential employees in its bargaining unit delineations.[3]

The restriction has not been unqualified. Confidential employees are those who, in the regular course of their duties, as-

---

[1] Hoover Co., 55 N.L.R.B. 1321 (1944).

[2] *Id.* at 1323.

[3] Swift & Co., 124 N.L.R.B. 899 (1959); ACF Industries, Inc., 115 N.L.R.B. 1106 (1956).

sist and act in a confidential capacity to persons who exercise managerial functions *in the field of labor relations*.[4] Matters concerning contract negotiations, disposition of grievances, instructions regarding employees' overtime allowances and reports concerning grievances are regarded as confidential matters in labor relations.[5] Furthermore, the employees' access to the information must be part of their regular duties. Employees who obtain the information in an informal manner [6] or who substitute occasionally for a confidential employee are not considered to be subject to the exclusion.[7]

The fact that employees have access to such confidential information as trade secrets [8] or unpatented products [9] does not prevent their inclusion in an appropriate bargaining unit. The secret information must relate to the labor relations policies of the employees' employer. Thus, in *National Cash Register Co.*,[10] the Board excluded the private secretaries of the employer's division managers from the production and maintenance unit. It was found that the managers had participated in contract negotiations and grievance procedures and that the private secretaries had custody of the grievance files from which the employer's contract proposals were made.

One of the more significant issues in the area of unit placement of confidential employees concerns the extent to which the employees' superior may affect management's labor policies. In the case of *Westinghouse Electric Corp.* v. *NLRB*,[11] the Sixth Circuit Court of Appeals affirmed a Board decision holding private secretaries to be exempt from the confidential employee rule. It was reasoned that the secretaries were not "confidential employees" because their bosses dealt with industrial relations matters only to a limited extent and did not "determine, formulate and effectuate" management's labor policies. Implicit in both the

---

[4] Swift & Co., 124 N.L.R.B. 899 (1959); ACF Industries, Inc., 115 N.L.R.B. 1106 (1956); B. F. Goodrich Co., 115 N.L.R.B. 722 (1956).

[5] *See, e.g.,* cases cited at notes 3 and 4, *supra.*

[6] Hughes Tool Co., 97 N.L.R.B. 1107 (1952).

[7] Heck's Inc., 156 N.L.R.B. 760 (1966).

[8] Sargent & Co., 95 N.L.R.B. 1515 (1951).

[9] Borg-Warner Corp., 61 N.L.R.B. 1178 (1945).

[11] 398 F.2d 669 (6th Cir. 1968).

[11] 398 F.2d 669, (6th Cir. 1968).

Board and court decisions was the need to provide the NLRB with a great deal of discretion and flexibility in determining the *extent* of a manager's involvement in labor relations issues. Further exercising this discretion, the NLRB has ruled that the confidential employee exclusion is not applicable to private secretaries to management personnel who participate in labor matters only to the extent of furnishing factual data representing their immediate problems.[12] Subsequent cases have attempted to distinguish between the furnishing of facts used in setting labor policies and their actual formation and effectuation. For example, in *Consolidated Papers, Inc.*,[13] a three-man panel of Chairman McCulloch and Members Brown and Zagoria was requested to clarify the existing office and clerical employees unit but adding to it certain private secretaries. The employer resisted, arguing the applicability of the confidential employee exclusion.

In granting the union's request, the Board panel reviewed the various functions performed by the secretaries' boss. It was found that the manager conducted or supervised studies which potentially affected the size of the work force and the pay scales proposed during contract negotiations. The manager also recommended to the industrial relations department "which way they should go" in regard to establishing pay scales. Based on these facts, the Board members reasoned that

> The foregoing summary of Bingham's responsibilities and duties make clear that he is not a person who "formulate(s), determine(s) and effectuate(s) managements policies in the field of labor relations." At most his duties entail the reporting of factual data and recommendations which may ultimately have an impact upon employment conditions but do not in themselves constitute labor relations policy.[14]

As in many other areas of labor law, the issue of inclusion of allegedly confidential employees presents the NLRB with conflicting policy interests. In one respect, the Board must preserve the employees' section 7 right to engage in collective bargaining.

---

[12] Vulcanized Rubber & Plastics Co., 129 N.L.R.B. 1256 (1961); Eastern Corp., 116 N.L.R.B. 329 (1956).

[13] 179 N.L.R.B. No. 21, 72 L.R.R.M. 1274 (1969).

[14] 179 N.L.R.B. No. 21, 72 L.R.R.M. at 1275. *Accord*, Ladish Co., 178 N.L.R.B. No. 5, 71 L.R.R.M. 1641 (1969) (first aid department employees were not confidential employees even though they may advise the employer on whether an employee's absence was justified).

But, the maintenance of industrial stability and the preservation of a fair and equitable system require the exclusion of confidential employees from bargaining units composed of rank-and-file employees. As noted earlier, it is distinctly unjust to require the employer to handle labor relations matters through employees who are represented by the union and who may obtain advance knowledge of the company's position with regard to contract negotiations. The decision in *Consolidated Papers* raises doubts as to the equality of the balancing process conducted by the Board. The realities of the corporate world would prevent the industrial relations department from substantially deviating from the manager's recommendations. The private secretary, who has now been included in the bargaining unit, will surely have "advance information of the company's position." [15]

The most recent issue confronted by the NLRB in the area of confidential employees involved the employees of an employers' association. In *Pacific Maritime Ass'n*,[16] a 1970 case, Members Fanning, Brown, and Jenkins were confronted with a representation petition requesting bargaining rights for the employees of an association established to represent its member-employers in labor relations matters. In response to the union's petition, the employer contended that all of its employees must be excluded as confidential employees and that therefore there could exist no unit appropriate for the purposes of collective bargaining.

Reviewing the development of the applicable law, the Board panel reaffirmed the rule that "an employee who directly aids or assists managerial personnel in the formulation, determination, and effectuation of an employer's labor relations policies should not be included in a bargaining unit of rank-and-file employees." [17] In almost all of these instances, the Board observed, the context was that of an employer developing and implementing labor relations policies for its own employees. Thus the current case could be distinguished in that the employees of the association developed and implemented labor relations policies affecting the employees of the member-employers.

Turning to precedents, the members referred to the 1961 decision in *Air Line Pilots Ass'n*,[18] in which it was held that em-

---

[15] See note 2 and accompanying text, *supra*.

[16] 185 N.L.R.B. No. 114, 75 L.R.R.M. 1195 (1970).

[17] 185 N.L.R.B. No. 114, 75 L.R.R.M. at 1196.

[18] 97 N.L.R.B. 929 (1951).

ployees of labor organizations were not confidential unless they had legal access to the labor organization-employer's labor relations policies concerning its own employees. Seeing no persuasive reason for not extending the rule, the Board concluded:

> Accordingly, we find that only employees who assist and act in a confidential capacity to persons who formulate, determine, and effectuate labor relations policies affecting directly the Employer's own employees are confidential employees and excluded from the unit hereinafter found appropriate.[19]

If one again refers to the underlying policy behind the confidential employee exclusion, the NLRB's decision in *Pacific Maritime* appears to be correct. Weighing the conflicting interests, the Board found no persuasive reason for denying to all of the association's employees the congressionally guaranteed right to join or not to join a labor organization. Employee freedom was equitably balanced with stability in labor relations.

Clerical Employees

As with confidential employees, the NLRB has developed special rules applicable to clerical employees. For purposes of representation issues, clerical employees are categorized as either office clerical or plant clerical. The former are considered to be the "white collar" office workers, while the latter have interests more closely associated with production than with administrative functions. To aid in distinguishing the two groups the Board has developed certain relevant factors. Those applicable to plant clericals would be such as the relation of their work to production operations, their relative location in the plant, their supervision, method of pay, similarity of working conditions, and working contacts with production employees.[20] In determining if a group of employees are office clericals, considered are such factors as the relation of their work to company-wide duties; their method of supervision and pay; and whether they work in a separate location.[21]

Subsequent to a finding that the requested employees comprise office clericals, the Board will deny their inclusion in a production

---

[19] 185 N.L.R.B. No. 114, 75 L.R.R.M. at 1196.

[20] Swift & Co., 131 N.L.R.B. 1143 (1961); Pabst Brewing Co., N.L.R.B. Case No. 13-RC-7883, 48 L.R.R.M. 1728 (1961).

[21] Vulcanized Rubber & Plastics Co., 129 N.L.R.B. 1256 (1961); E. I. duPont de Nemours & Co., 107 N.L.R.B. 734 (1954).

and maintenance unit and find for a separate unit.[22] Separate representation has been granted despite a past history of collective bargaining in which the office clericals had been represented as part of a larger unit.[23] Cognizant of the other bargaining unit factors, the Board has been willing to make exceptions to the office clerical rules. Thus, in *Boston Consolidated Gas Co.*,[24] the office clericals were consolidated with other employees whom the Board found to share a strong community of interests.

Similarly, the NLRB has refused to grant a separate bargaining unit where the requested office clericals constituted only a fraction or segment of a larger group of clerical employees.[25] Refusing to adhere to a mechanistic rule, the Board considered such other factors as similar skills, duties, working conditions, and interests. Finally, the Board has allowed office clericals or plant clericals to be represented by the same union which represents the employer's production and maintenance unit.[26]

Plant clericals, because of their common community of interests with production employees, are generally included in the production and maintenance bargaining unit.[27] Under appropriate circumstances, however, the Board has granted representation rights to plant clericals on a separate unit basis.[28] In those situations where the plant clericals were originally excluded from the production and maintenance unit but subsequently desire inclusion, the Board has made frequent use of the *Globe* election process.[29] When a question of representation exists among all the production and maintenance employees, the secret ballot election is held for all employees and the plant clericals are denied a separate unit.[30] This same rule is applicable to an unrepresented group of fringe employees.[31]

---

[22] Cases cited note 21, *supra.*

[23] International Smelting & Refining Co., 106 N.L.R.B. 223 (1953).

[24] 107 N.L.R.B. 1565 (1954).

[25] Ryan Aeronautical Co., 121 N.L.R.B. 1502 (1958).

[26] Birmingham Elec. Co., 89 N.L.R.B. 1342 (1950).

[27] Columbia Cabinet Corp., 146 N.L.R.B. 1039 (1964); Equipment Sales Co., 146 N.L.R.B. 865 (1964).

[28] Cases cited note 20, *supra.*

[29] Robbins & Myers, Inc., 144 N.L.R.B. 295 (1963).

[30] D. V. Displays Corp., 134 N.L.R.B. 568 (1961). For a discussion of this and other relevant cases see Chapter II, *infra.*

[31] *Id.*

Confidential and clerical employees have not presented any significant problems in the NLRB's determination of the appropriate bargaining unit. The Board has successfully categorized the types of employees and developed rules which enable it to conduct an equitable balancing process between conflicting interests. Although some decisions may be questionable, the Board generally has provided the desired consistency and stability.

MANAGERIAL AND SUPERVISORY EMPLOYEES

The legal significance of supervisory employees in industrial relations has had a vascillating history. The growth of union organization among nonsupervisory personnel, especially in the mass production industries, had profound effects upon supervisors. On one side, the increasing power of union stewards usurped much of the responsibility previously delegated to the foremen. On the other side, top management, whether due to shortsightedness or uncertainty, ignored the dual role played by their supervisory personnel. The inevitable result was that foremen found themselves to be "in the middle, the target of union labor without support from top management, devoid of consideration or respect from either." [32]

Many of the industrial relations problems confronted by supervisors may be traced back to the absence of congressional guidelines in the Wagner Act of 1935. Section 2(3) of the Act defined employee as "any employee." At the same time, section 2(2) defined employer as "any person acting in the interest of an employer, directly or indirectly." The dual status of supervisors aggravated the overlap between the two sections. NLRB decisions, accepting this overlap, equated foremen with management and held the latter liable for the former's unfair labor practices. At the same time, supervisors were allowed representation privileges [33] and protected against discriminatory discharges.[34] It was not until 1942 that the NLRB was confronted with the legal status of supervisors in an organizational campaign in a mass production industry.

---

[32] H. R. Northrup, *The Foremen's Association of America*, 23 Harvard Business Review 187, 188 (1945).

[33] Delaware-New Jersey Ferry Co., 1 N.L.R.B. 85 (1935).

[34] Fruehauf Trailer Co., 1 N.L.R.B. 68 (1935).

In *Union Colleries Co.*,[35] the sole issue was whether supervisors were protected by the law in the exercise of their right to organize and bargain collectively. A majority of the Board, over the emphatic dissent of Member Gerard Reilly, reasoned that since Congress did not specifically exclude them and since their status as "employees" was self-evident, the guarantees of the Act should be extended to cover supervisors. Dissenting Member Reilly argued that his colleagues' decision was a prelude to industrial strife and not a promotion of labor relations stability. Since in many instances foremen acted in the interest of management, an employer would be involved in unfair labor practices which, in fact, he was practically powerless to avoid.[36]

The NLRB's decision in *Union Colleries* was to be of short duration. For in 1943, less than a year later, the issue was again presented in the case of *Maryland Drydock Co.*[37] During the intervening period, Member William Leiserson left the Board to return to the National Mediation Board and was replaced by John Houston. The new member joined Gerard Reilly to form the majority in *Maryland Drydock.*

Basing their argument on policy considerations, the two members reversed the earlier decision, reasoning that the law did not specifically require a finding that supervisors were "employees." Not wishing to disturb the existing collective bargaining agreements covering supervisors, the majority attempted to distinguish between craft and mass production industries.[38] They reasoned that the Wagner Act was promulgated primarily due to the conditions existing in the mass production industries and that traditionally the interests of supervisors were more closely allied with those of management.

The decision in *Maryland Drydock* notwithstanding, the parties continued to argue over the legal status of supervisors. The unions claimed that the Act's definition of "employee" was sufficiently broad so as to allow supervisory personnel access to its

---

[35] 41 N.L.R.B. 961 (1942).

[36] The Board subsequently ruled that the right of supervisors to organize could not be denied "merely because they have selected a representative which is an affiliate of the same parent organization as is the spokesman for subordinate employees." Godchaux Sugars, Inc., 44 N.L.R.B. 874, 877 (1942).

[37] 49 N.L.R.B. 733 (1943).

[38] Bargaining units composed entirely of supervisors were considered to be the prevailing practice in the maritime and printing industries. Delaware-New Jersey Ferry Co., 1 N.L.R.B. 68 (1935).

guarantees. Employers, on the other hand, contended that foremen were more closely associated with management and thus
could not be considered "employees." The Board, in *Soss Manufacturing Co.*,[39] sought to avoid the issue. As one commentator
observed:

> Reduced to its essence, the policy articulated in the *Soss* case
> made it clear that supervisors were, in fact, "employees" and were
> entitled to the protection of Sections 8(1) and (3) of the Act
> (those sections prohibiting interference and discrimination based
> on union activity) but were denied access to Section 9 (the repre-
> sentation procedure) and Section 8(5) (the bargaining obliga-
> tion).[40]

The decision in *Maryland Drydock* and the seemingly inconsistent treatment provided supervisors were to last for a period
of less than two years. In *Packard Motor Car Co.*,[41] Member
Houston reversed his earlier position and joined Chairman Millis
in ruling that supervisors were employees within the meaning of
the Act and thus entitled to its protections. The majority, over
the dissent of Member Reilly, reviewed the role of the foreman
in the industrial setting and concluded that the policies of the
Act would best be served by allowing supervisors to organize
within the processes established by federal law. On appeal, the
Supreme Court affirmed the Board's decision without commenting
on the favorability, or lack thereof, of supervisory organization.[42]
Noting that the policies and mandates of the Wagner Act did not
deny coverage to supervisory personnel, the Court commented:

> Even those who act for the employer in some matters, including
> the service of standing between management and manual labor,
> still have interests of their own as employees. Though the foreman
> is the faithful representative of the employer in maintaining a
> production schedule, his interest may properly be adverse to that
> of the employer when it comes to fixing his own wages, hours,
> seniority rights or other working conditions. He does not lose
> his right to serve himself in these respects because he serves his
> master in others.[43]

---

[39] 56 N.L.R.B. 348 (1944).

[40] J. Moore, *The National Labor Relations Board and Supervisors*, 21 Labor
Law Journal 195, 200 (1970).

[41] 61 N.L.R.B. 4 (1945).

[42] Packard Motor Car Co. v. NLRB, 330 U.S. 485 (1947).

[43] *Id.* at 489-490.

The decision in Packard had an even less lasting effect than did the earlier cases. In June of 1947, Congress promulgated the Taft-Hartley Amendments and therein expressly excluded "supervisors" from the definition of the term "employee." In so doing, Congress did not outlaw union representation or collective bargaining on behalf of supervisors. In fact, section 14(a) of the Act as amended provides that

> Nothing herein shall prohibit any individual employed as a supervisor from becoming or remaining a member of a labor organization, but no employer subject to this Act shall be compelled to deem individuals defined herein as supervisors as employees for the purpose of any law, either national or local, relating to collective bargaining.

Although settling one conflict, the Taft-Hartley Amendments gave rise to another. The National Labor Relations Board was now confronted with the problem of determining whether a particular individual was an "employee" and thus entitled to the benefits of the law or a "supervisor" and thus excluded from those rights. To aid in this determination, Congress provided in section 2(11) the following definition:

> The term "supervisor" means any individual having authority, in the interest of the employer, to hire, transfer, suspend, lay off, recall, promote, discharge, assign, reward, or discipline other employees, or responsibly to direct them, or to adjust their grievances, or effectively to recommend such action, if in connection with the foregoing the exercise of such authority is not of a merely routine or clerical nature, but requires the use of independent judgment.

The onerous burden of applying the definition to a given factual situation fell upon the NLRB.

The majority of the Board decisions dealing with the supervisory status of an employee center upon the degree of judgment exercised by the individual. For example, in *Mid-State Fruit, Inc.*,[44] the employer challenged the ballot of an alleged supervisor in an election which resulted in a six to five vote in favor of the union. The company contended, and the hearing officer concluded, that employee Barrons had authority "of more than a routine kind." Specifically, he was authorized to instruct the night crew and the drivers, to rearrange the order of deliveries if necessary, and to recruit substitute drivers in case of illness.

---

[44] 186 N.L.R.B. No. 11, 75 L.R.R.M. 1280 (1970).

On appeal, Chairman Miller, joined by Members Fanning and Brown, reversed the hearing officer and ordered the ballot counted. After reviewing the employee's responsibilities, the members concluded:

> It is apparent from the record that Barrons issues instructions and directs other employees in the performance of their tasks. However, it is clear that any such instructions or directions either originated directly with Besteman (the president) or conformed to guidelines established by him. In these circumstances, *we find that Barrons is not free to use his own independent judgement and therefore does not responsibly direct the work of other employees.*
>
> Barrons does not possess any of the other statutory indicia of a supervisor. We find that he is not a supervisor within the meaning of Section 2(11) of the Act. Accordingly, we shall overrule the challenge to his ballot.[45]

It is evident from the Board's decision in *Mid-State Fruit* that there may exist an infinite number of gradations of authority in any given industrial setting. By necessity, the Board must examine the actual power distributions in an enterprise and then draw the line between the personnel of management and the rank-and-file workers.[46] The task is difficult, but necessary and important. Although the Act gives an employer the right to have supervisory employees excluded from bargaining units, caution must be exercised so as not to construe the term supervisor too broadly since the employee who is deemed a supervisor is denied the employee rights which the Act is intended to protect.

An interesting compromise between these conflicting statutory policies was reached in *Westinghouse Electric Corp.*[47] Westinghouse employed certain "field engineers" who installed and serviced steam turbine equipment at customer locations. Under one type of agreement, the field engineer supervised the installation which was performed by the customer's own labor. The second type of agreement required Westinghouse to furnish all necessary labor, as well as supplies. In this situation, one field engineer was designated to supervise the group and, for the length of the project, was classified as a "lead engineer." Each of the engineers had spent a varying amount of time as a lead engineer.

---

[45] 186 N.L.R.B. No. 11, 75 L.R.R.M. at 1281 (emphasis supplied).

[46] NLRB v. Metropolitan Life Ins. Co., 405 F.2d 1169, 1172 (2nd Cir. 1968).

[47] 163 N.L.R.B. 723 (1967).

Based on these facts, the employer contended that the field engineers were supervisors as defined by section 2(11) and should therefore be excluded from the bargaining unit. The Board, and subsequently the Seventh Circuit Court of Appeals,[48] disagreed. Regarding the supervisory functions over the customer's employees, it was reasoned that "Although there are many ways in which one person can 'direct' and 'assign' another, only if the individual 'directs' or 'assigns' *qua* employer, or *qua* representative of the employer, such as a foreman might do, does the individual 'supervise' within the meaning of Section 2(11)."[49]

Turning to the next issue, the Board considered whether every field engineer who had worked as a lead engineer during the year must be excluded from the unit as a supervisor. The crux of the problem was that the actual distribution of power varied from time period to time period. The Board noted that among the six engineers the percentage of time spent by each as a lead engineer varied from 15 percent to 95 percent. Three spent more than one-half their time and three less. This latter group, the Board reasoned, "are primarily attached to the non-supervisory work force and that they share a substantial community of interest with fellow non-supervisory engineers in the conditions governing the performance of unit work."[50] To accommodate both of the conflicting interests, the Board resolved the issue by including in the unit each engineer who, during the preceding year, spent 50 percent or more of his working time performing nonsupervisory duties. It was specified, however, that any bargaining representative may not represent any engineer with respect to his supervisory functions. The Board's decision, although probably creating serious practical problems, did represent a good, legalistic compromise to a difficult situation.

Managerial Employees

An issue closely related to that of supervisory personnel is the legal status of "managerial employees." Although the Act contains no exemption for managers, as it does for supervisors, they have long been excluded from coverage as a matter of Board

---

[48] Westinghouse Elec. Corp. v. NLRB, 424 F.2d 1151 (7th Cir. 1970).

[49] *Id.* at 1156. Citing International Ladies' Garment Workers' Union v. NLRB, 339 F.2d 116, 121 (2nd Cir. 1964).

[50] 424 F.2d at 1157.

policy.[51] Managerial employees are not considered employees for the purposes of the NLRA and have no bargaining rights either as a group or in conjunction with rank-and-file employees.[52] Managerial employees are defined generally as those who formulate, determine, and effectuate management policies. As set forth in *Illinois State-Journal-Register, Inc.* v. *NLRB*,[53] the fundamental tests to be used in determining whether an individual is such a managerial employee are: (1) whether the employee is "so closely related to or aligned with management as to place the employee in a position of potential conflict of interest between his employer on one hand and his fellow workers on the other" and (2) "whether the employee is formulating, determining and effectuating his employer's policies or has discretion, independent of an employer's established policy, in the performance of his duties." [54] They do not need to have access to confidential information or supervisory authority over employees.

In various cases, the NLRB has laid down general rules applicable to the determination of managerial status. Thus, it has been held that mere attendance at staff meetings where managerial policy is discussed is not sufficient to warrant exclusion from a bargaining unit.[55] Alternatively, management trainees who take part in management conferences are excluded since their interests are more closely allied with management than with the employees.[56] Furthermore, the ownership of stock in a small corporation would serve to exclude the stockholder-employee because of his influence on management policies.[57]

Reviewing these and other Board decisions [58] dealing with managers reveals a commendable attempt to balance the needs of both employers and employees. Although some of the results may be

---

[51] Ford Motor Co., 66 N.L.R.B. 1317 (1946).

[52] Allied Super Markets, Inc., 167 N.L.R.B. 361 (1967).

[53] 412 F.2d 37 (7th Cir. 1969).

[54] *Id.* at 41.

[55] Newark Stove Co., 143 N.L.R.B. 583 (1963).

[56] Banco Credito y Ahorro Poncenso, 160 N.L.R.B. 1504 (1966).

[57] Union Furniture Co., 67 N.L.R.B. 1307 (1946).

[58] *See, e.g.,* Puget Sound Power & Light Co., 117 N.L.R.B. 1825, 1827 (1957); Westinghouse Elec. Corp., 92 N.L.R.B. 871 (1950); Palace Laundry Dry Cleaning Corp., 75 N.L.R.B. 320 (1947).

subject to doubt, the cases, on the whole, appear to have provided considerable stability in an area subject to much confusion.

PROFESSIONAL EMPLOYEES AND GUARDS

As originally enacted, the National Labor Relations Act (the Wagner Act of 1935) gave no special recognition to representational problems involving professional employees and guards. With the growth of mass production industries and the greater utilization of these types of employees, it became obvious that congressional action would be needed to clarify existing and potential problems. Consequently, the Taft-Hartley Amendments of 1947 provided certain affirmative standards to be used by the NLRB in unit cases involving either professionals or guards. In addition to setting forth these standards, this section will briefly review the rules as developed by the Board and applied in these types of bargaining unit cases.

Professional Employees

When promulgating the Wagner Act of 1935, Congress was aware that the interests of professional employees differed from those of nonprofessionals. Nevertheless, the resolution of the problems involved in the unit placement of these employees was left to the National Labor Relations Board. Generally, the Board followed the policy of excluding professional employees from all bargaining units of production and maintenance workers.[59] The many exceptions to the rule, however, caused considerable debate at the hearings preceding the 1947 amendments.

The legislative history accompanying the Taft-Hartley Amendments revealed an acute awareness of the increasing importance of professionals in the mass production industries.[60] It was further noted that as employment of professionals increased it became apparent that they could not be subject to the same working standards as nonprofessionals. The method of pay, the hours worked and the need to maintain professional standards all served to distinguish the two groups of employees. Representatives of various professional organizations testified that a forced grouping of professional and nonprofessional employees in any plant or-

---

[59] H. R. Northrup, *Unionization of Professional Engineers and Chemists*, p. 22 *et seq*, Industrial Relations Counselors, Monograph No. 12 (1946).

[60] *Hearings before the House Committee on Education and Labor*, 80th Cong., 1st Sess. (1947).

ganization could not possibly constitute an appropriate bargaining unit. With regard to the Board's awareness of these problems, one witness testified:

> Some groups of professional employees have been recognized as appropriate bargaining units under existing laws, but usually such recognition has been accomplished only after long and costly controversy, entailing litigation and appeal and fundamental disturbance of employer-employee relationships. Frequently, however, professional employees have been grouped arbitrarily in heterogenous bargaining units. In such cases the professional employees are usually a small minority in a large bargaining unit or trade-union local, the majority of whose members have no community of thought or interest with professional employees.[61]

The result of this and other testimony was the Taft-Hartley amendment to section 9(b).

The proviso to section 9(b) states, in part, that "the Board shall not (1) decide that any unit is appropriate for [collective bargaining] if such unit includes both professional employees and employees who are not professional employees unless a majority of such professional employees vote for inclusion in such a unit . . . ." In determining the applicability of the restriction, reference must be made to section 2(12) which provides that

> The term "professional employee" means—
>
> (a) any employee engaged in work (i) predominantly intellectual and varied in character as opposed to routine mental, manual, mechanical, or physical work; (ii) involving the consistent exercise of discretion and judgment in its performance; (iii) of such a character that the output produced or the result accomplished cannot be standardized in relation to a given period of time; (iv) requiring knowledge of an advanced type in a field of science or learning customarily acquired by a prolonged course of specialized intellectual instruction. . . .

The NLRB decisions applying section 9(b)(1) interpreted the proviso to restrict unit determinations only with respect to units containing both professionals and nonprofessionals. Since the mandate made no reference to purely professional units, the Board has remained unrestricted in its determinations as to the size and nature of such units.[62] A professional unit may be limited to one profession and may exclude other professions having dissimilar

---

[61] *Id.* at 2785-2786.

[62] Western Elec. Co. v. NLRB, 236 F.2d 939 (3rd Cir. 1956).

interests. Similarly, if the factors used in determining an appropriate bargaining unit indicate that two or more professional groups share a common community of interests, the Board will consolidate them into one bargaining unit.[63] Thus, in *Western Electric Co.*,[64] the Board found a nationwide unit of professionals to be appropriate; while in *Standard Oil Co.*,[65] it excluded some professionals from a unit of professional employees since the former had a separate community of interests. A slight exception to this may be found when the requested unit is confined to previously unrepresented professionals. So as not to delay the collective bargaining rights of these employees, the Board has held that it is not improper to exclude other professionals who share a community of interests if they are currently represented in another unit and if, at the proper time, they may determine whether they desire inclusion in the professional unit.[66]

Although the statutory proviso does not cover purely professional units, it does restrict the inclusion of professionals in a unit containing nonprofessionals. Before certifying such a mixed unit, the Board must direct a self-determination election among the professionals to determine if they desire to be included with the nonprofessionals in a single unit. Initially, the Board construed the statute as not prohibiting a mixed unit, even without an election, where the unit was predominantly professional and would not be substantially affected by the inclusion of the nonprofessionals.[67] The United States Supreme Court, however, in the 1958 case of *Leedom* v. *Kyne*,[68] reversed this policy on the grounds that it exceeded statutory authority. The Court enjoined the Board from including nonprofessionals in the same unit as professionals, unless the latter were first given an opportunity to vote on inclusion. This voting requirement has been held to be mandatory even where the professionals, on an earlier occasion, had voted against separate representation.[69]

---

[63] Ryan Aeronautical Co., 132 N.L.R.B. 1160 (1961).

[64] 98 N.L.R.B. 1018 (1952).

[65] 107 N.L.R.B. 1524 (1954).

[66] Western Elec. Co., 98 N.L.R.B. 1018 (1952).

[67] Westinghouse Elec. Corp., 111 N.L.R.B. 497 (1955).

[68] 358 U.S. 184 (1958).

[69] Westinghouse Elec. Corp., 116 N.L.R.B. 1545 (1956).

Unlike the restrictions placed on the representation of guards, section 9(b)(1) does not limit professional employees in the choice of their bargaining representative.[70] Accordingly, the self-determination election ordered by the Board will generally pose two questions: (1) do the professionals desire separate representation or inclusion in a mixed unit; and (2) which union, if any, do they desire to be represented by. Should a majority of the professional employees wish to be included with the non-professional employees, their votes on the second question will be counted with the votes from the nonprofessional workers to determine which union, if any, will represent the overall unit. If a majority of the professionals vote for their own bargaining unit, their votes will be counted separately to determine which union, if any, will represent them in a separate unit.[71]

A final issue pertaining to representation of professional employees involves a requested severance of professionals from a broader unit. Unlike the craft severance rules,[72] the Board has held that professional employees may be severed from an existing broader bargaining unit, notwithstanding a well established history of bargaining for the broader unit.[73] When, however, a group of professionals historically represented in a mixed unit seeks to decertify the representative and sever themselves, the Board will deny the request. Ostensibly, it has been reasoned that a representation proceeding is distinguishable from a decertification proceeding because the former will result in continued union representation for purposes of collective bargaining while the latter will not.[74] Such a policy undoubtedly is subject to serious question. Section 7 of the Act, as amended by Taft-Hartley, guarantees employees the right to join a labor organization and engage in collective bargaining or to refrain therefrom. Surely the preservation of employee freedom requires the NLRB to allow professionals to sever themselves from a mixed unit regardless of the nature of the proceeding. That a requested severance pursuant to a decertification proceeding might result in a discontinuance of union representation should not be used as

---

[70] Huron Portland Cement Co., 112 N.L.R.B. 1465 (1955).

[71] Firestone Tire & Rubber Co., N.L.R.B. Case No. 26-RC-3633 (April 1, 1970).

[72] See Chapter III, *infra*.

[73] S. S. White Dental Mfg. Co., 109 N.L.R.B. 1117 (1954).

[74] Campbell Soup Co., 111 N.L.R.B. 234 (1955).

a rationalization for denying the freedom of choice guaranteed to all employees by the NLRA.

Guards

As with professional employees, the 1947 Taft-Hartley Amendments sought to impose certain restrictions upon the representation of guards. In promulgating section 9(b)(3), Congress revealed an awareness that employees performing the functions of a guard shared a community of interests distinct from that of other employees. Moreover, a bargaining unit which combined guards, who might well have the responsibility of enforcing rules against employees, with those employers would be, *per se*, inappropriate. Consequently, Congress mandated that

> the Board shall not . . . decide that any unit is appropriate for [collective bargaining] if it includes, together with other employees, any individual employed as a guard to enforce against employees and other persons rules to protect property of the employer or to protect the safety of persons on the employer's premises; but no labor organization shall be certified as the representative of employees in a bargaining unit of guards if such organization admits to membership, or is affiliated directly or indirectly with an organization which admits to membership, employees other than guards.[75]

The statute thus imposes two important restrictions upon the representation of guards. First, they may not be included in a bargaining unit which is composed of other employees, regardless of their desire to do so. Second, and probably more restrictive, a union may not be certified to represent guards if it admits to membership, or is affiliated directly or indirectly with a labor organization which admits to membership, employees other than guards. This latter prohibition specifically overruled earlier Board decisions which generally allowed a rank-and-file union to represent guards.[76] It should be noted that although the Act does not outlaw this situation, it does deny the union certification and allows the employer to refuse to bargain.[77] Such a result has been reached even where the petitioning union is only indirectly affiliated with another labor organization which represents non-

---

[75] National Labor Relations Act, § 9(b)(3).

[76] NLRB v. Jones & Laughlin Steel Corp., 331 U.S. 416 (1947).

[77] Mack Mfg. Co., 107 N.L.R.B. 209 (1953); Chrysler Corp., 79 N.L.R.B. 462 (1948).

guard employees.[78] Assistance by a nonguard union to a guard union does not amount to indirect affiliation.[79]

Unlike the term "professional," the NLRA does not separately define the term "guards." Nevertheless, Congress clearly enunciated the intended coverage of the proviso by specifying therein the functions performed by employees considered to be guards. Thus, any individual who is responsible for enforcing rules intended to protect the property of the employer or any persons thereon are within the ambit of the restriction.

In applying the section, the NLRB has tended to focus upon the duties performed by the employees and not the amount of time spent in performing them. For example, in *Kolcast Industries,*[80] the Board excluded certain employees from the requested unit despite the fact that only 25 percent of their time was spent performing guard duties. Moreover, it is generally agreed that to be a guard an employee need not be armed, deputized, or uniformed.[81] Finally, the Board has found that the statute is broad enough to cover employees who work for a company which furnishes guard services to other employers.[82] Subsequent to a finding that the requested employees are guards and that the labor organization is a pure guard union, the Board will apply the relevant factors to determine the appropriateness of the requested unit configuration.[83]

MULTIEMPLOYER BARGAINING UNITS

The utilization of multiemployer bargaining units for purposes of collective bargaining long has been recognized as an accepted means of establishing wages, hours, and working conditions. Authorities have argued that "better organization for bargaining means more intelligent and responsible negotiation on the part of

[78] Schenley Distillers, Inc, 77 N.L.R.B. 468 (1948).

[79] International Harvester Co., 81 N.L.R.B. 374 (1949).

[80] 114 N.L.R.B. 1311 (1955).

[81] Lone Star Boat Co., N.L.R.B. Case No. 4-RC-4605, 48 L.R.R.M. 1262 (1961).

[82] Armored Motor Service Co., 106 N.L.R.B. 1139 (1953); *reversing the contrary rule of* Brink's Inc., 77 N.L.R.B. 1182 (1948).

[83] *See, e.g.,* Pinkerton's Inc., 170 N.L.R.B. No. 108, 67 L.R.R.M. 1559 (1968); O'Neill Int'l Detective Agency, 115 N.L.R.B. 760 (1956); Burns Detective Agency, 110 N.L.R.B. 995 (1954); Joseph E. Seagram & Sons, Inc., 101 N.L.R.B. 101 (1952).

management and labor alike." [84] Theoretically, such high-level bargaining will encourage compromise settlements by increasing the cost of economic struggle. Furthermore, the broader based discussion will encourage the use of experienced professionals aided by staffs of experts who seem more aware of the long range effects of the various proposals.

The parties in the bargaining process also recognize the advantages of employer associations. Labor organizations realize that successive negotiations with a number of employers may create a considerable waste of manpower. Moreover, in addition to standardizing wages and working conditions, multiemployer bargaining may allow the union to secure gains which no one employer could grant for fear of a competitive disadvantage. The security of the incumbent union is assured too in that a rival union must organize a larger group of employees in an attempt to unseat the incumbent. Finally, the union leaders certainly are aware that a high degree of centralization provides added strength to their control over the rank-and-file.

Employers, especially small businessmen, are not unmindful of the benefits of association bargaining. Competitive disadvantages caused by a disparity of labor costs are diminished. The increased economic bargaining power aids in obtaining a better settlement and assures a greater ability to withstand the threat of a work stoppage. Lastly, bargaining as a group serves to protect the employer-members from being struck while their competitors gain the lost business.

The benefits of multiemployer bargaining combined with the advent of mass production industries led to increased use of this practice. This tremendous growth [85] coupled with the fear that a unit-wide strike could cripple the national economy caused considerable debate during the hearings preceeding the Taft-Hartley Act.[86] The House version of the labor bill imposed severe restrictions on multiemployer bargaining, but this, and other such proposals, were never enacted.[87] Noting this legislative history, the United States Supreme Court has commented:

---

[84] A. Cox and D. Bok, *Cases and Materials on Labor Law*, 6th ed. (Brooklyn The Foundation Press, 1965), p. 330.

[85] *See* Pierson, *Prospects for Industry-Wide Bargaining*, 3 Industrial and Labor Relations Review 341, 349 (1950).

[86] 93 Cong. Rec. 4574 (1947) (remarks of Senator Kilgore).

[87] H.R. 3020, 80th Cong., 1st Sess. 9(f)(1) (1947).

The debates over the proposals demonstrate that Congress refused to interfere with such bargaining because there was cogent
evidence that in many industries the multi-employer bargaining
basis was a vital factor in the effectuation of the national policy
of promoting labor peace through strengthened collective bargaining. The inaction of Congress with respect to multi-employer bargaining cannot be said to indicate an intention to leave the resolution of this problem to future legislation. Rather, the compelling
conclusion is that Congress intended "that the Board should continue its established administrative practice of certifying multiemployer units, and intended to leave to the Board's specialized
judgement the inevitable questions concerning multi-employer bargaining bound to arise in the future." [88]

Thus having obtained congressional and Supreme Court approval,
the NLRB has developed principles applicable to the creation of
multiemployer bargaining units and withdrawal therefrom.

Appropriateness of Multiemployer Units

The question of the NLRB's authority to find a multiemployer
unit "appropriate" was resolved as far back as 1938. In *Shipowners' Ass'n of the Pacific Coast*,[89] the Board reasoned that the
term "employer unit" as used in section 9(b) was sufficiently
broad to cover multiemployer associations. Only in a few instances has this decision been challenged.[90]

The appropriateness of a requested multiemployer unit primarily is dependent upon the history of collective bargaining.
The Board has followed the policy that a single-employer unit is
presumptively appropriate, and that to establish a claim for a
broader unit, the petitioner must show a controlling bargaining
history on the broader basis.[91] Consequently, the initial formation of a multiemployer unit must result from a voluntary agreement. With respect to an employer already engaged in multiemployer bargaining, the Board requires evidence of two criteria
in order to establish a desire to participate in joint rather than
individual action. The employer must have participated for a

---

[88] NLRB v. Truck Drivers Local 449, 353 U.S. 87, 95-96 (1957).

[89] 7 N.L.R.B. 1002 (1938).

[90] Note, *Multi-Employer Bargaining and the National Labor Relations
Board*, 66 Harvard Law Review 886, 888 (1953).

[91] Cab Operating Corp., 153 N.L.R.B. 878 (1965); John Brenner Co., 129
N.L.R.B. 394 (1960).

"substantial period of time" in joint bargaining negotiations and must have uniformly adopted the agreements resulting from such negotiations.[92] A substantial period has generally been interpreted as a period of no less than one year.[93] Thus, the Board has held that a 19 month history of multiemployer bargaining is sufficiently long to preclude the establishment of a single-employer unit, notwithstanding a prior 16 year history of single-unit bargaining.[94]

The nature of the history used in multiemployer unit cases is not unlike that of the traditional bargaining history factor.[95] The most persuasive history is that of the particular employer involved. Nevertheless, consideration is given to the history of bargaining of those employees who are similarly situated to the requested employees. Thus, in *Arden Farms,*[96] the Board held that a multiemployer unit of a class of employees was appropriate. This decision was based on the fixed pattern of multiemployer bargaining for other employees and the fact that the unit sought was coextensive with the unit established for the other employees. Although persuasive, the bargaining history for a group of organized employees does not invariably control the bargaining pattern for every other group of unorganized employees.[97] This limitation has been felt especially where the unrepresented employees sought by the petitioning union constituted a homogeneous, separately identifiable group.[98] In fact, this "indirect" bargaining history has been given almost controlling weight in those cases in which the employees sought comprised only "a miscellaneous grouping of unrepresented employees lacking any internal homogeneity or cohesiveness."[99]

Using the principles adopted by the NLRB, an employer will be included in a multiemployer bargaining unit if the employer has indicated an unequivocal intent to be bound in collective bar-

---

[92] Quality Limestone Products, Inc., 143 N.L.R.B. 589 (1963); Morgan Linen Service, Inc., 131 N.L.R.B. 420 (1961).

[93] Miron Building Products Co., 116 N.L.R.B. 1406 (1956).

[94] Consolidated Iron-Steel Mfg. Co., 98 N.L.R.B. 481 (1952).

[95] See Chapter II, *infra.*

[96] 118 N.L.R.B. 117 (1957).

[97] Joseph E. Seagram & Sons, Inc., 101 N.L.R.B. 101 (1952).

[98] John McShain, Inc., 185 N.L.R.B. No. 39, 75 L.R.R.M. 1108 (1970); Charles H. Tompkins Co., 185 N.L.R.B. No. 38, 75 L.R.R.M. 1106 (1970).

[99] Los Angeles Statler Hilton Hotel, 129 N.L.R.B. 1349 (1961).

gaining by group, rather than individual action. It is not a prerequisite that there exist an employer association with formal organizational structure, or that the members delegate to the association final authority to bind them, or that the association membership be nonfluctuating.[100] An employer's participation in joint negotiations, either directly or through an authorized agent, is a sufficient indication of his desire to be bound by joint action.[101] This participation occurs when there is a delegation to the employer group, either formal or informal, of the power to bargain for the employer.[102]

Since the controlling factor for inclusion is the employer's participation in joint negotiations, the Board has held that it is insignificant that the employer refuses to agree in advance to be bound by any agreement.[103] Furthermore, whether an employer historically has signed separate or group contracts is irrelevant in determining participation and thus inclusion. Alternatively, the mere adoption by an employer of the terms of an agreement negotiated by its union and an existing multiemployer association does not require the employer's inclusion in the multiemployer unit. Again, the determinative factor is the presence or absence of the employer's participation in the joint negotiations.[104]

Withdrawal from Multiemployer Bargaining

After the establishment of multiemployer bargaining, changes in economic environment may cause the union or an employer to wish to return to single-employer bargaining. Under current Board policy, an employer may withdraw from the unit, regardless of the reason, provided that the withdrawal request is unequivocal and appropriately timed, or is made with the express or implied consent of the union or under unusual circumstances.[105] A withdrawal is deemed to be unequivocal if it contemplates "a sincere abandonment, with relative permanency, of the multi-

---

[100] York Transfer & Storage Co., 107 N.L.R.B. 139 (1953).

[101] Kroger Co., 148 N.L.R.B. 569 (1964).

[102] Rose Exterminator Co., 143 N.L.R.B. 59 (1963).

[103] Atlas Storage Division, 100 N.L.R.B. 1443 (1952).

[104] Colonial Cedar Co., 119 N.L.R.B. 1613 (1958); Jewish Baking Ass'n, 100 N.L.R.B. 1245 (1952).

[105] Halquist Lannon Stone Co., 156 N.L.R.B. 694 (1966); Galdeen's Inc., 134 N.L.R.B. 770 (1961); Abbott Laboratories, 131 N.L.R.B. 569 (1961).

employer unit and the embracement of a different cause of bargaining on an individual-employer basis." [106]

The Board's requirement pertaining to the timing of the requested withdrawal is based on the need to preserve industrial relations stability. Once the NLRB has certified a unit to be appropriate, the parties cannot thereafter challenge the unit size for a one-year period under section 9(c)(3) of the Act. If a contract has been negotiated, the unit configuration cannot be changed for three years or until the termination date of the contract, whichever is first. [107] A withdrawal filed outside of the certification or contract bar periods is considered timely if an adequate written notice is given prior to the date set by the contract for modification, or prior to the date upon which negotiations are to commence. [108] The rule that withdrawal must occur before negotiations have begun received strong judicial endorsement in *NLRB v. Sheridan Creations, Inc.* [109] The Second Circuit Court of Appeals affirmed the Board's decision that an employer's withdrawal was untimely despite evidence of bad faith and a showing that there had been an adverse effect upon the bargaining process.

An employer's requested withdrawal, even though untimely filed, may be effective if it is based upon mutual consent. It is now accepted policy that the union's consent may be either expressed or implied. In *John J. Corbett Press, Inc.*, [110] the Board, in finding no implied consent to withdraw, adopted the findings of the trial examiner who stated:

> "Consent," in legal contemplation, arises only from express statement or as an implication from conduct. Where implied from conduct, that conduct must normally involve a course of positive action clearly antithetical to a claimed position. Typical of such antithetical conduct is union resort to individual bargaining with an employer following his asserted withdrawal from multiemployer unit bargaining, and this is the, or a, key fact indicative of consent to withdrawal. . . . [111]

---

[106] Retail Ass'ts, Inc., 120 N.L.R.B. 388, 394 (1958).

[107] Auburn Rubber Co., 140 N.L.R.B. 919 (1963). For the exceptions to this rule, see Cox & Bok, *supra* note 84, at 313-316.

[108] Kroger Co., 148 N.L.R.B. 569 (1964); C & M Construction Co., 147 N.L.R.B. 843 (1964).

[109] 357 F.2d 245 (2nd Cir. 1966), *cert. denied*, 385 U.S. 1005 (1967).

[110] 163 N.L.R.B. 154 (1967).

[111] *Id.* at 158. *Accord*, Joseph C. Collins & Co., 184 N.L.R.B. No. 113 (1970).

In addition to the doctrine of implied consent, the Board, with court approval, has also relied on the presence of "unusual circumstances" to find an untimely withdrawal to be effective. For example, in *U.S. Lingerie Corp.*,[112] an employer's untimely withdrawal was justified on the grounds that the employer: withdrew from the association in order to relocate its plant; unsuccessfully sought help from the union in its effort to overcome difficult economic straits; and was in the status of a debtor under the bankruptcy laws. The Board members reasoned that the employer's intention to relocate raised issues inherently more amenable to resolution through single-employer collective bargaining than association-wide bargaining. And in the case of *NLRB* v. *Spun-Jee Corp.*,[113] the Second Circuit Court of Appeals remanded a Board decision for having failed to consider the "unusual circumstances" of an employer's decision, for economic reasons, to close down part of its plant. It should be noted that the Board and courts have given the "unusual circumstances" exception a narrow interpretation. Thus, it has been held that the fact that an employer no longer has any union employees does not make an untimely withdrawal effective.[114]

Prior to 1965, the NLRB had maintained a distinction between the right of the employer and that of the union to withdraw from a multiemployer bargaining unit. The basis of this distinction was that a withdrawal by an employer, as opposed to the union, would not affect the rights of the remaining employers to continue to bargain as a group. However, in *Evening News Ass'n*,[115] "the Board rendered a decision calculated to cripple the effectiveness of association bargaining." [116]

For many years, the Detroit newspapers which employed members of the same Printing Pressman's local were represented in collective bargaining by a local publishers' association. This form of multiemployer bargaining had resulted in a series of contracts

---

[112] 170 N.L.R.B. No. 77, 67 L.R.R.M. 1482 (1968).

[113] 385 F.2d 379, 381-382 (2nd Cir. 1967).

[114] NLRB v. John J. Corbett Press, Inc., 401 F.2d 673 (2nd Cir. 1968). *Accord,* Service Roofing Co., 173 N.L.R.B. No. 44, 69 L.R.R.M. 1384 (1968).

[115] 154 N.L.R.B. 1494 (1965).

[116] P. Abodeely, *Compulsory Arbitration and the NLRB*, Labor Relations and Public Policy Series, Report No. 1 (Philadelphia: Industrial Research Unit, Wharton School of Finance and Commerce, University of Pennsylvania, 1968), p. 45.

over a 25 year period. In 1963, when the association contract was about to expire, the union served notice of termination and proposed thereafter to conduct negotiations on an individual employer basis. The employers refused to negotiate on any basis other than that of multiemployer. A majority of the NLRB reversed precedent and held the newspapers in violation of section 8(a) (5).

In sustaining the charges, the Board reasoned that continuing consent was the basis of a multiemployer relationship. Consequently, either an employer or the union could terminate its consent by filing a timely notice of withdrawal. Any other result, according to the majority, would have meant the application of "more restrictive rules governing union withdrawal from multiemployer bargaining units than are applicable to employers." [117] In thus ruling, the Board rejected the argument that union and employer withdrawals warrant different treatment because only the former involved destruction of the multiemployer unit.

Dissenting Member Brown would have maintained the distinction between the parties' rights of withdrawal. The dissenter offered the following analysis.

> The term "union withdrawal" is misleading, for a union does not withdraw unilaterally, but compels an employer to forego group action and pursue an independent course. Thus, when a union withdraws, it remains unaffected as an entity while requiring a change in the very identity, nature, and composition of the employer with whom bargaining is to be conducted. In contrast, an employer's withdrawal has no impact on the union as an entity in any way. In this respect one could equate an employer participation in multiemployer bargaining with a single union's engagement in multiunion (e.g., through a council) bargaining. Where a group of unions representing different units of a single employer wish to consolidate, a single combined unit can be achieved only with the employer's agreement. Once a broad unit is established by mutual consent, an employer could not refuse to bargain with the multiunion group as the representative of his employees. . . .[118]

Unfortunately, the NLRB has been unwilling to accept the opinion proffered by Member Brown. To the contrary, the Board in *Hearst Consolidated Publications, Inc.*,[119] reaffirmed the rule and disregarded the employer's contention that the long history

---

[117] 154 N.L.R.B. at 1496.

[118] *Id.* at 1503.

[119] 156 N.L.R.B. 210 (1965).

of multiemployer bargaining rendered the separate units inappropriate. Moreover, in 1967, the NLRB again extended the bargaining tactics available to unions bargaining on a multiemployer basis. In *Pacific Coast Association of Pulp and Paper Manufacturers*,[120] the Board granted the union the right to withdraw from a multiemployer unit with respect to one or more employers while continuing to bargain with the remaining employers on an associationwide basis. Thus, in permitting partial withdrawal, the union was provided with the power to determine the scope of the multiemployer unit. Historically and legislatively, the determination of the appropriate bargaining unit should be performed by the NLRB, and not by one of the parties.

Multiemployer bargaining associations have long been recognized by both labor and management representatives as being "uniquely suited to meet the specific structural problems of many bargaining situations." [121] It is unfortunate that the NLRB's decisison in *Evening News* endangers the future worth of these associations. Strategically, the Board's rulings will leave employers at the mercy of the whipsaw strike. "The union can use the whipsaw to force reluctant employers to form multiemployer units, or alternatively it can withdraw from such a unit and whipsaw employers to achieve results it could not obtain from the formal unit." [122] Such a result is unequitable and inconsistent with harmonious industrial relations. In the words of Circuit Court Judge Kaufman, the Board's decisions have disrupted the history of "more than 50 years of multiemployer bargaining . . . upon the whim of one of the parties without any reasons assigned and with more abrasiveness sure to follow as a result." [123]

---

[120] 163 N.L.R.B. 882 (1967). *Accord*, Washington Post Co., 165 N.L.R.B. 819 (1967).

[121] Abodeely, *supra* note 116, at 45.

[122] Note, *Extending the Multi-Employer Lockout to Less than Formal Units*, 53 Virginia Law Review 1189, 1200 (1967).

[123] Publishers' Ass'n v. NLRB, 364 F.2d 293 (2nd Cir. 1966) (concurring opinion).

CHAPTER VII

Summary and Conclusion

As the country enters a new decade, the very heart of the nation's labor policies—the free system of collective bargaining —is being questioned. Can the process of collective bargaining protect not only the interests of labor and management, but also those of the public? If it cannot, the destruction of the system is inevitable. The resolution of this vital issue lies not only with the actions of the parties to the system, but also with the National Labor Relations Board. This government agency has been delegated the responsibility for balancing the needs of the employers, the employees, the labor organizations and the public. It is a responsibility of immeasurable difficulty; but one which, within an overall policy of promoting free and effective collective bargaining, can be met.

The initial step in the preservation of this collective bargaining system is the determination of the appropriate bargaining unit. The delineation of the unit configuration has two distinct, but equally important, consequences. First, since the unit determination is, "by (its) nature an exercise in political science," [1] it has the effect of defining that group of people within which the "majority" will determine the issues of which union, if any, will gain representation rights. If one grouping is favored over another those members constituting the necessary majority will change accordingly. In thus possessing the power to determine who will constitute the "majority," the Board has indirect, but significant, control over which labor organization, if any, will prevail. Indeed, in a case decided in February of 1970,[2] the NLRB's unit decision effectively determined the issue of union representation. The Board had initially ordered an election in a

---

[1] R. Hall, *The Appropriate Bargaining Unit: Striking a Balance Between Stable Labor Relations and Employee Free Choice*, 18 Western Reserve Law Review 479, 481 (1967).

[2] Liberty Coach Co., 181 N.L.R.B. No. 32, 73 L.R.R.M. 1322 (1970).

production and maintenance unit. The result of the balloting was 94 votes for the union and 94 against, with two votes being challenged. These challenges concerned the unit placement of two mechanics. If the Board ruled for inclusion, the entire complement of employees would come under union representation. A contrary ruling would result in no representation.

The more significant consequence of the NLRB's unit determinations is its effect upon the structure of collective bargaining. This structure and the accompanying scope of the collective bargaining process are determined, to a great extent, by the initial unit determination. As former Secretary of Labor George P. Shultz has commented, " 'Appropriate unit' and 'structure' are . . . not synonymous, but the former is at least one of the more important determinants of the latter." [3] As such, the unit determinations can greatly affect the opportunity for efficient, effective, and stable collective bargaining. In order to effectuate the realization of the relevancy of unit determinations to successful collective bargaining, the NLRB has developed certain factors to be applied in unit cases.

The most influential of these unit factors is the community of interests. Although lacking a consistently precise definition, a community is generally considered as common skills, wages and working conditions. Interwoven in the determination of the presence or absence of a common community of interests are the factors of geographical location, functional integration, employee interchange and administrative territory. Moreover, where two or more of these distinct communities are functionally integrated or where they actively interchange employees, an interdependence is created which generally leads to a single unit finding. Where there has been a prior determination of a bargaining unit, the success of the resulting bargaining relationship could well justify the denial of a change in the unit configuration. And finally, where the various factors indicate the appropriateness of two or more units, the desires of the employees will be given determinative consideration.

The NLRB's application of the factors in determining the appropriate unit in the initial, organizing phase of unionization has been, and will continue to be, of primary significance. Notwith-

---

[3] D. Brown and G. Shultz, "Public Policy and the Structure of Collective Bargaining," in A. Weber (editor), *The Structure of Collective Bargaining* (New York: Free Press of Glencoe, 1961), p. 308.

standing this, recent trends reveal that the Board has become more heavily involved in post-bargaining unit issues. The growth of this new involvement, one commentator has observed, may be attributed to "the dynamic and continuing interaction among market forces, individual needs and desires, and organizational survival factors."[4] Regardless of the causes, these recent demands have forced the NLRB into areas involving a level of complexity heretofore unknown. Such institutional changes as the growth of conglomerates occasioned by corporate mergers and acquisitions have challenged the relevance of historical doctrines and stimulated the search for future policies. The decision in *Mallinckrodt Chemical Works*,[5] the "new use" of the unit clarification petition, and recently revised successor employer principles are the results of that search.

An examination of the historical development and current application of the policies used in determining appropriate units reveals a number of deeply entrenched, far-reaching problems. With regard to the unit factors, the Board's decisions indicate not only an absence of precise definitions, but also an inconsistent application of these factors. Moreover, there has never been a concise indication of the relative significance of each of the standards. Each factor taken by itself can be the basis for a given result; but it is also true that if weight is given to one factor over another, a different or inconsistent result might evolve.[6] Admittedly, there are factual differences in each case. "These legitimate differences do not, however, absolve the Board of its responsibility to hand down clearly written opinions in which the established relevant factors are discussed and the Board's conclusions are supported by precise factual information."[7] Absent the meeting of this responsibility, the factors can be used to *support* a conclusion rather than to *reach* it.

This problem becomes more acute when viewed in light of the power struggle between union and management. "Covertly, if not overtly, NLRB representation cases involve this power struggle, notwithstanding the rational and logical articulation utilized

---

[4] B. Samoff, *Law School Education in NLRB Representation Cases*, 21 Labor Law Journal 691, 699 (1970).

[5] 162 N.L.R.B. 387 (1966).

[6] *See* NLRB v. Puritan Sportswear Corp., 385 F.2d 142 (3rd Cir. 1967).

[7] Hall, *supra* note 1, at 539.

by the parties." [8] For an administrative agency—the so-called headless fourth branch of the government—to externally influence the relative economic bargaining power of the parties is most surely inconsistent with the nation's labor policies. The Kennedy-Johnson Board, with its Democratic majority, has reversed earlier unit decisions in a manner which is apparently consistent with union objectives.[9] A regulatory agency responsible for governing much of the country's labor force should not be so easily influenced by the political breeze. Objectively reasoned change is necessary, but change without reason must be avoided.

The effect of bargaining unit policies on the labor-management relationship may be seen in many of the decertification petition cases. For example, in a recent case involving General Electric,[10] the petitioner, an employee, requested the NLRB to order a decertification election in the production and maintenance unit at the company's Bettendorf, Iowa plant. The Board members first set forth the prevailing rule that: "[T]he unit appropriate in a decertification election must be coextensive *with either the unit previously certified* or the one recognized in the existing contract unit." [11] Despite the fact that the Bettendorf plant was the previously certified bargaining unit, the Board dismissed the petition. It was reasoned that because the company had historically bargained on the basis of a single multiplant unit—a somewhat questionable finding [12]—the decertification election in the single unit would be inappropriate. Since the Board consistently espouses the policy of promoting employee freedom of choice when the union requests a certification election, why then not adhere to this same policy when a decertification is involved? The employees at the Bettendorf plant—the previously certified appropriate bargaining unit—must continue to work under union representation despite their possible desires to the contrary. Fur-

[8] B. Samoff, *Law School Education in NLRB Representation Cases*, 21 Labor Law Journal 691, 703-704 (1970).

[9] K. C. McGuiness, *The New Frontier NLRB* (Washington: Labor Policy Association, 1963), p. 93.

[10] General Elec. Co., 180 N.L.R.B. No. 162, 73 L.R.R.M. 1193 (1970).

[11] *Id.* at 1193-1194 (emphasis supplied).

[12] The Board noted that "there are factors which might tend to support the Petitioner's and Employer's contentions that bargaining has not been on the basis of a single multiplant basis." *Id.* at 1194.

thermore, in certification cases, the Board, in order to enhance the "rights of the employees," will allow an election in "any" unit which is appropriate. But here, despite the general rule allowing a decertification election in *either* the certified or recognized unit,[13] the Board dismissed the employees' request.[14]

Many of the problems with the NLRB's bargaining unit policies may be attributed to an overly legalistic approach.[15] An examination of the Board's unit decisions provide substantial evidence to support this contention. The fault does not lie with the labor attorney who, working under an adversary system, must seek that which is best for his client. The considerations applied in determining an appropriate unit were developed by the Board, not Congress or the parties involved. It is, therefore, the responsibility of the Board to develop standards which reflect the realities of industrial relations and the needs of collective bargaining.

With these objectives in mind, a general solution might be proposed. Traditionally, the NLRB's appropriate unit decisions have been predominantly structured for purposes of *organization*. Using the terminology set forth at the outset of this study, the unit configurations have been used simply as an "election district" and the parties have regularly shifted to a "negotiation unit."[16] Consequently, it is submitted that future unit decisions be structured for purposes of *bargaining*. This shift in the emphasis of public policy, while leaving the Board with wide discretion, would provide for greater consideration of "the needs of the industrial organization as a whole."[17] The unit delineations would more nearly reflect the anticipated scope of collective bargaining and the needs of both unions and employers to improve the effectiveness of their relationships. The NLRB has the power to promote, protect, and preserve the system of free collective bargaining. Future unit determinations may well play an intricate part in the success or failure of the Board's exercise of this power.

---

[13] W. T. Grant Co., 179 N.L.R.B. No. 114, 72 L.R.R.M. 1434 (1969)

[14] *Compare* Univac Div., Sperry Rand Corp., 158 N.L.R.B. 997 (1966), *with* Univac Div. of Remington Rand Div. of Sperry Rand Corp., 137 N.L.R.B. 1232 (1962).

[15] Discussion, "Public Policy and the Structure of Collective Bargaining" in A. Weber, *supra* note 3, at 327.

[16] See Chapter 1, *infra.*

[17] Brown and Shultz, *supra* note 3, at 318.

Index

Abbott Laboratories, 131 N.L.R.B. 596 (1961), 220
Abbotts Dairies, Inc., 97 N.L.R.B. 1064 (1952), 81
ABC, 112 N.L.R.B. 605 (1956), 123
ACF Indus., Inc., 136 N.L.R.B. 594 (1962), 73
ACF Indus., Inc., 115 N.L.R.B. 1106 (1956), 198-199
ACF-Wrigley Stores, 124 N.L.R.B. 200 (1959), 11
Aerojet-General Corp., 163 N.L.R.B. No. 23 (1967), 99
Air California, 170 N.L.R.B. No. 1 (1968), 48
Air Line Pilots Ass'n, 97 N.L.R.B. 929 (1951), 201
Alabama Drydock & Shipbldg. Co., 5 N.L.R.B. 149 (1938), 10
Alcan Aluminum Corp., 178 N.L.R.B. No. 55 (1969), 109-110
S.L. Allen & Co., 1 N.L.R.B. 714 (1936), 89
Allied Chem. Corp., 165 N.L.R.B. No. 23 (1967), 99
Allied Chem. & Dye Corp., 116 N.L.R.B. 1784 (1956), 44
Allied Chem. & Dye Corp., 71 N.L.R.B. 1217 (1946), 90
Allied Stores, 175 N.L.R.B. No. 162 (1969), 38
Allied Stores, 150 N.L.R.B. 799 (1965), 28
Allied Super Mkts., Inc., 167 N.L.R.B. 361 (1967), 210
Allis-Chalmers Mfg. Co., 4 N.L.R.B. 159 (1937), 67-69, 89
Allstate Ins. Co., 118 N.L.R.B. 855 (1957), 12
Aluminum Co. of America, 44 N.L.R.B. 1111 (1942), 9
American Automobile Ass'n, 172 N.L.R.B. No. 131 (1968), 39
American Bosch Arma Corp., 163 N.L.R.B. No. 23 (1967), 99
American Brass Co., 6 N.L.R.B. 723 (1938), 9
American Can Co., 13 N.L.R.B. 1252 (1939), 42, 69-70, 89-91, 99

American Cyanamid Co., N.L.R.B. Case No. 2-UC-34 (1970), 145
American Cyanamid Co., 131 N.L.R.B. 909 (1961), 7
American Potash & Chem. Corp., 107 N.L.R.B. 1418 (1954), 76, 92-95, 98, 101, 106
American Seating Co., 106 N.L.R.B. 250 (1953), 195-196
American Stores Co., 130 N.L.R.B. 678 (1961), 117
Amfac, Inc., ——— N.L.R.B. ——— (1969), 38
Anheuser-Busch, Inc., 170 N.L.R.B. No. 5 (1968), 103-104
Arden Farms, 118 N.L.R.B. 117 (1957), 219
Armored Motor Service Co., 106 N.L.R.B. 1139 (1953), 216
Armour & Co., 5 N.L.R.B. 535 (1938), 66
Arnold Constable Corp., 150 N.L.R.B. 788 (1965), 28
Atlas Storage Div., 100 N.L.R.B. 1443 (1952), 220
Auburn Rubber Co., 140 N.L.R.B. 919 (1963), 221

P. Ballantine & Sons, 141 N.L.R.B. 1103 (1963), 83-86
P. Ballantine & Sons, 120 N.L.R.B. 86 (1958), 83-86
Baltimore Transit Co., 92 N.L.R.B. 688 (1950), 150
Banco Credito y Ahorro Ponceno, 167 N.L.R.B. 397 (1967), aff'd, 390 F.2d 110 (1st Cir. 1968), cert. denied, 393 U.S. 832 (1968), 30, 33
Banco Credito y Ahorro Ponceno, 160 N.L.R.B. 1504 (1966), 210
Barrington Plaza & Traginew, Inc., 185 N.L.R.B. No. 132 (1970), 193
Bartlett & Snow Co., 4 N.L.R.B. 113 (1937), 10
Bath Iron Works Corp., 154 N.L.R.B. 1069 (1965), 134-135
Beaunit Fibers, Inc., 153 N.L.R.B. 987 (1965), 130

Beechnut Foods Div. of the Beechnut Life Savers Co., 118 N.L.R.B. 123 (1957), 44

Bell Tel. Co., 118 N.L.R.B. 371 (1957), 115-116

Birmingham Elec. Co., 89 N.L.R.B. 1342 (1950), 203

Black & Decker Mfg. Co., 147 N.L.R.B. 825 (1964), 51, 70, 153

Bluff City Transfer & Storage Co., 184 N.L.R.B. No. 83 (1970), 196

Boeing Co., 169 N.L.R.B. No. 33 (1968), 71

Borden Co., Hutchinson Ice Cream Div., 89 N.L.R.B. 227 (1950), 40-41

Borg-Warner Corp., 61 N.L.R.B. 1178 (1945), 199

Boston Consol. Gas Co., 107 N.L.R.B. 1565 (1954), 203

Boston Gas Co., 136 N.L.R.B. 219 (1962), 119

Bowman Transp., Inc., 166 N.L.R.B. 982 (1967), 58, 60

John Brenner Co., 129 N.L.R.B. 394 (1960), 218

Bricklayers Local No. 3, 162 N.L.R.B. 476 (1966), 193

Brink's Inc., 77 N.L.R.B. 1182 (1948), 216

Brockton Taunton Gas Co., 132 N.L.R.B. 940 (1961), 73, 125

Brown Equip. & Mfg. Co., 93 N.L.R.B. 1278 (1951), *enf'd*, 205 F.2d 99 (1st Cir. 1953), 17

Buckeye Cellulose Corp., 184 N.L.R.B. No. 84 (1970), 196

Buckeye Village Mkt., Inc., 175 N.L.R.B. No. 46 (1969), 57, 61-64, 105

Buddy L Corp., 167 N.L.R.B. 808 (1967), 74, 101, 106

Burns Detective Agency, 110 N.L.R.B. 995 (1954), 216

William J. Burns Int'l Detective Agency, 182 N.L.R.B. No. 50 (1970), 149, 168, 185-197

Busch Kredit Jewelry Co., 97 N.L.R.B. 1386 (1952), 18

Cab Operating Corp., 153 N.L.R.B. 878 (1965), 218

Harry T. Campbell Sons' Corp., 164 N.L.R.B. 247 (1967), *enf. denied*, 407 F.2d 969 (4th Cir. 1969), 35, 47-48

Campbell Soup Co., 111 N.L.R.B. 234 (1955), 214

Carey v. Westinghouse Elec. Co., 15 App. Div.2d 7 (1961), *aff'd*, 11 N.Y.2d 452 (1962), *rev'd*, 375 U.S. 261 (1964), 114, 122-124, 126-128

B.J. Carney Co., 157 N.L.R.B. 1285 (1966), 120

Carson Pirie Scott & Co., 173 N.L.R.B. No. 48 (1968), 42

J.I. Case Co., 87 N.L.R.B. 692 (1949), 70

Central Wisconsin Motor Transp. Co., 85 N.L.R.B. 287 (1949), 50

Century Elec. Co., 146 N.L.R.B. 232 (1964), 10, 72

Chrysler Corp., 79 N.L.R.B. 462 (1948), 215

Chrysler Corp., 76 N.L.R.B. 55 (1948), 7

Chrysler Corp., 42 N.L.R.B. 1145 (1942), 133

Cities Service Oil Co., 182 N.L.R.B. No. 6 (1970), 143-144

Cities Service Oil Co., 145 N.L.R.B. 467 (1963), 71

City Auto Stamping Co., 3 N.L.R.B. 307 (1937), 66

Clay & Bailey Mfg. Co., 106 N.L.R.B. 210 (1953), 11

C & M Construction Co., 147 N.L.R.B. 843 (1964), 221

Coca-Cola Bottling Co., 156 N.L.R.B. 450 (1965), 57

Coca-Cola Bottling Co., 133 N.L.R.B. 762 (1961), 117-118, 154

Joseph C. Collins & Co., 184 N.L.R.B. No. 113 (1970), 221

Colonial Cedar Co., 119 N.L.R.B. 1613 (1958), 220

Columbia Cabinet Corp., 146 N.L.R.B. 1039 (1964), 203

Community Publications, Inc., 162 N.L.R.B. 855 (1967), 74

Consolidated Iron-Steel Mfg. Co., 98 N.L.R.B. 481 (1952), 219

Consolidated Papers, Inc., 179 N.L.R.B. No. 21 (1969), 200-201

Continental Baking Co., 99 N.L.R.B. 777 (1952), 7, 9-11

Continental Can Co., 171 N.L.R.B. No. 99 (1968), 13

Continental Ins. Co. v. NLRB, 409 F.2d 727 (2nd Cir. 1969), 35

Cook Paint & Varnish Co., 127 N.L.R.B. 1098 (1960), 77
John J. Corbett Press, Inc., 163 N.L.R.B. 154 (1967), 221
Corn Products Ref. Co., 80 N.L.R.B. 362 (1948), 92
Joseph Cory Warehouse, Inc., 184 N.L.R.B. No. 73 (1970), 154-155
Crown Drug Co., 108 N.L.R.B. 1126 (1954), 18
Crown Simpson Pulp Co., 163 N.L.R.B. No. 109 (1967), 109

Davenport Insulation, 184 N.L.R.B. No. 114 (1970), 193-194
Dayton Power & Light Co., 137 N.L.R.B. 337 (1962), 117
Delaware-New Jersey Ferry Co., 1 N.L.R.B. 85 (1935), 204
Delaware-New Jersey Ferry Co., 1 N.L.R.B. 68 (1935), 205
Diamont T. Utah, Inc., 124 N.L.R.B. 966 (1959), 11, 93
Dixie Belle Mills, Inc., 139 N.L.R.B. 629 (1962), 18, 26
Drug Fair-Community Drug Co., 180 N.L.R.B. No. 94 (1969), 20-22
Dundee Cement Co., 170 N.L.R.B. No. 66 (1966), 100
E.I. duPont de Nemours & Co., 162 N.L.R.B. 413 (1966), 98, 102-103, 107, 110
E.I. duPont de Nemours & Co., 126 N.L.R.B. 885 (1960), 94
E.I. duPont de Nemours & Co., 107 N.L.R.B. 734 (1954), 202
D.V. Displays Corp., 134 N.L.R.B. 568 (1961), 72, 203

Eastern Corp., 116 N.L.R.B. 329 (1956), 200
Eaton Mfg. Co., 121 N.L.R.B. 813 (1958), 54
Electric Sprayit Co., 67 N.L.R.B. 780 (1946), 158
El Paso Elec. Co., 168 N.L.R.B. No. 136 (1967), 48
Emerald Maintenance, Inc., N.L.R.B.-TXD-620-70, No. 23-CA-3597 (1970), 195
Emerson Elec. Co., 176 N.L.R.B. No. 98 (1969), 174
Equipment Sales Co., 146 N.L.R.B. 865 (1964), 203
Equitable Life Ins. Co., 138 N.L.R.B. 529 (1962), 18-19

Evening News Ass'n, 154 N.L.R.B. 1494 (1965), 222-224

Father & Son Shoe Stores, Inc., 117 N.L.R.B. 1479 (1957), 12, 22, 24
Federal Elec. Corp., 167 N.L.R.B. No. 63 (1967), 179-180
Federal Elec. Corp., 162 N.L.R.B. 512 (1966), 151
Felix Half & Bros., Inc., 132 N.L.R.B. 1523 (1961), 77-78
Firestone Tire & Rubber Co., N.L.R.B. Case No. 26-RC-3633 (April 1, 1970), 214
Firestone Tire & Rubber Co., 185 N.L.R.B. No. 11 (1970), 145-146
Firestone Tire & Rubber Co., 103 N.L.R.B. 1749 (1953), 55
Fisher Body Corp., 7 N.L.R.B. 1083 (1938), 9
Fleming & Sons, Inc., 118 N.L.R.B. 1451 (1957), 73
Ford Motor Co., 66 N.L.R.B. 1317 (1946), 210
Foreman & Clark, Inc., 97 N.L.R.B. 1080 (1952), 54
Foreman & Clark, Inc. v. NLRB, 215 F.2d 396 (9th Cir. 1954), 81
Formica Corp., 142 N.L.R.B. 433 (1963), 120
Fort Worth Stockyards, 109 N.L.R.B. 1452 (1954), 71
Fox Co., 158 N.L.R.B. 320 (1966), 12, 73, 125
Frankel Shops, Inc., N.L.R.B. Case No. 29-RC-1139 (1969), 38
Fremont Hotel, Inc., 168 N.L.R.B. No. 23 (1967), 102
Frisch's Big Boy Ill-Mar, Inc., 147 N.L.R.B. 551 (1964), *rev'd and remanded*, 356 F.2d 895 (7th Cir. 1966), 19, 27-28, 33, 37
Frito-Lay, Inc., 177 N.L.R.B. No. 85 (1969), 151-152
Freuhauf Corp., 157 N.L.R.B. 28 (1966), 73
Freuhauf Trailer Co., 1 N.L.R.B. 68 (1935), 204
FWD Corp., 131 N.L.R.B. 404 (1961), 130

Galdeen's Inc., 134 N.L.R.B. 770 (1961), 220
Gas Service Co., 140 N.L.R.B. 445 (1963), 73, 125

General Box Co., 82 N.L.R.B. 678 (1949), 118, 146

General Dynamics Corp., 184 N.L.R.B. No. 71 (1970), 195-196

General Elec. Co., 185 N.L.R.B. No. 4 (1970), 159

General Elec. Co., 180 N.L.R.B. No. 162 (1970), 228

General Elec. Co., 173 N.L.R.B. No. 64 (1968), 42

General Elec. Co., 144 N.L.R.B. 88 (1963), 117

General Elec. Co., 119 N.L.R.B. 1233 (1958), 130

General Elec. Co., 106 N.L.R.B. 364 (1953), 156

General Elec. Co., 58 N.L.R.B. 57 (1944), 69, 90

General Instrument Corp. v. NLRB, 319 F.2d 420 (4th Cir. 1963), 81

General Motors Corp., 120 N.L.R.B. 1215 (1958), 54

Gerber Products Co., 172 N.L.R.B. No. 195 (1968), 48

Globe Mach. & Stamping Co., 3 N.L.R.B. 294 (1937), 65-76, 79, 82, 89, 138

Globe Oil & Refining Co., 63 N.L.R.B. 958 (1945), 151

Godchaux Sugars, Inc., 44 N.L.R.B. 874 (1942), 205

B.F. Goodrich Co., 115 N.L.R.B. 722 (1956), 199

Goodyear Tire & Rubber Co., 168 N.L.R.B. No. 25 (1967), 164

Goodyear Tire & Rubber Co., 3 N.L.R.B. 431 (1937), 8

Gould National Batteries, Inc., 157 N.L.R.B. 679 (1966), 129

Governale & Drew, Inc., 106 N.L.R.B. 1317 (1953), 156

Grand Union Co., 176 N.L.R.B. No. 28 (1968), 37

W.T. Grant Co., 179 N.L.R.B. No. 114 (1969), 229

Great Atlantic & Pacific Tea Co., 128 N.L.R.B. 342 (1960), 12

Haag Drug Co., 169 N.L.R.B. No. 111 (1968), 36-37

Hackney Iron & Steel Co., 167 N.L.R.B. 613 (1967), *remanded*, 395 F.2d 639 (D.C. Cir. 1968), *reaff'd*, 182 N.L.R.B. No. 53 (1970), 168, 190

Halquist Lannon Stove Co., 156 N.L.R.B. 694 (1966), 220

Harrington Bottling Co., N.L.R.B. Case No. 19-UC-46 (September 24, 1968), 116-117

Hearst Consol. Publications, 156 N.L.R.B. 210 (1965), 223

Heck's Inc., 156 N.L.R.B. 760 (1966), 199

Hilton-Burns Hotel Co., 167 N.L.R.B. 221 (1967), 71

Holmberg, Inc., 162 N.L.R.B. 407 (1966), 99-100

Home Furniture Co., 174 N.L.R.B. No. 113 (1969), *remanded*, 419 F.2d 179 (3rd Cir. 1969), 181-182

Hoover, Co., 55 N.L.R.B. 1321 (1944), 198

Hotel Employees v. Joden, Inc., 262 F. Supp. 390 (D. Mass. 1966), 176

Hot Shoppes, Inc., 130 N.L.R.B. 144 (1961), 53

Howmet Corp., 162 N.L.R.B. No. 143 (1967), 117

Hudson Hosiery Co., 74 N.L.R.B. 250 (1947), 80, 82

Hudson Pulp & Paper Corp., 117 N.L.R.B. 416 (1957), 73

Hughes Tool Co., 97 N.L.R.B. 1107 (1952), 199

Huron Portland Cement Co., 112 N.L.R.B. 1465 (1955), 214

Illinois State-Journal-Register, Inc. v. NLRB, 412 F.2d 37 (7th Cir. 1969), 210

Industrial Rayon Corp., 128 N.L.R.B. 514 (1960), *enf. denied*, 291 F.2d 809 (4th Cir. 1961), 93

Interchemical Corp., 116 N.L.R.B. 1443 (1956), 44

International Furniture Co., 119 N.L.R.B. 1462 (1958), 43

International Harvester Co., 119 N.L.R.B. 1709 (1958), 93

International Harvester Co., 81 N.L.R.B. 374 (1949), 216

International Ladies' Garment Workers' Union v. NLRB, 339 F.2d 116 (2nd Cir. 1964), 209

International Minerals & Chem. Corp., 71 N.L.R.B. 878 (1946), 69, 90

International Paper Co., 171 N.L.R.B. No. 89 (1968), 57

International Smelting & Refining Co., 106 N.L.R.B. 223 (1953), 203

Interscience Encyclopedia, Inc., AAA Case No. L-45577-NY-L-138-65 (August 7, 1970), 172, 183-185, 189

Jay Kay Metal Specialties Corp., 163 N.L.R.B. 719 (1967), 74, 105-106

Jewel Food Stores, 111 N.L.R.B. 1368 (1955), 18, 22

Jewish Baking Ass'n, 100 N.L.R.B. 1245 (1952), 220

Johnson Ready Mix Co., 142 N.L.R.B. 437 (1963), 185

Jordan Marsh Co., 174 N.L.R.B. No. 187 (1969), 99

Kaiser Aluminum & Chem. Corp., 100 N.L.R.B. 107 (1952), 57

Kaiser Co., 59 N.L.R.B. 547 (1944), 129

Kalamazoo Paper Box Corp., 136 N.L.R.B. 134 (1962), 2, 43-47

Kennecott Copper Corp., 176 N.L.R.B. No. 13 (1969), 162-163

Kolcast Indus., 114 N.L.R.B. 1311 (1955), 216

Kostel Corp., 172 N.L.R.B. No. 167 (1968), 36-37, 39

Kota Div. of Dura Corp., 182 N.L.R.B. No. 51 (1970), 168, 189-190, 197

Krambo Food Stores, Inc., 119 N.L.R.B. 369 (1957), 71

Kroger Co., 148 N.L.R.B. 569 (1964), 220-221

Kroger Co., 88 N.L.R.B. 243 (1950), 151

KVP Sutherland Paper Co., 146 N.L.R.B. 1553 (1964), 53

Ladish Co., 178 N.L.R.B. No. 5 (1969), 200

Lear-Siegler, Inc., 170 N.L.R.B. No. 114 (1968), 100

Leedom v. Kyne, 358 U.S. 184 (1958), 82, 213

Libbey-Owens-Ford Glass Co., 169 N.L.R.B. No. 2 (1968), *injunction granted*, 131 U.S. App. D.C. 190 (1968), *rev'd*, 403 F.2d 916 (D.C. Cir. 1968), *cert. denied*, 393 U.S. 1016 (1969). *Election certified*, 173 N.L.R.B. No. 187 (1968), 74-75, 113, 131-147

Libby, McNeill & Libby, 159 N.L.R.B. 677 (1966), 120-121

Liberty Coach Co., 181 N.L.R.B. No. 32 (1970), 225

Liebman Breweries, Inc., 142 N.L.R.B. 121 (1963), 50-51

Lockheed Aircraft Corp., 100 N.L.R.B. No. 147 (1952), 54

Lockheed Aircraft Corp., 73 N.L.R.B. 220 (1947), 43

Bhd. of Locomotive Firemen & Enginemen, 145 N.L.R.B. 1521 (1964), 115-116

Lone Star Boat Co., N.L.R.B. Case No. 4-RC-4605 (1961), 216

Lord & Taylor, 150 N.L.R.B. 812 (1965), 28

Los Angeles Statler Hilton Hotel, 129 N.L.R.B. 1349 (1961), 219

LTV Aerospace Corp., 170 N.L.R.B. No. 40 (1968), 153

Lufkin Foundry & Mach. Co., 174 N.L.R.B. No. 90 (1969), 130

McCord Corp., 169 N.L.R.B. No. 7 (1968), 99

McDonnell Co., 163 N.L.R.B. No. 31 (1968), 123

McGuire v. Humble Oil & Refining Co., 355 F.2d 352 (2nd Cir. 1966), *cert. denied*, 384 U.S. 988 (1966), 178-180

John McShain, Inc., 185 N.L.R.B. No. 39 (1970), 219

Mack Mfg. Co., 107 N.L.R.B. 209 (1953), 215

Mallinckrodt Chem. Works, 162 N.L.R.B. 387 (1966), 64, 74, 76, 94-110, 227

Mallinckrodt Chem. Works, Uranium Div., 129 N.L.R.B. 312 (1960), 94

Maryland Cup Corp., 171 N.L.R.B. No. 71 (1968), 57-58

Maryland Drydock Co., 49 N.L.R.B. 733 (1943), 205-206

Mason & Hanger—Silas Mason Co., 180 N.L.R.B. No. 63 (1969), 111

Matt's Shop-Rite, Inc., 174 N.L.R.B. No. 157 (1969), 38

May Dep't Stores, 175 N.L.R.B. No. 97 (1968), 37

Meijer Supermkts, Inc., 142 N.L.R.B. 513 (1963), 53-55

Melbet Jewelry Co., 180 N.L.R.B. No. 24 (1969), 166

Merner Lumber & Hardware Co., 145 N.L.R.B. 1024 (1964), *enforced,* 345 F.2d 770 (9th Cir. 1965), *cert. denied,* 382 U.S. 942 (1966), 36

Mesta Mach. Co., 167 N.L.R.B. No. 10 (1967), 101-102

Metro Beverages, —— N.L.R.B. ——, 46 LRRM 1492 (1960), 11

Metropolitan Life Ins. Co. v. NLRB, 328 F.2d 820 (3rd Cir. 1964), 82

Metropolitan Life Ins. Co., 138 N.L.R.B. 512 (1962), *enforced,* 330 F.2d 62 (6th Cir. 1964), *vacated and remanded,* 380 U.S. 525 (1965), 53

Mid-State Fruit, Inc., 186 N.L.R.B. No. 11 (1970), 207-208

Miron Bldg. Products Co., 116 N.L.R.B. 1406 (1956), 219

Mobil Oil Corp., 169 N.L.R.B. No. 35 (1968), 100-101

Monogram Industries, Inc., Arbitrator's decision, December 1969, 165

Monongahela Power, 176 N.L.R.B. No. 123 (1969), 39

Monroe Sander Corp. v. Livingston, 377 F.2d 6 (2nd Cir. 1967), 171-172

Montana-Dakota Utils. Co., 110 N.L.R.B. 1056 (1954), 71

Morand Bros. Beverage Co., 91 N.L.R.B. 409 (1950), 70, 83

Morgan Linen Service, Inc., 131 N.L.R.B. 420 (1961), 219

Morgan Transfer & Storage Co., 131 N.L.R.B. 1434 (1961), 73

Motor City Dodge Co., 185 N.L.R.B. No. 88 (1970), 178

Mountain State Woodworkers Ass'n, 118 N.L.R.B. 806 (1957), 72

Murray Co., 107 N.L.R.B. 1571 (1954), 150

Murray Corp. of America, 101 N.L.R.B. 313 (1952), 17

Myers Drum Co., 165 N.L.R.B. 1060 (1967), 71, 102

National Cash Register Co., 168 N.L.R.B. No. 130 (1967), 111, 199

National Tube Co., 76 N.L.R.B. 1199 (1948), 57, 91-95, 106-107, 109-110

Newark Stove Co., 143 N.L.R.B. 583 (1963), 210

New England Tel. & Tel. Co., N.L.R.B. Case Nos. 1-RC-10718, 10719, 10720, 10721 (1970), 195

News Syndicate Co., 164 N.L.R.B. No. 69 (1967), 117

Niagara Hudson Power Corp., 79 N.L.R.B. 1115 (1948), 23

NLRB v. Adams Drug Co., 414 F.2d 1194 (D.C. Cir. 1969), 29

NLRB v. Capital Bakers, Inc., 351 F.2d 45 (3rd Cir. 1965), *dec. on remand,* 168 NLRB No. 119 (1967), 33

NLRB v. John J. Corbett Press, Inc., 401 F.2d 673 (2nd Cir. 1968), 222

NLRB v. Davis Cafeteria, Inc., 358 F.2d 98 (5th Cir. 1966), *reaff'd,* 160 N.L.R.B. 1141 (1966), *enf. denied,* 396 F.2d 18 (5th Cir. 1968), 33-34

NLRB v. Food Employees Council, 399 F.2d 501 (9th Cir. 1968), 161

NLRB v. Ideal Laundry & Dry Cleaning Co., 330 F.2d 712 10th Cir. 1964), 65

NLRB v. Jones & Laughlin Steel Corp., 331 U.S. 416 (1947), 215

NLRB v. Metropolitan Life Ins. Co., 405 F.2d 1169 (2nd Cir. 1968), 208

NLRB v. Metropolitan Life Ins. Co., 380 U.S. 438 (1965), 81

NLRB v. Moss Amber Mfg. Co., 264 F.2d 107 (9th Cir. 1959), 49

NLRB v. Pinkerton's, Inc., 416 F.2d 627 (7th Cir. 1969), 51-52

NLRB v. Pittsburgh Plate Glass Co., 270 F.2d 167 (4th Cir. 1959), 93

NLRB v. Puritan Sportswear Corp., 385 F.2d 142 (3rd Cir. 1967), 227

NLRB v. Sheridan Creations, Inc., 357 F.2d 245 (2nd Cir. 1966), *cert. denied,* 385 U.S. 1005 (1967), 221

NLRB v. Smythe, 212 F.2d 664 (5th Cir. 1954), 14

NLRB v. Solis Theatre Corp., 403 F.2d 381 (2nd Cir. 1968), 34-35

NLRB v. Spartans Indus., Inc., 406 F.2d 1002 (5th Cir. 1969), 126

NLRB v. Spun-Jee Corp., 385 F.2d 379 (2nd Cir. 1967), 222

NLRB v. Truck Drivers Local 449, 353 U.S. 87 (1957), 218

NLRB v. Valleydale Packers, 402 F.2d 768 (5th Cir. 1968), 173

Olinkraft, Inc., 179 N.L.R.B. No. 61 (1969), 46-47
O'Neill Int'l Detective Agency, 115 N.L.R.B. 760 (1956), 216
Overnite Transp. Co., 157 N.L.R.B. 1185 (1966), *aff'd*, 372 F.2d 765 (4th Cir. 1967), *cert. denied*, 389 U.S. 838 (1967), 173, 175, 185

Pabst Brewing Co., N.L.R.B. Case No. 13-RC-7883 (August 10, 1961), 202
Pacific Coast Ass'n of Pulp & Paper Mfrs., 163 N.L.R.B. 882 (1967), 224
Pacific Maritime Ass'n, 185 N.L.R.B. No. 114 (1970), 201-202
Pacific States Steel Corp., 134 N.L.R.B. 1325 (1961), 73, 125
Pacific Tel. & Tel. Co., 23 N.L.R.B. 280 (1940), 90
Packard Motor Car Co., 61 N.L.R.B. 4 (1945), *aff'd*, 330 U.S. 485 (1947), 29, 36, 206
Palace Laundry Dry Cleaning Corp., 75 N.L.R.B. 320 (1947), 210
Paxton Wholesale Grocery Co., 123 N.L.R.B. 316 (1959), 12, 18, 23-24
Pennsylvania Edison Co., 36 N.L.R.B. 432 (1941), 9
Pep Boys, 172 N.L.R.B. No. 23 (1968), 38
Permanente Metals Corp., 89 N.L.R.B. 804 (1950), 92
Perma Vinyl Corp., 164 N.L.R.B. 968 (1967), 173-175, 185
Perma Vinyl Corp., 151 N.L.R.B. 1679 (1965), 173-175, 185
Pinkerton's Inc., 170 N.L.R.B. No. 108 (1968), 216
Pittsburgh Plate Glass Co. v. NLRB, 313 U.S. 146 (1941), 65
R.L. Polk & Co., 91 N.L.R.B. 443 (1950), 11
Portland Gas & Coke Co., 2 N.L.R.B. 552 (1937), 89
Potlatch Forests, Inc., 165 N.L.R.B. No. 89 (1967), 108-109
Potter Aeronautical Corp., 155 N.L.R.B. 1077 (1965), 40-41
PPG Indus., Inc., 180 N.L.R.B. No. 58 (1969), 142-144
PPG Indus., Inc., N.L.R.B. Case No. 6-UC-8 (December 9, 1966), 140-142

Primrose Super Mkt., Inc., 148 N.L.R.B. 610 (1964), *enforced*, 353 F.2d 675 (1st Cir. 1965), *cert. denied*, 382 U.S. 830 (1966), 36
Publishers' Ass'n v. NLRB, 364 F.2d 293 (2nd Cir. 1966), 224
Puget Sound Power & Light Co., 117 N.L.R.B. 1825 (1957), 210
Purity Food Stores, Inc., 150 N.L.R.B. 1523 (1965), *enf. denied*, 354 F.2d 926 (1st Cir. 1965), *reaff'd*, 160 N.L.R.B. 651 (1966), *enf. denied*, 376 F.2d 497 (1st Cir. 1967), *cert. denied*, 389 U.S. 959 (1968), 29-33, 37

Quality Limestone Products, Inc., 143 N.L.R.B. 589 (1963), 219

Radio Corp. of America, 173 N.L.R.B. No. 72 (1968), 101-102
Radio Corp. of America, 66 N.L.R.B. 1014 (1946), 43
Ranch-Way, Inc., 183 N.L.R.B. No. 116 (1970), 192-194
R.B.P., Inc., 176 N.L.R.B. No. 22 (1969), 39
Reichold Chems., Inc., 126 N.L.R.B. 619 (1960), 43
Remington Rand Div. of Sperry Rand, 132 N.L.R.B. 1093 (1961), 130
Republican Co., 169 N.L.R.B. No. 167 (1968), 42
Retail Associates, Inc., 120 N.L.R.B. 388 (1958), 221
Reynolds Metals Co., 108 N.L.R.B. 821 (1954), 93
Richmond Greyhound Lines, Inc., 65 NLRB 234 (1946), 151
Robbins & Myers, Inc., 144 N.L.R.B. 295 (1963), 203
Rohlik, Inc., 145 N.L.R.B. 1236 (1964), 185
Rohm & Haas Co., 183 N.L.R.B. No. 20 (1970), 143-144
Rose Exterminator Co., 143 N.L.R.B. 59 (1963), 220
Royal McBee Corp., 117 N.L.R.B. 741 (1957), 74
Royal McBee Corp. v. NLRB, 302 F.2d 330 (4th Cir. 1962), 93
Ryan Aeronautical Co., 132 N.L.R.B. 1160 (1961), 213

Ryan Aeronautical Co., 121 N.L.R.B. 1502 (1958), 203
Ryan Indus., Inc., 100 N.L.R.B. 1455 (1952), 73

Saco-Lowell Shops, 107 N.L.R.B. 590 (1953), 73
Safety Cabs, Inc., 173 N.L.R.B. No. 4 (1968), 57
Safeway Stores, Inc., 178 N.L.R.B. No. 64 (1969), 104-105
Safeway Stores, Inc., 174 N.L.R.B. No. 189 (1969), 164
Safeway Stores, Inc., 96 N.L.R.B. 998 (1951), 16-17, 22
St. Regis Paper Co., N.L.R.B. Case No. 6-R-1193 (1967), 133-134
Sangamo Elec. Co., 112 N.L.R.B. 1310 (1955), 135
Sargent & Co., 95 N.L.R.B. 1515 (1951), 199
Sav-On Drugs, Inc., 138 N.L.R.B. 1032 (1962), 12, 14, 17-19, 24-30, 36, 38, 41, 50
Schenley Distilleries, Inc., 77 N.L.R.B. 468 (1948), 216
Joseph E. Seagram & Sons, Inc., 101 N.L.R.B. 101 (1952), 216, 219
Sears, Roebuck & Co., 172 N.L.R.B. No. 132 (1968), 42
Service Roofing Co., 173 N.L.R.B. No. 44 (1968), 222
Sheraton-Kauai Corp. v. NLRB, 429 F.2d 1352 (9th Cir. 1970), 167
S-H Food Service, Inc., 183 N.L.R.B. No. 124 (1970), 191-192
Shipowners' Ass'n of the Pacific Coast, 7 N.L.R.B. 1002 (1938), 218
Shoe Corp. of America, 117 N.L.R.B. 1208 (1957), 11
Simmons Co., 126 N.L.R.B. 656 (1960), 180
Sioux City Brewing Co., 63 N.L.R.B. 964 (1945), 43
Smith Steel Workers, 174 N.L.R.B. No. 41 (1969), 131
Solomon Johnsky, 184 N.L.R.B. No. 94 (1970), 194
Soss Mfg. Co., 56 N.L.R.B. 348 (1944), 206
Southern Conference of Teamsters v. Red Ball Motor Freight, Inc., 374 F.2d 932 (5th Cir. 1967), 180-181

Southland Mfg. Corp., 186 N.L.R.B. No. 111 (1970), 175
Southland Mfg. Corp., N.L.R.B.-TXD No. 397-69 (July 22, 1969), 174-175
Sparkle Mkts. Co., 113 N.L.R.B. 790 (1955), 22
Spartan Dept's Stores, 140 N.L.R.B. 608 (1963), 53
Spartans Indus., Inc., 169 N.L.R.B. No. 47 (1968), *enforced*, 406 F.2d 1002 (5th Cir. 1969), 160-162
Sperry Rand Corp., 116 N.L.R.B. 137 (1956), 72
Square D Co., 169 N.L.R.B. No. 140 (1968), 104
Standard Oil Co., 146 N.L.R.B. 1189 (1964), 117, 119, 130
Standard Oil Co., 107 N.L.R.B. 1524 (1954), 213
Standard Oil Co., 5 N.L.R.B. 750 (1938), 9
Standard Plumbing & Heating Co., 185 N.L.R.B. No. 63 (1970), 194
Star Mkt. Co., 172 N.L.R.B. No. 130 (1968), 38, 52
Star Union Products Co., 127 N.L.R.B. 1173 (1960), 43
Stauffer Chem. Co., 113 N.L.R.B. 1255 (1955), 76
Sun Drug Co., 147 N.L.R.B. 669 (1964), *enf'd*, 359 F.2d 408 (3rd Cir. 1966), 36
Sunset House, 167 N.L.R.B. 870 (1967), 166
Super Mkts. General Corp., 170 N.L.R.B. No. 61 (1968), 160
Sutherland Paper Co., 55 N.L.R.B. 38 (1944), 43
Swift & Co., 131 N.L.R.B. 1143 (1961), 202
Swift & Co., 124 N.L.R.B. 899 (1959), 198-199
Symns Grocer Co., 109 N.L.R.B. 346 (1954), 173

Tennessee Copper Co., 5 N.L.R.B. 768 (1938), 9
Texas Eastman Co., 175 N.L.R.B. No. 105 (1969), 174
Texas Pipe Line Co., 129 N.L.R.B. 705 (1961), *aff'd*, 296 F.2d 208 (5th Cir. 1961), 48
Textron, Inc., 117 N.L.R.B. 19 (1957), 17

Thalhimer Bros., Inc., 83 N.L.R.B. 664 (1949), 81
Timber Products Co., 164 N.L.R.B. No. 109 (1967), 107-109
Todd-Johnson Dry Docks, Inc., 18 N.L.R.B. 973 (1939), 90
Charles H. Tompkins Co., 185 N.L.R.B. No. 38 (1970), 219
Transcontinental Bus System, Inc., 178 N.L.R.B. No. 110 (1969), 60
Transportation-Communication Employees Union v. Union Pacific R.R., 349 F.2d 408 (10th Cir. 1965), *remanded to NRAB*, 385 U.S. 157 (1966), 126-127
Travelodge Corp., 182 N.L.R.B. No. 52 (1970), 168, 190-191

Union Colleries Co., 41 N.L.R.B. 961 (1942), 205
Union Furniture Co., 67 N.L.R.B. 1307 (1946), 210
Uniroyal Merchandising Co., N.L.R.B. Case No. 5-RC-6688 (March 14, 1969), 157-158
U.S. Lingerie Corp., 170 N.L.R.B. No. 77 (1968), 222
United States Plywood-Champion Papers, Inc., 174 N.L.R.B. 48 (1969), 108-109
United States Plywood-Champion, Papers, Inc., 68-1 CCH Labor Arbitration Awards, ¶ 8273 (1968), 11-12
United States Smelting, Refining & Mining Co., 116 N.L.R.B. 661 (1956), 44
United Steel Workers v. Reliance Universal, Inc., 335 F.2d 891 (3rd Cir. 1964), 170-171, 176-177
Univac Div. of Remington Rand Div. of Sperry Rand Corp., 137 N.L.R.B. 1232 (1962), 229
Univac Div., Sperry Rand Corp., 158 N.L.R.B. 997 (1966), 229
U-Tote-Em Grocery Co., 185 N.L.R.B. No. 6 (1970), 37

Vulcanized Rubber & Plastics Co., 129 N.L.R.B. 1256 (1961), 200, 202

Wackenhut Corp. v. United Plant Guard Workers, 332 F.2d 954 (9th Cir. 1964), 107-171, 177
Waikiki Biltmore Inc., 127 N.L.R.B. 82 (1960), 77-78

Warehouse Mkts., Inc., 174 N.L.R.B. No. 70 (1969), 164
Ware Laboratories, Inc., 98 N.L.R.B. 1141 (1952), 73
S.D. Warren Co., 144 N.L.R.B. 204 (1963), *aff'd on other grounds*, 353 F.2d 494 (1st Cir. 1965), 41-42
Washington Post Co., 165 N.L.R.B. 819 (1967), 224
Weis Mkts., Inc., 152 N.L.R.B. 708 (1963), 26-28, 52
Wells Dairies Cooperative, 107 N.L.R.B. 1445 (1954), 11
Wells Fargo Bank, 179 N.L.R.B. No. 79 (1969), 39
West Coast Wood Preserving Co., 15 N.L.R.B. 1 (1939), 90
Western Elec. Co. v. NLRB, 236 F.2d 939 (3rd Cir., 1956), 212
Western Elec. Co., 98 N.L.R.B. 1018 (1952), 23, 213
Western Union Tel. Co., 61 N.L.R.B. 110 (1945), 133
Westinghouse Elec. Corp., 173 N.L.R.B. No. 51 (1968), 73, 125
Westinghouse Elec. Corp., 173 N.L.R.B. No. 43 (1968), 130
Westinghouse Elec. Corp., 163 N.L.R.B. 723 (1967), *aff'd*, 424 F.2d 1151 (7th Cir. 1970), 208-209
Westinghouse Elec. Corp., 162 N.L.R.B. 768 (1967), 73, 123
Westinghouse Elec. Corp., 142 N.L.R.B. 317 (1963), 119
Westinghouse Elec. Corp., 116 N.L.R.B. 1545 (1956), 213
Westinghouse Elec. Corp., 111 N.L.R.B. 497 (1955), 213
Westinghouse Elec. Corp., 108 N.L.R.B. 556 (1954), 76
Westinghouse Elec. Corp., 92 N.L.R.B. 871 (1950), 210
Westinghouse Elec. Corp. v. NLRB, 398 F.2d 669 (6th Cir. 1968), 199
West Virginia Pulp & Paper Co., 53 N.L.R.B. 814 (1943), 133
Weyerhaeuser Timber Co., 87 N.L.R.B. 1076 (1949), 92, 107
S.S. White Dental Mfg. Co., 109 N.L.R.B. 1117 (1954), 214
John Wiley & Sons, Inc. v. Livingston, 203 F. Supp. 171 (S.D.N.Y. 1962), *rev'd*, 313 F.2d 52 (2nd Cir. 1963), *aff'd*, 376 U.S. 543 (1964), 168-190, 196-197

Window Glass Cutters League of America v. American St. Gobain Corp., 428 F.2d 353 (3rd Cir. 1970), *affirming* 47 F.R.D. 255 (W.D. Pa. 1969), 128

F.W. Woolworth Co., 144 N.L.R.B. 307 (1963), 14, 28

Worthington Corp., 155 N.L.R.B. 222 (1965), 73, 125

Worthington Pump & Mach. Corp., 4 N.L.R.B. 448 (1937), 66

York Transfer & Storage Co., 107 N.L.R.B. 139 (1953), 220

K.B. & J. Young's Super Mkts. Inc., 157 N.L.R.B. 271 (1966), *aff'd*, 377 F.2d 463 (9th Cir. 1967), 177

Zenite Metal Corp., 5 N.L.R.B. 509 (1938), 10

Zia Co., 108 N.L.R.B. 1134 (1954), 72

DATE DUE

DEC 08 '93			
			PRINTED IN U.S.A.